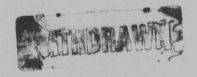

Financial Management in Public Organizations

Financial Management in Public Organizations

Alan Walter Steiss
University of Michigan

Brooks/Cole Publishing Company
Pacific Grove, California

Brooks/Cole Publishing Company
A Division of Wadsworth, Inc.

Library of Congress Cataloging in Publication Data

Steiss, Alan Walter.
  Financial management in public organizations.

  Includes index.
  1. Finance, Public. 2. Finance, Public—Accounting.
3. Administrative agencies—Management. I. Title.
HJ192.S73 1988   350.72   88-14476
ISBN 0-534-09438-4

Sponsoring Editor: *Cynthia C. Stormer*
Editorial Assistant: *Mary Ann Zuzow*
Production Editor: *Linda Loba*
Manuscript Editor: *Peggy Tropp*
Permissions Editor: *Carline Haga*
Interior and Cover Design: *Sharon L. Kinghan*
Art Coordinator: *Lisa Torri*
Typesetting: *Bookends Typesetting, Ashland, Oregon*
Printing and Binding: *The Maple-Vail Book Manufacturing Group, York, Pennsylvania*

Preface

It has been said that "If you don't know where you are going, any road will get you there." It can also be said "If an organization doesn't know where it wants to go, no road will get it there." A dynamic process of management is a critical prerequisite for any organization to know where it wants to go and how to get there.

A basic purpose of management should be to provide focus and consistency regarding the action programs of the organization. Management should involve a blending and directing of available human, physical, and financial resources in order to achieve organizational objectives. In the public sector in particular, the effectiveness of such an approach must be measured by the results achieved and by the people served; that is, in terms of performance.

The concept of performance suggests a melding of the basic management objectives of *efficiency* and *effectiveness*. In this context, efficiency can be equated with doing things right, whereas effectiveness involves doing the right things. Moreover, effectiveness must be measured in terms of the response time required to make critical adjustments when things go wrong. In responding to the variety of decision situations encountered in complex organizations, the functions of management must be carried out as a balanced blend of objective methods and subjective ability.

This book examines a major set of components in the management process—those relating to the management of organizational resources, and in particular, the management of financial resources. A basic management tenet is that resource commitments should be made only if by so doing, the organization can expect to move toward the achievement of its goals and objectives. Since the common denominator among the various resources of any organization is the cost involved in their utilization, the focus most often is on the management of financial resources.

Effective financial management requires appropriate mechanisms for recording and disseminating information about revenues and expenditures, procedures for the allocation of resources and the management of costs, and techniques for financial planning and resource acquisition. An overview of the financial management process, building on these basic components, is provided in Chapter 1. While local government serves as a focal point of this book, the principles and techniques have application to all public organizations—for example, voluntary associations, schools, health and welfare organizations.

Financial accounting data form the basis for much of the cost–analysis conducted in complex organizations. For this reason, the two basic approaches to accounting in the public sector—fund accounting and budgetary accounting—are the first topics to be examined in detail (Chapter 2). Accounting data, however, provide a retrospective view of the consequence of past decisions. The conceptual framework of financial management adopted in this book demands analytical techniques that can accommodate dimensions of risk and uncertainty that are inevitable in future–oriented decision environments.

Managerial accounting focuses on financial estimates of future performance (the planning and budgeting processes) and, subsequently, on the analysis of actual performance in relation to these estimates (program evaluation and performance auditing). Various accounting mechanisms must be maintained to ensure the proper recording of cost flow and the allocation of costs according to their variable, fixed, direct, and indirect components. These mechanisms, for the most part, are embodied in the procedures of *cost accounting*. Techniques of managerial and cost accounting are examined in Chapter 3.

Effective *cost management* involves four basic elements: forecasting the organization's short- and long-range cash needs, managing the cash flow, developing and maintaining good relations with financial institutions, and formulating sound investment strategies. These elements of financial management are examined in Chapters 4 and 5. The basic objective of cost management is to incur minimum opportunity costs, while at the same time, holding a sufficient cash balance to meet the day-to-day needs of the organization.

Factors influencing future costs must be dealt with as part of the *financial planning* process, as outlined in Chapter 6. Monetary costs—research and development costs, investment costs, and the cost of operations, maintenance, and replacement— are commonly reflected in financial accounts. The first step in controlling costs is to determine how costs function under various conditions. This process involves an attempt to find predictable relationships (cost functions) between a dependent variable (cost) and one or more independent variables (organizational activities). In financial planning, however, it often is necessary to look beyond these monetary costs to what economists refer to as opportunity costs, associated costs, and social costs. The extended–time horizon adopted in financial planning leads to fuller recognition of the need for life-cycle costing and benefits analysis. Examining expenditures in terms of program objectives and the evaluation of total benefits for alternative program expenditures alongside of total costs can be important derivatives of *cost–benefit* techniques.

The *budget process* (Chapter 7) includes the application of analytical models for the allocation of scarce resources and the evaluation of alternative strategies at the program level. The traditional role of a budget is to serve as a control mechanism to ensure financial integrity, accountability, and legal compliance. The budget can provide an important tool for management when used to ascertain operating economies and performance efficiencies. A budget should also reflect organizational goals and objectives, and the overall effectiveness of programs in meeting client/community needs.

The commitment of public resources often involves relatively short-term decisions. If a particular program does not achieve the anticipated objectives, basic changes can be made or the activity can be abandoned altogether. Decisions affecting *capital facilities* are not so easily altered or adjusted. Once the resources are committed, the location of elementary school or firehouse can be changed only at considerable public expense. Furthermore, since conditions seldom remain static during the life span of such facilities, as discussed in Chapter 8, the planning and programming of major capital investments must be undertaken as a function of changing public requirements and facility capacity.

Few governments have the capability to finance vital public facilities strictly on a "pay-as-you-go" basis through annual tax yields. Therefore, the power to borrow is one of the most important assets of government. Like all government powers, however, the capacity to borrow must be used with critical regard for its justifiable purposes, with a clear understanding of its safe and reasonable limits, and with sound procedures for debt administration (Chapter 9). An effective borrowing policy seeks to conserve rather than exhaust credit. The ability to borrow when necessary on the most favorable terms afforded by the market is an objective that applies to governments just as it does in the private sector.

The final chapter seeks to place the concepts and techniques of financial management in the broader context of strategic management. Strategic management is a process by which policies are formulated and strategies are selected to achieve organizational goals and objectives. Strategic managers must: (a) identify the long-range needs of the organization, (b) explore the ramifications of policies and programs designed to meet these needs, and (c) formulate strategies that maximize the positive aspects and minimize the negative aspects of the foreseeable future. Strategic management offers a framework by which an organization can adapt to the vagaries of an unpredictable environment and an uncertain future.

Many of the tasks identified in this conceptual framework of financial management are assigned to various sectors in a complex organization. Planners plan; financial analysts prepare budgets; accountants maintain ledgers and prepare financial reports; program personnel schedule and control resources for specific activities; and administrators monitor and evaluate performance. Some of these tasks are undertaken on a grand scale, while others are fairly routine. With the increasing complexity of organizational operations, however, the "division of labor" established to deal with complexity may well become the major impediment to the effective management of financial resources. The underlying premise of this book is that, unless a more comprehensive framework is created to provide guidance and coordination, the sum of the parts may be far less than an integrated whole.

The author would like to thank the following reviewers for their helpful comments: Dr. Harry Fuchs, Tennessee State University; Dr. Patricia Ingraham, The Maxwell School, Syracuse University; Prof. Fred Kramer, University of Massachusetts; Dr. Jeremy Plant, George Mason University, Fairfax, Virginia; Prof. Syedur Rahman, Pennsylvania State University; Prof. Richard Sylves, University of Delaware; and Prof. James Wilson, University of Hartford, Hartford, Connecticut. The author would like to acknowledge the contributions of Chukwuemeka O'Cyprian Nwagwu for his background research on the techniques of cash management in local government and the continued patience and guidance of Leo Herbert in dealing with the intricacies of financial accounting.

Improved managerial performance in government is one of this nation's more pressing needs, now and in the future. Therefore, this book is dedicated to those professionals who have dedicated their knowledge, skills, and talents to meeting this challenge.

Alan Walter Steiss

Contents

CHAPTER 4

Cash Management 80

CHAPTER 5

Investment Strategies 103

CHAPTER 6

Financial Planning and Cost Analysis 121

Exhibits

*Financial Management
in Public Organizations*

Financial Management: An Overview

Significant changes have taken place in recent years in the size and complexity of both private and public organizations. Today's managers are faced with an accelerating rate of evolution in technical, social, political, and economic forces. As a result, the management process has become more difficult, requiring greater skills in planning, analysis, and control—skills aimed at guiding the future course of an organization in an uncertain world. This book is devoted to an examination of a major segment of these management skills: the theory and practice of financial management in public organizations and, in particular, in local government.

The Resource Management Problem

In theory, the problem of managing resources is quite simple; it is difficult only in practice. One merely has to decide what is wanted (specify goals and objectives), measure these wants (quantify benefits sought), and then apply the means available to achieve the greatest possible value of the identified wants (maximize benefits). In contemporary society, the *means* often are the resources of complex organizations. Therefore, the problem is to *maximize benefits* for any given set of *resource inputs*.

Managing Public Resources

Government exists to provide valuable services that businesses or individuals are unable or unwilling to provide for themselves. The benefits to society from any government action should exceed the cost of that action to society. Determining whether the commitment of governmental resources really improves the conditions of the broader community can get complicated, however, particularly when no basis exists for assessing the value of such actions to individuals. The Pareto criterion suggests that the welfare of a community is improved if some members are made better off while no one is made worse off. This criterion has no logical flaws and does not require interpersonal comparisons of utility. Since not all members of the community are likely to benefit equally from a given action, however, many choices are still open to political decision. Despite rigor and sophistication, scientific analysis cannot provide definitive answers to many of the questions involved in the allocation of government resources.

Nevertheless, a continuous search must be maintained for more productive ways to operate public organizations and to assess their capacity to meet changing environmental conditions. The concern must be with the effective allocation of public resources to those organizational units that will carry out plans, strategies, and programs. *Resource management* can provide the critical link between the formulation of goals and objectives and the actual performance of organizational activities.

The common denominator among the various resources of any organization is the cost involved in their utilization. The production of public and quasi-public goods and services requires the acquisition and allocation of relatively scarce resources, the values of which are measured and compared in the common unit of dollars. Consequently, the focus of management most often is on *financial resources.*

The tendency is to think of costs strictly in terms of quantifiable inputs—the financial resources required to support personnel, equipment, materials, and so forth. Costs that cannot be conveniently measured in dollars all too often are dismissed as noncost considerations. Future costs may have important economic implications beyond their measurable monetary value, however. A basic tenet in resource management is that costs should be incurred only if, by so doing, the organization can expect to move toward the achievement of agreed-upon goals and objectives.

Techniques for Financial Management

Financial management has an impact on all segments of an organization. It is involved in the acquisition and allocation of resources and in the tracking of performance resulting from such allocations. In a profit-oriented enterprise, financial statements form the basis for the assessment by stockholders of management's record. In a not-for-profit organization, management seeks to satisfy the desires of its constituents within a set of financial (budgetary) constraints. In either case, financial resources are the focal point for managerial decision making, action, and accountability. Methods and techniques utilized in the performance of these financial functions are relevant to managers in all types of organizations.

Financial management in the public sector borrows liberally from the tools and concepts of business management. The transfer of techniques cannot be complete, however, because of the basic nature of services provided by government. Since private enterprise is unable or unwilling to provide appropriate levels of these services, it must be assumed that some features distinguish them from the goods and services provided privately. These features include the need to provide for the public safety and common welfare of the community and to allocate basic public services on the basis of criterion other than the ability to pay. These same features limit the extent to which business management techniques can be applied in the management of public resources.

Several functions are common to financial management, however, whether in the private or public sector. The objective of this initial chapter is to provide a broad overview of these basic functions.

Keeping Score: Accounting and Control Mechanisms

A traditional role for financial management is that of scorekeeping. In this function, reports of past performance are prepared for internal management as well as outside groups, such as stockholders, creditors, and the general public. These reports may pinpoint responsibility for deviations from previously approved plans. The extent to which these deviations can be attributed to specific components of the organization depends on the degree of sophistication built into the accounting and related control mechanisms. Good financial management requires careful consideration of alternative scorekeeping and reporting methods.

Although scorekeeping is an important function for all types of organizations, to remain effective it must always be viewed as a tool and not as an end in itself. If control systems become overly rigid and lose sight of their operating objectives, countermeasures and subterfuges will emerge that may destroy the effectiveness of the system (and possibly the organization itself). To remain effective, scorekeeping functions must achieve organizational compliance by demonstrating their utility to all levels of management.

Allocation and Management of Existing Resources

The allocation of existing resources and the management of costs to derive future benefits are key responsibilities of financial managers. The relationship between resource allocations and future benefits is asymmetrical, however. Whereas existing resources are expended with certainty, the anticipated stream of benefits is not guaranteed—it is uncertain. This stream may fall considerably short of the expected results or may exceed initial estimates. In financial management, this deviation from expected returns provides an important definition of *uncertainty* and *risk*.

Determining the financial feasibility and desirability of resource commitments requires an analysis of *future* costs and benefits rather than the mere reconciliation of past expenditures. Because traditional methods of financial accounting are not well suited to this task, financial management is based on microeconomic theory. In the allocation of resources, the following question must continually be examined: Are anticipated long-run benefits (adjusted for risk) of a given project commensurate with the long-run costs that may be incurred?

Long-Term Organizational Assets

Beyond the daily problems of cost management, financial managers must be concerned with the long-term asset requirements of the organization. A prime function of financial management is to identify the resources required to attain the overall objectives of the organization. The financial plan is a key ingredient in any organization's strategies. The primary purposes of the financial plan are to project resource requirements for specific time periods and to identify the likely sources of the funds needed.

Before any plan can be formulated, a view of the future, or *forecast,* is required. This forecast lays out explicitly and implicitly the political, economic, and environmental conditions that are likely to affect the programs and activities of the organization. Because of the difficulty of predicting future conditions and events, sound professional judgment is an essential ingredient in the development of forecasts.

Financial management must identify the magnitude of future needs, determine the timing, and negotiate with potential sources of external capital. Decisions of whether to engage in short-term bank borrowing or long-term bond issues are dependent on cash flow expectations, capital structure determination, and cost-of-capital considerations. To discharge these functions effectively, financial managers must maintain close contact with financial markets and be sensitive to macroeconomic developments that may influence the availability and cost of the capital to be acquired. Accuracy, timeliness, and tactfulness are primary characteristics required for these activities.

Given the increasing role that government and other not-for-profit organizations play in the economy, the stake that the public has in effective financial management of these organizations and institutions is mounting. Essential tools for managing public resources include appropriate mechanisms for keeping score and disseminating relevant financial information, rational procedures for allocating resources and managing costs, and techniques for assessing the long-term needs of the organization and for acquiring these resources. Linkages among these basic components are shown in Exhibit 1-1. In the absence of the verdict of the marketplace, the role and responsibilities of financial management in the public sector are even greater than those in profit-oriented organizations.

Financial managers are charged with a dual set of responsibilities. First, they deal with areas for which they have specific line responsibility, such as financial accounting or cost management. Second, they must function as energizers and motivators: through persuasion, education, and admonition, they must establish a climate within the organization that fosters the contributions of all members of the management team to financial decision making. Success in exercising the financial management function requires as much devotion to the second set of activities as to the first and depends, among other factors, on the tone of cooperation set by the chief executive for the rest of the organization.

The Accounting Control Cycle

Accounting has always been an important component of the record-keeping and fiscal control functions of governmental organizations. These accounting control systems, for the most part, are based on double-entry accounting practices developed in the private sector. The role of accounting in public organizations is

Exhibit 1-1 Linkages Among the Financial Management Cycles

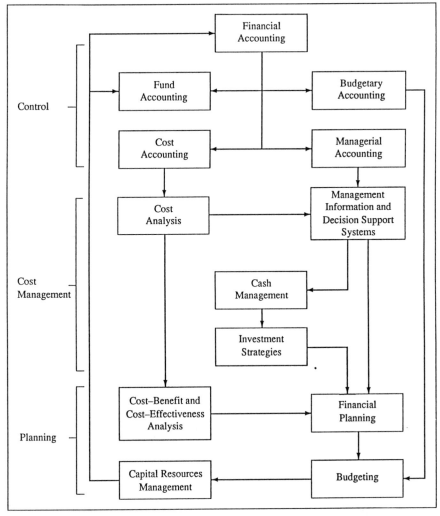

expanding, however, as a consequence of the increased attention in recent years to the need for greater economy, efficiency, and effectiveness in the operations of government. There is growing recognition that, in addition to the functions of financial record keeping and external reporting, accounting *can* and *should* serve as a tool for management planning, decision making, and control.

Financial Accounting

Financial accounting data form the basis for much of the cost analysis conducted in complex organizations. Although accounting data may be used as a basis for future plans (for example, for budget building), financial accounting is concerned primarily with the historical results of fiscal transactions and the consequent financial position of some organizational entity. Key concepts in financial accounting for public organizations are defined in Exhibit 1-2.

Exhibit 1-2 *Basic Accounting Vocabulary*

A *fund* is an independent fiscal, accounting, and often legal entity to which all resources and related liabilities, obligations, reserves, and equities are assigned.

Transactions are made between funds.

Separate *financial statements* are prepared for each of the major funds, and combined statements of funds with similar purposes often are distributed.

An *income statement* reflects the profit performance of an entity for some specific period of time.

Revenue represents an inflow of money and/or other representations of value in return for selling goods or providing some type of service.

Expense represents an outflow of resources, or incurring of obligations, for goods and services required to generate revenues.

Net income is simply the excess of revenue over expense.

A *balance sheet* shows the financial position of an entity at a particular time—resources available (assets) and obligations and debts outstanding (liabilities).

Owner's equity—sometimes called net worth, capital, or proprietorship—represents the residual interest in the entity after the various obligations have been deducted.

In accounting for governmental agencies, the concept of *fund equity* is substituted for owner's equity.

Equity is equal to the assets minus the liabilities of an entity. Claims for amounts due to creditors and employees (such as salaries payable) have legal priority.

A *trial balance* offers proof that a ledger is in balance, but it does not verify that transactions have been correctly analyzed and recorded in the proper accounts. Income and expense items that have been incurred during a fiscal period can be determined by comparing trial balances at the beginning and end of the period.

As further detailed in Chapter 2, the basic financial accounting equation can be expressed as follows:

$$\text{Assets} = \text{Liabilities} + \text{Fund Equity} + \text{Revenue} - \text{Expense}$$

Whereas profit entities seek to generate net income, not-for-profit organizations strive to "break even"—that is, to balance revenues and expenses.

Fund Accounting

The primary mechanisms for the control of governmental activities are provided through *fund accounting*. Eight standard fund designations recommended by the National Council on Governmental Accounting are shown in Exhibit 1-3. These funds are examined in some detail in Chapter 2.

Exhibit 1-3 *Standard Fund Designations*

> *General fund* is used to account for all financial resources, and activities financed by them, that are not accounted for in some special fund.
>
> *Special revenue funds* are used to account for taxes and other revenues (except special assessments) that are legally restricted for a particular purpose.
>
> *Debt service funds* account for the financing of interest and the retirement of principal of general long-term debt.
>
> *Capital project funds* account for those capital projects that are financed either on a "pay-as-you-go" basis or out of capital reserves, grants-in-aid, or transfers from other funds.
>
> *Special assessment funds* are established to account for special assessments levied to finance improvements or services deemed to benefit properties or individuals against which the assessments are levied.
>
> *Enterprise funds* are established to account for the financing of services rendered primarily to the general public for compensation.
>
> *Internal service funds* (working capital funds) are established to account for the financing of activities or services carried on by one department for other departments of the same governmental unit.
>
> *Trust and agency funds* account for cash and other assets held by a governmental unit as trustee or agent (for example, employee pension funds).

Revenues are controlled through the appropriation process, whereby public agencies are authorized to incur financial commitments based on estimated revenues to be collected. Proposed expenditures are controlled through budget line-items. Expenditures for any line-item—such as salaries, supplies and materials, travel, contractual services, or equipment—cannot exceed the dollar amount that has been appropriated or allocated to that particular line-item.

Two self-balancing groups of accounts constitute a second major component of governmental accounting. These account groups are not funds, because they do not contain resources that can be appropriated. These "holding areas" accomplish three important purposes: (1) fixed assets and long-term liabilities are segregated from each other, thereby avoiding the tracking of meaningless data on capital surplus; (2) most funds can be operated on the basis of *current* assets and liabilities; and (3) related accounts are brought together in one accounting compartment for control purposes.

Budgetary Accounting

The emphasis on budgetary control serves as a major distinction between governmental accounting and profit accounting in the private sector. Various types of budgets are found in public organizations. When concerned primarily with financial reporting, public activities are controlled primarily through the *line-item* or *object-of-expenditure budget*.

In most cases, actual expenditures should closely coincide with *budgetary appropriations;* the budget should serve as both a mandate for and a limitation on spending. The adoption of a budget by the legislative body represents the legal authority to spend. Appropriations may be subdivided according to agencies, programs, and classes of expenditures. These subdivisions, known as *allocations,* become the first accounting entries for the new fiscal period. Allocations may be made to specific line-items or object codes, and specific limitations may be imposed as to the deviations permitted within these expenditure categories.

Provision also may be made for an *allotment system* through which allocations are further subdivided into time elements—for example, monthly allotments for personal services (salaries and wages). Allotments are particularly useful where expenditures are contingent on future events, such as the availability of grants or the anticipated opening of a new capital facility. Allotment procedures that require monthly approvals of the governing body, however, can become cumbersome, can generate operational uncertainties, and may result in false economies.

Good budgetary accounting provides for *encumbrances* to record the placement of purchase orders or the letting of contracts as an obligation against the agency's allocation. By reserving a part of the allocation (or appropriation) as an encumbered expenditure, the entity is prevented from overspending the funds available during any fiscal period. In some cases, specific allocations are encumbered and are liquidated on an "as-billed" basis.

The expanded accounting equation for governmental funds can be expressed as follows:

Assets + Estimated Revenue + Expenditures + Encumbrances = Liabilities + Fund Balance + Revenue + Reserves for Encumbrances + Appropriations

This expanded equation is illustrated in considerable detail in the final portion of Chapter 2.

Managerial Accounting

Financial accounting focuses on the accurate and objective recording of fiscal transactions and on the preparation of financial reports largely for external distribution. Although these traditional outputs of financial accounting may be used for certain kinds of internal decisions, many management decisions must be based on other types of information. In recent years, the techniques of *managerial accounting* have been developed and refined to fulfill this informational need.

Managerial accounting involves the formulation of financial estimates of future performance and the subsequent analysis of actual performance in relation to these estimates (*program evaluation* and *performance auditing*). Managerial accounting provides information to support decisions about program costs. Significant features of managerial accounting are summarized in Exhibit 1-4. Chapter 3 is devoted to an exploration of possible applications of managerial accounting techniques in the public sector.

Exhibit 1-4 *Significant Features of Managerial Accounting*

1. Greater emphasis on the generation of information for planning and programming purposes, seeking to establish a balance with the control function of accounting.

2. Performance standards (workload and unit cost data) added to traditional control mechanisms based on legal compliance and fiscal accountability.

3. Experimentation and innovation in the types of information supplied to management at various levels.

4. Greater cost consciousness generated among operating units through the identification of cost and responsibility centers and the use of performance standards.

5. Linkage among management control, program budgeting, and performance auditing facilitated by cost analyses.

Costs can be measured in various ways, depending on the information requirements of management. Whatever the basis of measurement, costs must be weighed against anticipated benefits. The basic concepts of cost, summarized in Exhibit 1-5, are discussed in detail in Chapter 3. Techniques of cost–benefit analysis are examined in Chapter 6.

Exhibit 1-5 *Basic Concepts of Cost*

Cost can be defined as a release of value required to accomplish some goal, objective, or purpose.

Fixed costs do not change in total as the volume of activity increases but become progessively smaller on a per unit basis.

Variable costs are more or less uniform per unit, but their total fluctuates in direct proportion to the total volume of activity.

Costs also may be *semifixed*, described as a step-function, or *semivariable*, whereby both fixed and variable components are included in the related costs.

Overhead usually is defined as all costs other than direct labor and materials that are associated with the production process.

Direct costs represent costs incurred for a specific purpose that are uniquely associated with that purpose.

Indirect costs are costs associated with more than one activity or program that cannot be traced directly to any of the individual activities.

Controllable costs are defined as those costs subject to the influence of a given manager for a given time.

Noncontrollable costs include all costs that do not meet this test of "significant influence" by a given manager.

The first step in controlling costs is to determine how costs function under various conditions. This process—called *cost approximation* or *cost estimation*—involves an attempt to find predictable relationships between a dependent variable st) and an independent variable (some relevant activity), so that costs can be mated over time based on the behavior of the independent variable. Methods for approximating cost functions are discussed in detail in Chapter 3.

Cost Accounting

To determine the full cost of a service or product, costs must be allocated according to their variable, fixed, direct, and indirect components. Cost accounting procedures ensure the proper recording of cost flow by assembling and recording all elements of expense incurred to attain a purpose, to carry out an activity, operation, or program, to complete a unit of work or project, or to do a specific job. Basic terminology used in cost accounting is summarized in Exhibit 1-6.

Exhibit 1-6   *Cost Accounting Terminology*

Absorption or *full costing* considers all the fixed and variable costs associated with the provision of the goods or services in question.

Unit costs are often determined simply by dividing the current budget allocation for a given activity by the number of performance units.

Overhead includes the cost of various items that cannot conveniently be charged directly to those jobs or operations that are benefited.

Responsibility costing assigns to an operating department only those costs that its managers can control or at least influence.

Direct costing considers only the variable or incremental costs of a particular operation.

Job order costing is used by companies in which products are readily identifiable by individual units or batches.

Process costing is most often found in industries characterized by the mass production of like units, which usually pass in continuous fashion through a series of uniform production steps called operations or processes.

Standard costs relate the cost of production to some predetermined indices of operational efficiency to provide a means of cost control through the application of variance analysis.

Average unit costs may be determined by dividing accumulated costs by the quantities produced during the period. Unit costs for various operations can then be multiplied by the number of units transferred to obtain applicable total costs.

Workload measures focus on time-and-effect indices such as number of persons served per hour, yards of dirt moved per day, or more generally, volume of activity per unit of time.

Actual overhead costs incurred by an organizational unit typically are recorded by means of an overhead clearing account and some type of subsidiary record, such as a departmental expense analysis or overhead cost sheet.

Allocated or applied overhead (indirect costs) is distributed through the use of predetermined rates.

Cost accounting encompasses a body of concepts and techniques applicable in both financial accounting and managerial accounting, as suggested by the following schematic:

Financial Accounting

Cost Accounting

Managerial Accounting

Cost accounting seeks to assign accountability to those sectors of an organization in which day-to-day influence can be exercised over the costs in question. Passing the buck is an all-too-pervasive tendency in many large organizations; this tendency can be minimized when responsibility is firmly fixed. Nevertheless, a delicate balance must be maintained between the careful delineation of responsibility, on the one hand, and a too-rigid separation of responsibility, on the other.

The Cost Management Cycle

Effective cost management involves three basic elements: (1) forecasting short- and long-range resource needs based on thorough analyses of costs, (2) formulating sound investment strategies, and (3) managing the cash flow. A basic objective of cost management is to minimize opportunity costs. At the same time, however, a sufficient cash balance must be maintained to meet the day-to-day needs of the organization. The cost management cycle is summarized schematically in Exhibit 1-7.

Management Information

The timely flow of information is vital to effective cost management, as it is to other components of the financial management process. Management information systems often make use of computers to store and retrieve vast amounts of data. Many management problems are relatively short-lived, however, and traditional methods of building large management information systems may result in the delivery of "too much, too late." The fundamental objective should be to enhance the attributes of good decision making by providing *quality of information* rather than *quantity of data.*

Many managerial decisions require explicit attention to nonquantifiable inputs as well as to data that may result from computerized applications. Many excellent systems are based on relatively simple local data-processing operations, tailored to particular user needs. Hardware should be the last matter to be considered when thinking about a management information system. It is first necessary to decide what kind of information is needed—how much, how soon, and how often.

Cost Analysis

No program decision is free of cost, whether or not it leads to the actual commitment of financial resources. An organization is likely to encounter many different

Exhibit 1-7 *The Cost Management Cycle*

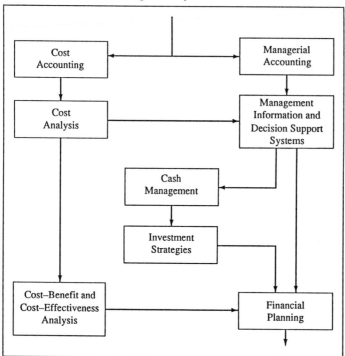

costs in choosing among alternate approaches to achieve its goals and objectives. Costs include not only the expenditure of money but also the consumption of physical resources, the employment of human resources, and the use of time. All of the factors identified in Exhibit 1-8 should be considered throughout the cost management process: (1) in the development of plans and programs; (2) in the preparation of budget requests; and (3) after commitments have been authorized, as programs or projects enter the implementation phase.

Exhibit 1-8 *Factors Influencing Future Costs*

1. Scope and quality of the services or products to be delivered.

2. Volume of activity required to deliver these services or products.

3. Methods, facilities, and organizational structure required to perform these activities.

4. Qualities and types of labor, materials, equipment, and other cost elements required by these programs.

5. Price levels of the various cost elements.

Research and development costs, investment costs, and the costs of operating, maintaining, and replacing programs and facilities are the monetary costs commonly reflected in financial accounts. At times, it may be appropriate to look beyond these monetary costs to what economists call *opportunity costs, associated costs,* and *social costs.* These classes of monetary and economic costs—discussed in some detail in Chapter 6—are summarized in Exhibit 1-9.

Exhibit 1-9 *Monetary and Economic Costs*

Research and development costs incurred explicitly for a given project should be included as a project expense. General R&D costs that benefit more than one project, however, are considered to be *sunk costs.*

Investment costs are incurred beyond the "start-up" phase to obtain future benefits. Frequently in the form of expenditures for construction or capital equipment, investment costs may be a function of the number of units planned (the greater the number, the higher the investment costs).

Sunk costs can become an *inheritable asset* if previous investments can be used to the particular advantage of one alternative over another.

Recurring costs include operating and maintenance costs that vary with both the size and duration of the program; they include salaries and wages, employee benefits, maintenance and repair of equipment, miscellaneous materials and supplies, transfer payments, insurance, and direct overhead costs.

Opportunity costs occur if the commitment of resources to one program preempts the use of these resources elsewhere.

Associated costs are any costs involved in utilizing facilities or services; for example, the costs that users must pay to travel to public recreational facilities, or the cost that government incurs to provide highway access to such facilities.

Social costs may be defined as the subsidies that would have to be paid to compensate persons adversely affected by a project or program for their suffering, or "disbenefits." Rarely is such compensation actually paid (except perhaps when affected individuals enter into litigation and are awarded damages). Social costs often carry emotional overtones and, therefore, may be difficult to evaluate.

As these definitions suggest, some program costs are *fixed*; that is, they are the same regardless of the size or duration of the program. Other costs are *variable* and may change significantly as the scope of the project or program is increased. Because total costs are often difficult to predict, particularly if the project has a relatively long duration, it is important to consider the *marginal,* or incremental, costs of increasing the size or scope of a program.

Forecasting

A forecast is an approximation of what will likely occur in the foreseeable future. The objective of forecasting is not to be 100 percent accurate, but to provide a basis on which to measure differences between actual events and the plan that was adopted to achieve certain objectives. In this way, problems can be identified quickly and the nature and extent of corrective actions clearly defined. Thus, forecasts provide management with a sound basis for action as the future unfolds and events begin to diverge from predictions. The techniques of forecasting, as applied to cash management procedures, are discussed in Chapter 4.

The notion that forecasting is impossible in the public sector is furthermost from the truth. Governmental cash requirements are based on budgeted expenditures, which are finite and known in advance. Revenues are tax-based and, therefore, estimable. Public organizations must develop reliable estimates of their cash flow positions in order to maximize returns on their financial assets.

Forecasts, in turn, form the basis for a *cash budget,* which is used to monitor how much money will be available for investment, when it will become available, and for how long. A cash budget tracks the movement of cash in and out of the treasury. An astute manager can use a cash budget to identify early signs of an impending cash problem and to indicate appropriate steps to avert the problem. The investment strategy of any organization must be strongly correlated with the accuracy and timeliness of its cash budget. Without a cash budget, a manager cannot obtain a long-term view of cash flow patterns and, therefore, cannot effectively plan future cash requirements and optimal investments. Decisions that can affect the flow of cash—in both the short and long term—are summarized in Exhibit 1-10.

Exhibit 1-10   *Decisions Affecting the Flow of Cash*

Operating decisions stem from the policies of the organization—such as the creation or elimination of a service unit or department, increases in the charges for services or in the tax rate in the case of local government, changes in the salaries and fringe benefits extended to staff, and so forth—and result in adjustments in the inflow and outflow of cash.

Capital expenditure decisions that affect the infrastructure of the organization give rise to the outward flow of cash. An organization's infrastructure involves the construction, repair, and maintenance of fixed, physical assets.

Credit decisions involve the length of time an organization takes to make payments to its vendors for goods and services provided, as well as the length of time a client/customer may take to make payment to the organization without penalty.

Investment decisions result in the use of inactive cash to purchase financial assets or the liberation of funds by the sale of such assets.

Financing decisions involve the acquisition of new money by selling bonds, borrowing, or increasing revenues (as by raising user charges, prices, or taxes).

Cash Mobilization

Cash mobilization falls into two areas: (1) acceleration of receivables and (2) control of disbursements. *Receivables* are funds that come into the organization's treasury. *Disbursements* are funds paid out to vendors and others who have provided services to the organization.

The flow and availability of cash can be expedited by collection systems that provide for advance billing and payment on or before receipt of goods and services. Such systems provide for the processing of payments separate from accounting documentation. Successful techniques for the acceleration of collections and deposits are discussed in Chapter 4.

Delaying cash outflows enables an organization to optimize earnings on available funds. Good cash management practices generally dictate that disbursements are made only when due. The timing of disbursements is a very important decision that has implications for the liquidity position of any organization.

Public organizations may find some of these techniques for cash acceleration and disbursement unacceptable. A local government, for example, must evaluate the possible effects on its taxpayers and clients of aggressive collection and disbursement practices. The objectives of cash management must be artfully blended with the need to maintain good public relations with vendors and the community at large.

Adequate credit must be available if any public organization is to survive in the short term. Lines of credit are commitments by banks to make loans available subject to certain mutually agreed-upon conditions and are important hedges against unanticipated contingencies, such as temporary financing needs and short-term cash flow shortages.

Keeping a tight rein on bank balances has become increasingly popular as a principle of cash management. Organizations have come to realize that money not needed to meet operating costs or for compensating balances required by banks should be invested in interest-yielding securities. All receipts—checks, money orders, and cash—should be deposited as soon as possible. Idle funds, such as checks sitting in safes, cash registers, or desk drawers over the weekend or even overnight, could earn income for the organization if invested in short-term securities.

Investments

Local governments and other public organizations often hold short-term securities that can be readily converted into cash either through the market or through maturity. The most attractive instruments that meet these criteria are securities supported by the full faith and credit of the federal government. Other relatively risk-free securities are time deposits, time certificates of deposit, commercial paper, banker's acceptances, and repurchase agreements.

The ideal investment is one that yields a high return at no risk, offers promise of substantial growth, and is instantly convertible into cash if money is needed for other purposes. Unfortunately, this ideal does not exist in reality. Each form of investment has its own special virtues and shortcomings. A fundamental objective of financial management is to maximize yield and minimize risk. Several exogenous considerations influence the yield on any investment, including interest rates, minimum investment requirements, and the maturation dates of investments. Primary determinants in selecting a specific security are: (1) safety/risk, (2) price stability, (3) liquidity and marketability, (4) maturity, and (5) yield. Public officials accord safety the highest priority, followed by liquidity and yield. The money market instruments most widely used by local governments are arrayed against these characteristics in Exhibit 1-11. These investment options are discussed in detail in Chapter 5.

Exhibit 1-11   *Money Market Instruments Used by Local Governments*

Investment Instrument	Safety/ Risk	Stability	Market- ability	Maturities	Yield
United States Treasury bills	No default risk	Most stable investment	Excellent secondary market	3, 6, 9, and 12 months	Modest but safe
Repurchase agreements through commercial banks	Fixed return; principal guaranteed	Penalty for early liquidation	No secondary market	Overnight minimum; 1–21 days common	Negotiated on basis of maturity
Negotiable certificates of deposit	Backed by credit of issuing bank	High liquidity	Active secondary market	Unlimited 30-day minimum	Based on maturity
Nonnego- tiable certifi- cates of deposit	Backed by credit of issuing bank	Penalty for early with- drawal	Limited secondary market	30-day minimum	Based on maturity
Commercial paper from finance companies	Higher default risk	"Buy- back" agreements possible	No secondary market	5–270 days	Higher yields
Banker's acceptances	Backed by specific collateral	Tied to foreign trade activities	Good secondary market	Up to 6 months	Based on discounted value
U.S. agency securities	Low risk	Close sub- stitutes for T-bills	Good secondary market	30 days; 270 days; 1 year	Yield premiums over T-bills

Generally speaking, U.S. Treasury bills (T-bills) are the most stable of all money market instruments, principally because they are backed by the full faith and credit of the federal government. In addition, T-bills are usually issued on a short-term basis, maturing before new market conditions alter the assumptions on which the investment was based.

The concept of liquidity involves managing investments so that cash will be available when needed. Marketability varies among money market instruments, depending not only on the price stability of the instrument but, more importantly, on the availability of a secondary trading market. In managing an investment portfolio, the maturity dates of holdings must be synchronized with the dates on which funds will be required for capital or operating expenses.

In general, securities characterized by low risk, high liquidity, and short maturities will also produce low yields. For a security to provide high yields, one or more of the other relevant criteria must be compromised. Although some localities are beginning to invest in high-grade, high-yield corporate bonds, many local officials still rank yield as the least important of all the criteria in selecting an investment instrument.

Localities have tried to mitigate risk by diversifying investment holdings and avoiding investments in weak financial institutions. Smaller jurisdictions, located in remote areas with minimal amounts of funds available for investments, have minimized risk by joining state-managed investment pools. These pools resemble money market mutual funds in their portfolio composition.

In seeking to provide improved or expanded services, local governments face (1) the need to expand revenues, (2) already heavily burdened taxpayers, and (3) narrow restrictions on their ability to borrow to finance public expenditures. Under these circumstances, public officials can be expected to respond enthusiastically to any source of additional revenue that does not involve increased taxation or additional debt. The net return on investments can be an especially important source of revenue.

The Financial Planning Cycle

Effective financial management requires analytical techniques that can accommodate the risk and uncertainty that are inevitable in future-oriented decisions. Risk is taken no matter what the decision. Even the decision to do nothing involves the risk of lost opportunity. An effective financial manager, whether in the public or private sector, must be aware of how opportunity, innovation, and risk are interrelated and must be willing to take risks appropriate to his or her level of responsibility. The financial planning cycle is summarized schematically in Exhibit 1-12.

Financial Analysis

Various indicators have been developed in the private sector to measure the well-being of a business with respect to liquidity, leverage, profitability, and utilization of assets. The possible application of these indicators in the public sector is the initial topic covered in Chapter 6. Because liquidity is essential for the survival of an organization, it is often given priority in financial analysis. On the other hand, since most short-term assets do not produce significant returns, financial managers must try to keep the liquidity of the organization low, while ensuring that short-term obligations can be met.

A second type of financial analysis examined in Chapter 6 seeks to identify discretionary funds that might be used to implement new programs and strategies.

Exhibit 1-12*   *The Financial Planning Cycle

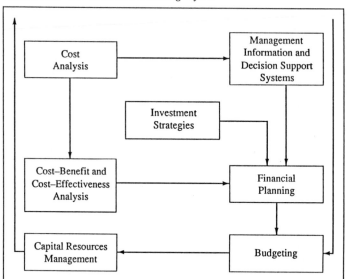

The first step is to determine how current financial resources are allocated between baseline funds and strategic funds. *Baseline funds* support the current, ongoing operations of the organization. They are used to pay current operating expenses, provide adequate working capital, or maintain current plant and equipment. *Strategic funds* are invested in new programs to meet the goals and objectives of the organization. They are used to purchase new assets, such as equipment, facilities, and inventory; to increase working capital; to support direct expenses for research and development, marketing, advertising, and promotions; and in the private sector, for mergers, acquisitions, and market development.

The strategic funds available to an organization can be determined by subtracting baseline funds from total assets (revenue or appropriations). Once estimates have been made, the available strategic funds should be allocated to each program in priority order according to its potential contribution to the achievement of identified goals and objectives.

Computer-Assisted Financial Planning

In recent years, computer-based methods of analysis have become a significant tool for financial planning (see Chapter 6). Interactive software facilitates the use of the computer as an on-line, real-time decision support system (DSS). Computer-assisted methods of financial planning provide a basis for the continuous fine tuning of plans, so as to anticipate things to come and adjust to unanticipated events that may arise as plans are implemented.

Various models can be used to project financial statements, to analyze cash flow requirements, to optimize financial leverage, to compare lease versus purchase options for different depreciation schedules, to evaluate the impact of proposed mergers or acquisitions, and to assess the impact of risk and uncertainty on financial decisions. Many of these models can be consolidated or combined so that managers in different functional areas can use the same financial planning assumptions to design models to meet their particular needs.

Cost–Benefit and Cost–Effectiveness Analysis

Techniques of cost–benefit and cost–effectiveness analysis can be used to determine if a proposed program is justified, to rank alternative approaches relative to a given set of objectives, and to ascertain an optimal course of action to attain these objectives. Such analyses are conducted within an extended time horizon and, insofar as possible, consider both the direct and indirect factors involved in the allocation of resources.

In general, two principal approaches can be taken to cost–benefit analysis. Under a *fixed cost* or *fixed budget* approach, the objective is to maximize benefits for an established level of costs or a predetermined budget allocation. The objective of a *fixed benefits* approach is to ascertain the minimum level of expenditures necessary to achieve some specified level of benefits. The fundamental components of both approaches are outlined in Chapter 6.

The basic components of cost–benefit analysis are outlined in Exhibit 1-13. All relevant components, reflecting the economic effects of the project, must be included for the results of a cost–benefit analysis to be valid and reliable. When important benefits are disregarded because they cannot be measured, the project will appear less efficient than it is. If certain costs are omitted, the project will seem more efficient. The results are misleading in either case.

Exhibit 1-13   Basic Components of Cost–Benefit Analysis

1. Selection of an *objective function* involves the quantification (in dollar terms, to the extent possible) of costs and benefits to facilitate the comparison of alternatives.

2. *Constraints* are the "rules of the game"—that is, the limitations within which a solution must be sought. Frequently, solutions that are otherwise optimal must be discarded because they do not conform to these imposed rules.

3. *Externalities* are side effects, or unintended consequences, that may be beneficial or detrimental. Often difficult to identify and measure, they may be excluded from the analysis initially in order to make the problem statement more manageable.

4. In examining the *time dimensions* of various alternatives, it is necessary to delineate life-cycle costs and benefits. Costs are not incurred on a uniform basis. A time lag often occurs between the initiation of a project and the realization of the first increment of benefits.

5. The *present value* of both costs and benefits must be determined by multiplying each by an appropriate *discount factor.* Benefits that accrue in the present are usually worth more to their recipients than benefits that may occur in the more distant future. Funds that must be invested today cost more than funds invested in the future, since one alternative would be to invest such funds at some rate of return that would increase their value.

Cost–effectiveness analysis can be viewed as an application of the economic concept of marginal analysis. The effectiveness of a program is measured by the extent to which, if implemented, some desired goal or objective will be achieved. The analysis must always move from some base that represents existing capabilities and existing resource commitments. The analytical task usually is to determine the most effective program, where the preferred alternative will either (1) produce the desired level of performance for the minimum cost or (2) achieve the maximum level of effectiveness possible for a given level of cost.

The objective of cost–effectiveness analysis is to determine what additional resources are required to achieve some specified increase in performance capability. Incremental costs, therefore, are the most relevant factors in such analyses. The supporting analyses required under the cost–effectiveness approach are summarized in Exhibit 1-14 and discussed in Chapter 6.

Exhibit 1-14   *Three Supporting Analyses Under the Cost–Effectiveness Approach*

1. *Cost–goal studies* are concerned with the identification of feasible levels of achievement. Cost curves are developed for each program alternative, approximating the sensitivity of costs (inputs) to changes in the desired level of achievement (outputs). Outputs are usually represented by nonmonetary indices, or *measures of effectiveness.*

2. *Cost–effectiveness comparisons* assist in the identification of the most effective program alternative by defining the *optimum envelope* formed by the cost curves. A desired level of effectiveness may be specified and cost minimized for that effectiveness level. Or effectiveness may be maximized for some level of resource allocation.

3. *Cost–constraint assessments* determine the cost of not adopting the most effective programs available. The impact of such factors as legal constraints, limits in technical capacity, employee rights, union rules, and so forth, are examined by comparing the cost of programs that might be adopted if these constraints were not present.

Cost–benefit and cost–effectiveness analysis can be applied at pivotal points in the evaluation of resource commitments. In the planning stage, such analyses may be undertaken on the basis of *anticipated* costs and benefits. After a program or project has been implemented and shown to have a significant impact, cost–benefit and cost–effectiveness analyses may be applied to assess whether the costs of the program can be justified by the magnitude of net outcomes. Such *after-the-fact* analyses should be based on detailed studies of available empirical data.

Budgeting

A budget traditionally has been used as a control mechanism to ensure financial integrity, accountability, and legal compliance. Budgets will inevitably be affected by past commitments, established standards of service, existing organizational structures, and current methods of operation. The basic differences among various budget formats are summarized in Exhibit 1-15. Approaches to public budgeting are examined in Chapter 7.

Exhibit 1-15 *Basic Differences Among Budget Orientations*

Characteristic	Objects of Expenditure	Performance Budget	Service Levels	Program Budget
Control responsibility	Central	Operating	Operating	Operating
Management responsibility	Dispersed	Central	Dispersed	Supervisory
Planning responsibility	Dispersed	Dispersed	Central	Central
Role of budget agency	Fiduciary	Efficiency	Effectiveness	Policy
Decision/ information flow	Bottom-up Aggregative	Bottom-up Aggregative	Bottom-up Aggregative	Top-down Disaggregative
Information focus	Objects	Activities	Service delivery	Programs
Decision basis	Incremental	Incremental	Programs	Programs
Key budget stage	Execution	Preparation	Priority rankings	Analysis
Personnel skills	Accounting	Administrative	Analysis	Economics

The object-of-expenditure budget has two distinct advantages: (1) accountability—an object classification establishes a pattern of accounts that can be documented, controlled, and audited; and (2) management control—control mechanisms for enforcing allocation and allotment limits are supplied through such devices as line-item allocations, periodic budget reports, and the independent audit at the end of the fiscal year. Since personnel requirements are closely linked with other budgetary requirements, the management of positions can be used to control the whole budget. The governing body also may insert control conditions on the use of specific funds and/or may require prior approval for proposed transfers between major budget items.

Although seldom practiced today in its pure form, many characteristics of *performance budgeting* have survived. Work-cost data are reduced to discrete, measurable units to determine the performance efficiency of prescribed activities. Performance measures—workload and unit cost measures—and the concept of levels of service have been incorporated into many contemporary financial management applications. The focus on cost-efficiency—a hallmark of performance budgeting—has its parallel emphasis in current budget and accounting formats. Cost accounting systems are also being used more widely in government and nonprofit organizations.

Service level analysis seeks to identify *essential* service levels so that a jurisdiction can maintain and deliver—and be held accountable for—such services in a more efficient and effective manner. Labeling a service as "essential" is not the same as defining its supporting expenditures as "fixed." Essential services can be provided more efficiently (at less cost) or more effectively (with greater benefits). The basic components of service level analysis are summarized in Exhibit 1-16. This analytical approach is applicable to all programs in which some discretion can be exercised as to the course of action pursued.

Exhibit 1-16   Basic Components of Service Level Analysis

1. *Identification of budget units:* designation of the basic building blocks within the organizational structure responsible for decision making; examination of goals and objectives, current purposes and methods of operation, ways of measuring performance and effectiveness, and relations with other budget units.

2. *Decision package analysis:* identification of alternative ways of providing essential services and justification of various levels of service at which each budget unit might operate. A decision package represents a discrete set of services, activities, and resources applicable to the performance of a given operation or achievement of a program goal.

3. *Priority ranking and evaluation:* the arrangement of levels of service in descending order of importance and the determination of a funding cutoff point. Ranking establishes an order or priority for each service level.

Program budgeting combines a planning framework with the basic functions of management and control. Under this approach, a *program* is a distinct organization of resources directed toward a specific objective: (a) eliminating, containing, or preventing a problem; (b) creating, improving, or maintaining conditions affecting the organization or its clientele; or (c) supporting or controlling other identifiable programs. Results to be accomplished within a specific time period should be specified. Program objectives must be consistent with the resources available (or anticipated).

The formulation of precise, qualitative statements of objectives is often difficult. The tendency is to describe what the organization does, instead of addressing the question of why these activities are appropriate to achieve the long-range goals of the organization. The "output" of many organizational activities may be difficult to define and measure. Therefore, secondary measures often must be used to test alternative approaches and evaluate costs.

Capital Facilities Planning and Programming

Resource commitments may involve relatively short-term decisions. If a particular public program does not achieve the anticipated results, basic changes can be made, or the activity can be abandoned altogether. Decisions affecting capital facilities are not so easily altered or adjusted, however. Once resources have been committed, the location of an elementary school or firehouse, for example, can be changed only at considerable public expense.

The term *capital facility* refers to any project having a long life (usually a minimum of 15 to 20 years), involving a relatively large investment of resources of a nonrecurring nature, and yielding a fixed asset for the community or organization. As a consequence of their relatively long life and substantial commitment of resources, capital facilities require a comprehensive approach in their planning, financing, programming, and debt administration.

Capital facilities planning should be built upon a continuous assessment of community/client preferences, demographic estimates, economic forecasts, and projections of development expectations. Demographic projections and other vital statistics should be analyzed to determine changes in client groups. Economic forecasts are an important factor in the preparation of demographic projections, since assumptions concerning population growth or decline are correlated with expected economic activities. Information concerning future economic conditions is also essential in determining the financial capacity of a community to pay for capital improvements.

In all likelihood, for any given budget period, the overall cost of capital projects proposed will exceed the available financial resources. Therefore, proposed projects must be evaluated and ranked in some manner. Preferably, each proposal should be rated against an explicit set of evaluation criteria.

Approaches to the assignment of priorities can be divided into two classes: (1) those that stress intangible values and (2) those that undertake to quantify various criteria to develop a numerical scoring system. Each approach has its merits and shortcomings, and to the extent possible, elements from each should be incorporated into a sound priority system. Procedures for capital facilities planning and criteria for the evaluation of capital projects are examined in detail in Chapter 8.

When all proposed projects have been examined and analyzed, a composite capital improvements program (CIP) should be prepared, usually spanning a five- to six-year period. Governments have found with experience that six years is a convenient period for the detail programming of capital expenditures. This time frame provides sufficient lead time for the design and other preliminary work required by such projects. Projects included in the CIP should be arrayed according to their priority ranking.

Debt Financing and Administration

Capital facilities can be financed in a number of ways, as summarized in Exhibit 1-17. These financing methods must be evaluated in terms of overall fiscal policies and in light of the particular capital facility involved. A sound long-range revenue program seeks to develop an appropriate mix among these three methods of financing capital improvements.

"Pay-as-you-go" financing encourages a community or organization to "live within its income." It minimizes premature commitment of funds and conserves the capacity to borrow for times of emergency when ample credit may be vital. The pay-as-you-go approach also avoids the added cost of interest payments, making it less costly than borrowing.

Exhibit 1-17 Methods for Financing Capital Facilities

Financing capital projects from current revenues—on a "pay-as-you-go" basis—is more feasible when capital expenditures are recurrent, either as to purpose or as to amount, as, for example, the paving of streets or the acquisition of neighborhood recreation areas. It may be easier to finance required public improvements out of current taxes once the infrastructure of the community has been established.

In financing capital facilities through a *reserve fund* (sometimes called a capital reserve), a portion of current revenue is invested each year in order to accumulate sufficient funds to initiate some particular project in the future.

Long-term borrowing may be appropriate under the following conditions: (1) where the project will not require replacement for many years, such as a major health facility or sewage disposal plant; (2) where the project can be financed by service charges to pay off revenue bonds; (3) where needs are urgent for public health, safety, or other emergency reasons; (4) where special assessment bonds are the only feasible means of financing improvements; (5) where intergovernmental revenues may be available to guarantee the security of the bonds; and (6) for financing projects in areas of rapid expansion, where the demands on municipal resources are comparatively large and unforeseen.

On the other hand, the burden of financing a facility may have to be spread over the life of the improvement to achieve *user-benefit equity.* The general assumption is that future economic and population growth will offset the increased liability and make the payment of debt service (principal and interest) more feasible. A sound borrowing policy is one that seeks to conserve rather than exhaust credit. The ability to borrow when necessary on the most favorable market terms is an objective that applies to governments just as it does to business and industry.

A *bond* is a promissory note ensuring that the lender will receive (1) periodic payments of interest (at some predetermined rate) and (2) at the due date, repayment of the original sum invested. The various types of municipal bonds, summarized in Exhibit 1-18, are examined in detail in Chapter 9. Interest earned on municipal bonds is exempt from federal taxes, and usually from state taxes in the state in which the bond is issued. As a consequence, municipal bonds carry lower interest rates than taxable corporate bonds.

Debt administration refers to the management of funds for the construction/acquisition of fixed assets. Capital project funds account for the resources used to build or buy specific capital facilities. These resources come from the issuance of bonds or other long-term obligations, from intergovernmental grants, or from transfers from other funds within the governmental unit. Upon completion of the project, the capital project fund is terminated, and the accounting results are transferred to other funds or account groups—the debt service fund and the general long-term debt and fixed assets accounting groups.

Debt service funds account for (1) the accumulation of resources from which the principal and interest on general long-term debt is paid and (2) the investment and expenditure of those resources. A sinking fund spreads the cost of repayment over the life of the bond issue to avoid large, irregular demands on the organization's

Exhibit 1-18 *Categories of Municipal Bonds*

> *General obligation bonds* are backed by the "full faith, credit, and taxing power" of the issuing government.
>
> *Revenue bonds* are backed by a pledge of revenues to be generated by the facility that is being financed.

Municipal bonds can also be classified into two general types according to the method of redemption.

Term bonds become due in a lump sum at the end of the term of the loan; all bonds in the issue reach maturity and must be paid off at the same time. The lump sum principal payment is met by making annual payments to a *sinking fund*.

Serial bonds are retired by annual installments directly from tax revenues or, in the case of revenue bonds, from earned income. Serial bonds have simpler retirement requirements and offer greater flexibility in marketing and in arranging the debt structure of the community.

- With *annuity serials*, the debt service payment is approximately the same each year (as with a home mortgage). The portion of the annual payment that covers interest is higher in the early years of the issue but declines as payments toward principal are made (that is, as the outstanding principal is retired).

- *Straight serial bonds* require annual payments of principal of approximately equal amounts. Interest payments are large in the early years and decline gradually as the bonds approach maturity.

annual budget. Sinking fund requirements should be recomputed on an annual basis. Should a surplus in excess of actuarial requirements develop, it may be possible to lower future requirements.

Maintaining accurate debt records is vital to short-term and long-term fiscal operations. Such records should include auditable ledgers as to the identity, purpose, and amount of debt commitments associated with capital projects and the principal and interest payments made. These records are used (1) to determine principal and interest requirements accurately, (2) to establish the financial capacity to meet future capital construction requirements, and (3) to plan the retirement schedule for any new borrowing. Accurate reporting develops confidence on the part of investors and the general public as to the management of the financial affairs of the jurisdiction or public organization. The relatively small investment of time and expense in preparing such reports may be repaid many times over through lower interest rates.

Maxwell's Demon

Many early contributors to the theory of complex organizations were influenced by the second law of thermodynamics, as formulated by William Thomson (Lord Kelvin). According to this basic principle of physics, the general trend of all physical events is toward an irreversible state of maximum disorder, with a leveling down of differences among component elements. Eventually, the process reaches a final state of equilibrium. Early writers postulated that conditions evident in the emerging urban society following the industrial revolution were the first stages of social degradation. According to these theorists, as society became more urbanized and more complex, differences in social characteristics would decline, and disorder would increase.

In all irreversible processes, the number of possible arrangements of elements—the randomness of the system—continually increases, and therefore, order is continually destroyed. This can be illustrated through the process of shuffling a deck of cards. If, at the beginning, the cards are in an orderly arrangement, the shuffling will tend to make the arrangement disorderly. If the shuffling is begun with a disorderly arrangement, it is very unlikely that, through shuffling, the cards will come into an orderly one. This is because there are many more "disorderly" than orderly arrangements, and therefore, a disorderly state is more probable.

James Clerk Maxwell, a contemporary of Lord Kelvin, suggested a very clever way to overcome the general trend toward maximum disorder. Maxwell envisioned a small but very intelligent creature—a demon—serving as "gatekeeper" between two containers of gas at equal temperature and pressure. By carefully opening and closing the gate, the demon could permit faster-moving molecules to pass into one container, while slower molecules remained in the other. Over time, the available energy in the system, as measured by the temperature differential between the two containers, would be increased without adding any new energy to the system (other than Maxwell's demon). Thus the second law of thermodynamics would be circumvented.

Maxwell's demon, of course, is an allegory for anything that contributes order to a disorganized or chaotic situation. Contemporary systems theory suggests that order can be restored to random arrangements of elements through feedback and adaptation. A complex system (community or organization) can react to its environment in ways that are favorable to its continued existence, and in so doing, it can avoid the continual increase of disorder. In the process, the system often develops toward states of higher order, heterogeneity, and organization.

Contemporary financial management activities are both *information-producing* and *information-demanding*. Important managerial feedback—soundings, scannings, and evaluations of changing conditions resulting from previous program decisions and actions—must be available to facilitate timely and effective decision making. Financial management procedures generate information that feeds forward to provide a basis for more informed decisions and actions over a range of time periods, locations, and perspectives. "Feedforward" information emerges from projections and forecasts; goals, objectives, and targets to be achieved; program analyses and evaluations; and the projection of outcomes and impacts of alternative programs.

In the context of financial management, the concept of Maxwell's demon refers to a positive genius, designed to address a host of problems within an organization. The objective is to satisfy the increasingly voracious appetite for management information applicable to strategic decisions, while reducing the cost of management in relation to total organizational costs. Maxwell's demon can also become a resource-demanding devil, an organizational black hole that can absorb considerable energy with little apparent payoff. The careful design and implementation of a financial management system that includes the elements outlined in this book can contribute significantly toward the demon-genius—or at least help avoid the demon-devil.

CHAPTER 2

Accounting Systems

An effective accounting system should provide management information for three broad purposes: (1) *external reporting* to various constituencies or client groups (for example, stockholders, elected officials, regulatory bodies, and the general public); (2) *internal reporting* for use in planning and controlling routine operations; and (3) assisting in the formulation of *policies and long-range plans.* This chapter will examine two basic approaches to accounting—fund accounting and budgetary accounting—that have served the first two of these broad purposes reasonably well as applied to governmental and other not-for-profit organizations. These accounting systems, however, provide relatively little direct assistance in the formulation of policies and plans. The principles and practices of managerial accounting, discussed in detail in Chapter 3, more fully address this third objective.

Basic Accounting Terminology

An accounting system measures and records financial data and converts those data to information that is then analyzed, interpreted, and reported to various groups both within and outside the organization. The intent of this chapter is not to prepare managers to carry out the complex responsibilities of accountants, but rather to provide a basic vocabulary and appreciation for the role of accounting in the financial management process.[1]

The Accounting Entity

One of the basic assumptions in providing accounting information to both internal and external users is that the information comes from a particular accounting entity. In both business and nonbusiness applications, the accounting entity often is related to the legal organization. The identity of the legal organization—the corporation, partnership, or individual proprietorship—is more clearly recognized in the private sector than in government and other nonbusiness situations. The city, for example, is not the appropriate accounting entity for financial reporting purposes. Neither is a college or university, hospital, health or welfare agency, labor union, or voluntary organization considered an accounting entity. Within such public organizations, other entities—called *funds*—are established for the purposes of maintaining accounting records and preparing financial statements.

Transactions are made between funds. Separate financial statements are prepared for each of the major funds. Often, combined statements of funds with similar purposes are distributed.

A sound accounting system for governmental and other not-for-profit organizations generally is built around four central components:

1. *Funds*—fiscal and accounting entities with self-balancing sets of accounts, together with all related liabilities, obligations, reserves, and equities.
2. Major nonfund, self-balancing groups of accounts that focus on *general fixed assets* and *general long-term debt*.
3. Unified records systems consisting of a *general ledger* that contains summary accounts (posted as totals), with supporting details maintained in *subsidiary ledgers*.
4. Basic *accounting classifications* that record revenues by fund and source and expenditures by fund, organizational unit, function, activity, character, and/or object.

The funds and account groups most commonly found in public organizations are summarized in Exhibit 2-1.

Financial Statements

The three most important financial statements are: (1) income statement, (2) balance sheet, and (3) statement of changes in financial position.

An *income statement* reflects the profit performance of an entity for some specific period of time. *Revenue* represents an inflow of money or other representations of value in return for selling goods or providing some type of service. *Expense* represents an outflow of resources, or the incurring of obligations, for goods and services required to generate revenues. A profit, or net income, is earned when revenue exceeds expense over some period of time.

A *balance sheet* shows the financial position of an entity at a particular time—that is, the amount of resources available (assets) and obligations and debts outstanding (liabilities). A simple example of a balance sheet for a university copy center is shown in Exhibit 2-2.

Owner's equity is an important concept in commercial accounting and is sometimes called net worth, capital, or proprietorship. In accounting for governmental agencies, the concept of *fund equity* is substituted for owner's equity. Equity is always equal to the entity's assets minus its liabilities. In effect, equity represents a residual interest of the fund in its assets. Claims for amounts due to creditors and employees (such as salaries payable) have legal priority. Equity comes from two sources: (1) contributed amounts resulting from investments made in the entity and (2) earnings that have been retained in the business or entity.

Exhibit 2-1 *Standard Funds and Account Groups*

Proprietary Funds

are used to account for the financing of services rendered primarily to the general public for compensation (such as the operation of a public utility).

Governmental Funds

General funds are used to account for all financial resources, and activities financed by them, that are not accounted for in some special fund. Among the revenues normally included are property taxes, licenses, fees, permits, penalties, and fines. Expenditures are authorized in the general budget.

Special revenue funds are used to account for taxes and other revenues (except special assessments) that are legally restricted for a particular purpose (such as schools, street improvements, parks).

Debt service funds are used to account for the financing of interest and the retirement of principal of general long-term debt.

Capital project funds are used to account for major improvements financed either on a "pay-as-you-go" basis or out of capital reserves, grants-in-aid, or transfers from other funds. Such funds are limited to an accounting of receipts and expenditures on capital projects paid out of current revenues.

Special assessment funds are used to account for the financing of improvements or services deemed to benefit properties against which special assessments are levied.

Fiduciary Funds

are used to account for assets held by a governmental unit as an agent or trustee for other governmental units, other funds, private organizations, or individuals (for example, employee pension funds).

Account Groups

General fixed assets account group records all fixed assets—long-term resources of the governmental unit—acquired through governmental funds.

Long-term debt account group records general long-term liabilities assumed by the governmental unit involving the commitment of governmental funds (except those associated with special assessment funds).

The *statement of changes in financial position* has come into general use because of the need for information concerning the financing and investing activities of an entity. This statement provides information about inflows and outflows of financial resources, including:

Sources
    Operations (revenue minus expenses)
    Sales of equipment used in operations
    Long-term loans
    Additional investment by the governing group

Uses
    Distribution of income
    Purchase of equipment
    Payment of loans

Such statements can be derived from analyses of the income statement and balance sheet (see Exhibit 2-3).

Exhibit 2-2   *University Copy Center Balance Sheet as of December 1, 1985*

Assets	
Cash	$20,000
Supplies	5,000
Space rental	6,000
Equipment	30,000
Total assets	$61,000
Liabilities	
Accounts payable	$10,000
Fund equity	51,000
Total liabilities and equity	$61,000

Exhibit 2-3   *Westview Golf Club Statement of Changes in Financial Position for the Year Ended December 31, 1985*

Cash generated		
From operations		
Cash revenue	$60,000	
Less: Cash expenses	44,000	
		$16,000
From other sources		
Sales of operating equipment	$14,000	
Sale of bonds	34,000	
		48,000
Total cash generated		$64,000
Cash used		
Purchase of building	$40,000	
Repayments of notes	16,000	
		$56,000
Increase in cash during year		$ 8,000

Basic Accounting Equation

The basic accounting equation can be expressed as follows:

$$\text{Assets} = \text{Liabilities} + \text{Fund Equity} + \text{Revenue} - \text{Expense}$$

Profit entities seek to generate net income—that is, to maximize the difference between revenues and expenses. Not-for-profit organizations strive to "break even" —that is, to balance revenues and expenses.

The logic for the debit and credit entries of accounting transactions can be derived from this equation, as follows:

Debits	Credits
Increases in: Assets Expenses	Decreases in: Assets Expenses
Decreases in: Liabilities Fund equity Revenue	Increases in: Liabilities Fund equity Revenue

The so-called *double-entry* or *T-form* was developed to provide a standardized method for recording increases and decreases in components of the accounting equation. A T-form account has a *debit* (or increase) side and a *credit* (or decrease) side. Since debits must equal credits, the effect on the accounting system is described in terms of double-entry mechanics.

To illustrate the double-entry mechanisms of the accounting equation, consider the following scenario. The state decides to establish an agency to make travel arrangements for state personnel. At the beginning of the fiscal year, $70,000 is allocated to the agency from the state budget. The agency purchases equipment costing $40,000 and leases office space, paying $2,400 in advance on the lease. Stationery and other forms are purchased from the state print shop at a cost of $1,000. These charges are recorded on an interdepartmental service form (are billed).

In recording these transactions, the initial budget allocation of $70,000 would be decreased (credited) by $40,000 for the equipment purchase and $2,400 for the prepaid rent. This would leave the "cash position" of the agency at $27,600. However, equivalent entries would record (debit) assets of $40,000 for equipment and $2,400 for the space rented. The forms and stationery would also represent an asset worth $1,000, offset by a liability in accounts payable of $1,000.

In the first month, the agency receives $10,000 in revenue for tickets sold and pays out $8,000 in expenses for personnel and in payments to airlines and other service providers. The $10,000 in revenue is recorded as a debit under assets, and the $8,000 is shown as a credit, increasing the cash position to $29,600. To bring the accounting equation into equilibrium, fund equity is recorded as $70,000 for the initial budget allocation, plus $10,000 for the revenue, minus $8,000 for the expenses (for a total of $72,000). Thus, the assets of the agency at the end of the first month of operation are $73,000, balanced by a like amount in liabilities and equities, as follows:

$$\text{Assets} = \$29,600 + \$2,400 + \$1,000 + \$40,000 = \$73,000$$
$$\text{Liabilities and Equities} = \$1,000 + \$72,000 = \$73,000$$

Each accounting transaction is recorded in a *general journal,* including the date of the transaction, the accounts to be debited and credited, an explanation of the transaction, the account number, and the financial effect on the accounts involved. Special journals are often established to separate functions and responsibilities and to improve management controls.

Trial Balances

Trial balances provide proof that ledgers are in balance. A trial balance does not verify that transactions have been correctly analyzed and recorded in the proper accounts, however. By comparing trial balances at the beginning and ending of a fiscal period (such as each month), it is possible to determine income and expense items that have been incurred during that period. A trial balance and year-end balance sheet for a water authority fund are shown in Exhibits 2-4 and 2-5.

Exhibit 2-4 *Water Authority Fund Trial Balance, June 30, 1986*

Cash	$ 1,045	
Accounts receivable	10,100	
Parts inventory	2,375	
Prepaid insurance	3,200	
Land	4,000	
Building	48,000	
Equipment	12,000	
Accumulated depreciation (building)		$ 400
Accumulated depreciation (equipment)		320
Accounts payable		3,795
Customer deposits		1,600
Contributed capital		50,000
Retained earnings		18,025
Operating revenue		10,250
Energy expense	680	
Truck expense	540	
Office expense	600	
Accounting expense	250	
Salary expense	1,600	
Totals	$84,390	$84,390

It may be noted that there is a difference of $5,500 between the trial balance and the year-end balance sheet. The value of the inventory was decreased by $910 in the year-end balance sheet to account for repair parts withdrawn and used in

Exhibit 2-5 *Water Authority Fund Balance Sheet, June 30, 1986*

Current Assets		
Cash	$ 1,045	
Accounts receivable	10,100	
Parts inventory	1,465	
Prepaid insurance	3,200	
Total Current Assets		$15,810
Property, Plant, and Equipment		
Land	$ 4,000	
Building	48,000	
Equipment	12,000	
	$64,000	
Less: Depreciation	$ 920	
Total Property, Plant, and Equipment		$63,080
Total Assets		$78,890
Liabilities		
Accounts payable	$ 3,795	
Customer deposits	1,600	
Total Current Liabilities		$ 5,395
Fund Equity		
Contributed capital	$50,000	
Retained earnings	23,495	
Total Equity		$73,495
Total Liabilities and Equity		$78,890

enterprise activities. This amount should be charged as an expense. Thus, expenses totaled $4,580 (that is, the $3,670 in expenses shown in the trial balance plus the $910 for the reduction of inventory). These expenses were subtracted from operating revenue, leaving a balance of $5,670. This balance, in turn, is added to the $18,025 in retained earnings shown in the trial balance. The other adjustment reflected an additional $200 in accumulated depreciation not recorded in the trial balance. Thus, the retained earnings on June 30 totaled $23,495 ($18,025 + $5,670 − $200), as reflected in the balance sheet.

Bases for Accounting

Several bases are used in accounting. On the revenue side, two bases are possible: cash and accrued revenue. On the commitment (outflow) side, four bases are used: cash, obligations, accrued expenditure, and accrued cost.

On a *strict cash basis,* revenues are recorded only when they are actually received, and expenditures are recorded when payments are made (as a cash disbursement). On a *strict accrual basis,* revenues are recorded as soon as the amounts are levied, billed, or earned, regardless of the fiscal period in which they are collected; expenditures are recorded (a) when goods are received or services are performed, (b) when a liability is incurred, or (c) when an invoice is received.

Various combinations are possible. A municipality may record revenues on a cash basis but accrue current expenditures and incurred obligations. On a *modified accrual basis,* revenues are recorded as received in cash, except for revenues susceptible to accrual (such as commitments from intergovernmental transfers); expenditures are recorded on an accrual basis, except for disbursements for inventory-type items, prepaid expenses, and long-term debt. On a *modified cost basis,* property taxes and other receivables are placed on the books for control purposes when they are levied but not accounted for as revenue until actually collected.

An example may help to clarify the distinctions among the various bases of accounting. The general fund of a city has taxes receivable during the year of $15 million, of which $12.5 million have been collected. During the year, the following transactions took place:

Expenditures	Paid	Owed	Total
Salaries and wages	$ 7,500,000	$ 200,000	$ 7,700,000
Equipment acquisition	3,000,000	500,000	3,500,000
Contractual services	1,000,000		1,000,000
Materials and supplies	1,000,000	500,000	1,500,000
Totals	$12,500,000	$1,200,000	$13,700,000

These transactions would be recorded as follows:

Cash Basis		Modified Accrual Basis	
Receipts	$12,500,000	Revenue	$15,000,000
Expenditures			
Salaries	$ 7,500,000		$ 7,700,000
Equipment	3,000,000		3,500,000
Contractual services	1,000,000		1,000,000
Materials	1,000,000		1,500,000
Total Expenditures	$12,500,000		$13,700,000
		Excess of revenue	
Net difference	$ 0	over expenditures	$ 1,300,000

Accounting becomes more refined as procedures shift in the following sequence: cash basis, modified cash basis, modified accrual basis, accrued expenditure basis, and finally, accrued cost basis. Reliable unit-cost data cannot be developed on a cash basis. Most governments have adopted a system under which obligations are recorded at the time they are incurred (as encumbrances).

If accounts are closed out and funds revert at the end of the fiscal year (on a cash basis), the agency may be tempted to overobligate or overspend to ensure that no monies are "left on the table." This can have significant consequences, however, if encumbrances are added to the system. Suppose a piece of equipment is ordered for $10,000 near the end of the fiscal year. The $10,000 is encumbered and cannot be spent for other commitments. The equipment is not delivered, and the encumbered funds revert. A new encumbrance is processed in the next fiscal year, and in effect, the agency has paid for the equipment twice. This problem is minimized under an accrued cost basis of accounting. Unspent funds are carried over to the next fiscal period, as are encumbered obligations.

Fund Accounting

Accounting and control of governmental activities are carried out through fund accounting. Revenue is controlled through the appropriation process, and proposed expenditures are controlled through a line-item budget. Expenditures for any line-item—such as salaries, supplies and materials, travel, contractual services, or equipment—cannot exceed the dollar amount that has been appropriated or allocated to that particular line-item. Usually, all revenue in each fund entity is expended during the fiscal period; that is, there is no surplus income or earnings. One of the basic principles of fund accounting is that financial statements must compare actual revenue and expenditures with those estimated in the budget.

Fund Designations

The National Council on Governmental Accounting (NCGA) has defined a fund as

> a fiscal and accounting entity with a self-balancing set of accounts recording cash and other financial resources, together with all related liabilities and residual equities or balances, and changes therein, which are segregated for the purpose of carrying on specific activities or attaining certain objectives in accordance with special regulations, restrictions or limitations.[2]

The eight standard fund designations recommended by the NCGA were identified in Exhibit 2-1.

Budgetary and accounting requirements tend to vary widely among these funds. However, these requirements can be summarized by considering four general groupings of funds:

1. Funds concerned with *current operations* (general funds, special revenue funds, debt service funds, and certain expendable trust funds) emphasize appropriated or allocated monies that are currently expendable. Fixed assets and long-term liabilities are excluded from the balance sheets of these funds. A modified accrual or encumbrance basis of accounting is often used in conjunction with these funds to record liabilities (expenditures) as they are incurred. Most types of revenue are not recorded, however, until they are received in cash. The result is a rather conservative statement of the balance currently available for approved activities.

2. Capital project funds and special assessment funds are concerned with *capital spending*. Budgetary restrictions normally are included in the ordinances that create these funds. As a consequence, these funds typically are not included in the annual appropriation ordinance.

3. *Commercial-type funds* record activities that are expected to earn a profit, or at least recover costs, and include proprietary or enterprise funds, internal service funds, and trust funds concerned with invested principal that earns income. These funds have complete balance sheets that include both fixed assets and long-term liabilities. Revenue and expenditures are recorded on an accrual basis. Budgets for these funds serve as guidelines for operations rather than as legal limits on expenditures.

4. *Custodial funds* are self-balancing liability accounts that record assets held for others. In some states, for example, certain fines collected by municipal courts are paid over to the school district. A custodial fund would account for these fines during the interval between collection and their transfer to the school district. Budgetary controls are unnecessary for such funds.

Two self-balancing groups of accounts—dealing with *general long-term debt* and *general fixed assets*—constitute a second major component of governmental accounting. They are not funds because they do not contain resources that can be appropriated. They are "holding areas" that accomplish three important purposes: (1) to segregate fixed assets and long-term liabilities from each other, thereby avoiding meaningless data on capital surplus; (2) to permit most funds to be operated on the basis of current assets and liabilities only; and (3) to bring together in one accounting compartment related accounts for control purposes.

The use of nonfund accounts can be illustrated by tracing the transactions that occur when a general obligation bond matures. The bond is recorded initially as part of the general long-term debt account. At maturity, the liability (in terms of a principal payment) becomes a current obligation of a debt service fund. Therefore, it is removed from long-term debt, and the total long-term debt is reduced accordingly. When the capital construction project funded by the bond issue is completed, it is recorded as a capital asset in the general fixed assets account. Should this asset subsequently be sold, the revenues would be recorded in the general fund, and the total general fixed assets of the government entity would be reduced accordingly.

Basic accounting classifications (or a chart of accounts) provide a uniform basis for cross-referencing both revenue and expenditures. Revenue is classified by fund and by source, and sometimes by collecting agency. Expenditure classifications are more elaborate, often providing details by fund, organizational unit, function, program, activity, character, and object (see Exhibit 2-6). Standard accounting classifications, promulgated by the NCGA, have helped bring about a degree of uniformity among state and local governments in the use of terminology and in account titles.

Illustrative Fund Accounting Transactions

Fund accounting has a built-in control through the use of budgetary transactions along with actual transactions. The accounting system will show when any expenditure category (line-item or object code) is about to exceed the amount appropriated or allocated for that purpose. When an order is placed for goods or services, for example, a legal commitment is made. By encumbering the funds necessary to meet

Exhibit 2-6 *Budget and Accounting Classifications*

Function	Broad classification of government responsibilities, such as public safety, health, education, welfare, recreation, and general government.
Program or Subprogram Classification	Used in program budgeting to group similar activities, often involving several organizational units, for purposes of analysis and evaluation, as well as the allocation of funds.
Activity Classification	Expenditure data organized according to the responsibilities of governmental units. The Police Department, for example, is responsible for crime investigation, traffic control, crowd control, and so forth.
Organizational Unit	Designated units or subunits within the organization, such as Police Department or Department of Parks and Recreation, authorized to hire personnel and make expenditures.
Character of Expenditure	Aggregates of expenditures that have certain specific qualities, such as current operating expenditures, capital expenditures, and debt service. Current operating expenditures represent the aggregate of personal services, contractual services, materials and supplies, and some types of equipment expenditures.
Object of Expenditure	Lowest level of classification. Objects of expenditure are the particular types of goods bought or services received for the expenditures. Examples are personal services (salaries, wages, and related employee benefits), contractual services, materials and supplies, equipment, property improvements, and debt service.

that commitment when the order is placed, the organizational unit will be assured that the allocation will not be overspent when the time comes to pay for the goods or services. Otherwise, there may not be any funds available to pay for the ordered goods when they arrive, along with an invoice.

Suppose the Public Works Department has placed an order for materials and supplies at an estimated cost of $22,000. The entry to encumber the funds for this order would be as follows:

	Debit	*Credit*
Encumbrance	$22,000	
Reserve for encumbrance		$22,000

The encumbrance account is debited and the reserve for encumbrances account is credited for the estimated cost. The amount of the encumbrance is subtracted from the department's budget allocation (usually in a subsidiary ledger), leaving the balance available for expenditure.

When materials and supplies are shipped, an invoice in the amount of $22,500 is received. The two above accounts are reversed at the estimated cost: the reserve for encumbrances account is debited, and the encumbrance account is credited. Then the actual amount of the order is placed in the expenditure and liability accounts, as follows:

	Debit	Credit
Expenditures	$22,500	
Accounts payable		$22,500

For all practical purposes, the encumbrance amount is added back to the budget allocation, and the actual amount is subtracted from it. In this manner, the budget allocation is kept under control at all times.

Most of the information needed for the control of expenditures—by department, by function, and by line-items or objects—is maintained in subsidiary ledgers. The control of expenditures by line-items for five typical governmental functions, is shown in summary fashion in Exhibit 2-7. Other functional categories or departments and other line-items and/or objects of expenditure could be added to this subsidiary ledger.

Personal services include not only salaries and wages but also such employee benefits as the city's share of retirement contributions, FICA payments, and hospitalization insurance. In addition, the city withholds state and federal taxes. As a rule, agency funds are established to account for withholding and retirement contributions for all funds, rather than accounting for these items in each fund.

Salaries and wages usually are not encumbered, because the amounts are fairly constant for the payroll periods as well as for the year. If the city budget reflects salaries and wages for the entire year, rather than for a fiscal year ending on pay periods, then an amount for salaries owed can be accrued at the end of the year.

Assume that the city pays approximately 5 percent of salaries and wages into a retirement fund and 7 percent for FICA payments, with the employees paying similar percentages. The employee's share is withheld from his or her salary or wages. Federal and state withholding taxes amount to 15 percent of the total salaries and wages paid. The amounts recorded for the fiscal year, in summary, are as follows:

Salaries and wages		$705,360
Retirement payments		35,265
FICA payments		49,375
Total personal services		$790,000
Salaries and wages		$705,360
Less: Employee's retirement and FICA payments	$ 84,640	
Withholding	105,805	190,445
Total salaries and wages payable		$514,915
Employee withholding	$190,445	
City's retirement and FICA contributions	84,640	
Agency funds		$275,085

Exhibit 2-7   Expenditure Ledger by Object of Expenditure, Fiscal Year 1986

Object of Expenditure by Function	Budget CR	Expenditure DR	Encumbrance DR	Under or (Over)
Personal services	800,000	790,000	0	10,000
General government	70,000	68,000	0	2,000
Public safety	60,000	62,000	0	(2,000)
Public works	150,000	140,000	0	10,000
Education	450,000	455,000	0	(5,000)
Health and welfare	70,000	65,000	0	5,000
Materials and supplies	200,000	205,000	6,000	(11,000)
General government	25,000	26,000	1,000	(2,000)
Public safety	25,000	24,000	1,000	0
Public works	40,000	38,000	2,000	0
Education	90,000	95,000	1,500	(6,500)
Health and welfare	20,000	22,000	500	(2,500)
Travel	50,000	50,000	1,500	(1,500)
General government	10,000	10,000	500	(500)
Public safety	10,000	9,000	500	500
Public works	10,000	11,000	0	(1,000)
Education	12,000	12,000	500	(500)
Health and welfare	8,000	8,000	0	0
Contractual services	60,000	54,000	4,000	2,000
General government	16,000	12,000	2,000	2,000
Public safety	10,000	9,000	1,000	0
Public works	10,000	8,500	0	1,500
Education	18,000	19,000	1,000	(2,000)
Health and welfare	6,000	5,500	0	500
Equipment	300,000	150,000	120,000	30,000
General government	50,000	0	25,000	25,000
Public safety	40,000	0	40,000	0
Public works	150,000	130,000	20,000	0
Education	30,000	20,000	10,000	0
Health and welfare	30,000	0	25,000	5,000
Debt servicing	250,000	225,000	25,000	0
General government	250,000	225,000	0	25,000

Detailed information on the amount of withholding for individual employees will have to be kept in a subsidiary ledger in the agency fund, so that W-2 forms can be prepared at the end of the year. Information concerning pensions and retirement for each employee must also be drawn from these ledgers.

Materials and supplies can be accounted for in one of three ways: (1) as a perpetual inventory, shown as expenditures when consumed; (2) as an expenditure when purchased, with physical inventory taken at the end of the year to determine the amount in the inventory account; or (3) as an expenditure when purchased, with no inventory account shown. When the amount of the inventory is large and needs to be shown in the balance sheet, only the following entry need be made:

Inventory (for amount of inventory or increase in inventory)
  Reserve for inventory (for amount or increase)

Thus an amount is reserved from the fund balance to take care of the amount set up as inventory. A reverse entry would be made when the inventory, once set up, decreases.

When purchases of materials and supplies are shown as expenditures that are reduced at the end of the year by setting up the inventory account, the following entries need to be made:

1. Inventory (an increase in inventory)
     Expenditures (a decrease in expenditures)
2. Fund balance (for the decrease in fund balance)
     Reserve for inventory (for the increase in inventory)

The reverse of the above entries would be made if the inventories decrease, thus increasing expenditures for the year.

The accounting for contractual services (services purchased outside the organizational unit, including telephone services, maintenance agreements on equipment, insurance, and the like), travel (sometimes included under contractual services), and equipment are fairly straightforward. The equipment category may be broadened to include all capital outlay expenditures and encumbrances (expenditures for fixed assets that have a relatively long life and cost more than a certain dollar amount). Such items as machinery, capital expansion or renovations of existing facilities, improvements and repairs of a capital nature, and land acquisitions may be included in this category.

Most of the money used for *debt servicing*—to pay off principal and interest on long-term debt—is transferred from the general fund to the debt service fund. Long-term liabilities and interest are then paid from this fund. Usually, the debt service fund is included in the budget of only one department. The amounts to be paid are usually known, so there is seldom any reason to accrue or encumber any of the funds.

During the year, the city paid out $225,000 of the $250,000 allocated for debt servicing. This amount is normally recorded as *transfers out,* rather than expenditures in the account debited, to make sure that expenditures and transfers are shown separately on the financial statements. Current principles of accounting require that *interfund transfers* include all transactions except loans or advances, quasi-external transactions, and reimbursements.

As shown in Exhibit 2-8, the subsidiary expenditure ledgers can be summarized by function or organizational unit. As these data show, expenditures in support of education are over budget in every line-item except equipment. Public safety also shows a negative balance overall as a consequence of the overcommitment for personal services. The other functional categories, however, show positive balances,

Exhibit 2-8   *Expenditure Ledger by Function/Organizational Unit, Fiscal Year 1986*

Function/ Organizational Unit	Budget CR	Expenditure DR	Encumbrance DR	Under or (Over)
General government	421,000	341,000	28,500	51,500
Personal services	70,000	68,000	0	2,000
Materials and supplies	25,000	26,000	1,000	(2,000)
Travel	10,000	10,000	500	(500)
Contractual services	16,000	12,000	2,000	2,000
Equipment	50,000	0	25,000	25,000
Debt servicing	250,000	225,000	0	25,000
Public safety	145,000	104,000	42,500	(1,500)
Personal services	60,000	62,000	0	(2,000)
Materials and supplies	25,000	24,000	1,000	0
Travel	10,000	9,000	500	500
Contractual services	10,000	9,000	1,000	0
Equipment	40,000	0	40,000	0
Public works	360,000	327,500	22,000	10,500
Personal services	150,000	140,000	0	10,000
Materials and supplies	40,000	38,000	2,000	0
Travel	10,000	11,000	0	(1,000)
Contractual services	10,000	8,500	0	1,500
Equipment	150,000	130,000	20,000	0
Education	600,000	601,000	13,000	(14,000)
Personal services	450,000	455,000	0	(5,000)
Materials and supplies	90,000	95,000	1,500	(6,500)
Travel	12,000	12,000	500	(500)
Contractual services	18,000	19,000	1,000	(2,000)
Equipment	30,000	20,000	10,000	0
Health and welfare	134,000	100,500	25,500	8,000
Personal services	70,000	65,000	0	5,000
Materials and supplies	20,000	22,000	500	(2,500)
Travel	8,000	8,000	0	0
Contractual services	6,000	5,500	0	500
Equipment	30,000	0	25,000	5,000

and as a result, the locality's budget as a whole shows a positive balance, as summarized in Exhibit 2-9.

Budgetary Accounting

Budgetary accounting can be applied to any of the governmental funds and to the accounts of other not-for-profit organizations. It is most appropriately used, however, in connection with those funds in which broader accountability is required, such as the general fund and special revenue funds.

Exhibit 2-9 *Expenditure Ledger, Fiscal Year 1986*

By Object of Expenditure	Budget CR	Expenditure DR	Encumbrance DR	Under or (Over)
Personal services	800,000	790,000	0	10,000
Materials and supplies	200,000	205,000	6,000	(11,000)
Travel	50,000	50,000	1,500	(1,500)
Contractual services	60,000	54,000	4,000	2,000
Equipment	300,000	150,000	120,000	30,000
Debt servicing	250,000	225,000	0	25,000
Totals	1,660,000	1,474,000	131,500	54,500
By Function/ Organizational Unit				
General government	421,000	341,000	28,500	51,500
Public safety	145,000	104,000	42,500	(1,500)
Public works	360,000	327,500	22,000	10,500
Education	600,000	601,000	13,000	(14,000)
Health and welfare	134,000	100,500	25,500	8,000
Totals	1,660,000	1,474,000	131,500	54,500

The Accounting Equation for Governmental Funds

The general classes of accounts in business accounting are: (1) assets and liabilities, both long- and short-term; (2) owner's equity; (3) revenue; and (4) expenses. In accounting for governmental funds, however, the general classes of accounts are: (1) short-term assets and liabilities; (2) fund balance; (3) revenue; and (4) expenditures. An expense is a resource consumed during the accounting period—used-up assets. Once written off as an expense, the resource has expired as an asset. An expenditure, on the other hand, is an amount of cash spent or to be spent during the accounting period. Since governmental funds do not include long-term assets or liabilities, expenditures and not expenses are measured in these accounts. Expenditures are made at the time the fixed assets are purchased and when a long-term liability expires (for example, when a term bond reaches maturity and the principal is repaid to the investors).

Only those *assets* that can be converted into cash in a relatively short period of time—no more than one year—are included in governmental funds. Similarly, *liabilities* in governmental funds are only those that would be paid in cash in a relatively short period of time. Exceptions to this general rule are bonds payable over an extended time period, which may be found in special assessment funds.

Revenue is the equity in resources (other than proceeds from bond issues or transfers from other funds) that is received during the fiscal period and is available to be spent in that fiscal period. *Expenditures* are the resources that are expended during the fiscal year. Thus, if the city has only a certain amount of resources available to expend during the accounting cycle, management must make certain that this amount is not overspent, or overcommitted for expenditure, during that fiscal period.

The *fund balance* is the difference between assets and liabilities and comes from the excess of revenue over expenditures during this or the prior fiscal year. The fund balance may also include other resources, such as bond proceeds or transfers from other funds. This remaining fund balance can be used to provide resources for expenditures in this or future years.

As identified previously, the basic accounting equation used in double-entry accounting for business activities is:

$$\text{Assets} = \text{Liabilities} + \text{Owner's Equity} + \text{Revenue} - \text{Expense}$$

In dealing with governmental funds, the basic accounting equation must be changed to show revenue and expenditures instead of revenue and expenses. In addition, there is no owner's equity as such in governmental funds. Instead of owner's equity, the residual portion of the equation would be the fund balance. Thus, the equation for governmental funds would read:

$$\text{Assets (current)} =$$
$$\text{Liabilities (current)} + \text{Fund Balance} + \text{Revenue} - \text{Expenditures}$$

For budgetary accounting, four new items must be added to the equation, as outlined below.

Estimated revenue is the amount of revenue anticipated over and above current assets that can be used as expendable resources for the fiscal period. *Appropriations* are the amounts of estimated resources provided by the legislative body for expenditure during the period and should be included on the liability and fund balance side of the equation. *Encumbrances* are used to obligate amounts for goods and services ordered but not yet received. Encumbrances are subtracted (shown as a minus figure) from the liability and fund balance side of the equation, much as expenditures are. The *reserve for encumbrances* is used to allocate a portion of the appropriations for the goods and services ordered but not yet received and represents an addition to the fund balance side of the equation.

A new equation for budgetary accounting for governmental funds can be developed by using these new budgetary terms and the accounting equation for governmental funds. To make the equation easier to follow, single letters will be used to designate actual accounting elements, and double letters will be used for budgetary elements within the equation, as shown below:

Actual Elements	*Budgetary Elements*
A = Assets L = Liabilities R = Revenue E = Expenditures	ER = Estimated revenue AP = Appropriations FB = Fund balance EN = Encumbrances RE = Reserve for encumbrances

Because the fund balance account often includes budgetary amounts, it is shown as a budgetary element (with double letters). Thus, the expanded equation is:

$$A + ER = L + FB + R - E + AP + RE - EN$$

The debit and credit conditions under budgetary accounting are shown in Exhibit 2-10.

Exhibit 2-10 *Debits and Credits to Accounts Under Budgetary Accounting*

Debits	Credits

Increases in:
  Assets (A)
  Estimated revenue (ER)
  Expenditures (E)
  Encumbrances (EN)
	Decreases in:
	  Assets (A)
	  Estimated revenue (ER)
	  Expenditures (E)
	  Encumbrances (EN)

Decreases in:
  Liabilities (L)
  Fund balance (FB)
  Revenue (R)
  Appropriations (AP)
  Reserve for encumbrances (RE)
	Increases in:
	  Liabilities (L)
	  Fund balance (FB)
	  Revenue (R)
	  Appropriations (AP)
	  Reserve for encumbrances (RE)

Budget and Accounting Classifications

It is important that the data presented in budget requests be compatible with data available within the accounting system. This compatibility facilitates comparisons between actual expenditures in previous fiscal periods and proposed future expenditures. It is also essential for performance evaluation and financial reporting purposes.

Generally accepted accounting principles require that financial statements follow certain standards. One standard is that expenditures be classified by functions or programs. Another standard is that, in all cases in which a budget is used to appropriate monies to funds, there be a statement that compares *actual* revenue and expenditures with *budgeted* revenue and expenditures (see Exhibit 2-11). Therefore, whenever possible, the budget classification system should follow the accounting classification system.

The basic control device for the line-item budget is the *object of expenditure*— the fundamental elements of an organization's operations in terms of the goods and services procured. *Object codes*—three- or four-digit numbers—are used to budget and record expenditures in considerable detail (see Exhibit 2-11). These object codes can be further subdivided into subobject classifications; for example, 1200 Contractual Services can be broken down into 1210 General Repairs, 1220 Utility Services, 1230 Motor Vehicle Repairs, 1240 Travel, and so forth. These categories of

Exhibit 2-11 *Comparison of Actual and Budgeted Expenditures Through Eight Months of the Fiscal Year*

DEPARTMENT: Financial Management				
Object Classifications	Budgeted	Expenditures to Date	Estimated Annual Expenditures	Difference
Personal Services				
1100 Salaries	278,020	188,345	282,520	4,500
1120 Wages	0	1,050	1,575	1,575
1130 Special Payments	0	0	0	0
1140 Overtime Payments	5,250	2,200	3,300	(1,950)
Subtotal: Personal Services	$283,270	$191,595	$287,395	$ 4,125
Contractual Services				
1210 General Repairs	700	445	668	(32)
1220 Utility Services	3,600	2,500	3,750	150
1230 Motor Vehicle Repairs	500	600	750	250
1240 Travel	2,100	1,400	2,100	0
1250 Professional Services	5,725	3,250	4,875	(850)
1260 Communications	6,780	4,600	6,900	120
1270 Printing	1,000	500	1,000	0
1280 Computing Services	64,725	44,200	66,300	1,575
1290 Other Contractual Services	3,000	2,000	3,000	0
Subtotal: Contractual Services	$ 88,130	$ 59,495	$ 89,343	$ 1,213
Supplies and Materials				
1310 Office Supplies	29,440	20,000	30,000	560
1320 Fuel Supplies	0	200	300	300
1330 Operating Supplies	1,000	700	1,050	50
1340 Maintenance Supplies	900	500	750	(150)
1350 Drugs and Chemicals	0	0	0	0
1360 Food Supplies	0	75	110	110
1370 Clothing and Linens	0	0	0	0
1380 Educational and Recreational Supplies	0	50	50	50
1390 Other Supplies	1,500	900	1,350	(150)
Subtotal: Supplies and Materials	$ 32,840	$ 22,425	$ 33,610	$ 770
Subtotal: Equipment	$ 17,020	$ 15,000	$ 15,800	(1,220)
Subtotal: Current Obligations	$ 10,940	$ 4,000	$ 5,600	(5,340)
Subtotal: Employee Benefits	$ 27,800	$ 18,780	$ 28,170	$ 370
TOTAL	$460,000	$311,295	$459,918	(82)

contractual services can be subdivided even further; for example, 1240 Travel might be broken down as follows:

1241   Mileage (use of private vehicles)
1242   Automobile Rentals
1243   Fares for Airlines and Other Public Conveyance
1244   Tolls and Parking
1245   Subsistence and Lodging
1246   Convention and Education Expenses

Objects of expenditure can be aggregated under broad expenditure characteristics, such as current operations, capital expenditures, and debt service. They also can be attributed to, and recorded as, the expenditures of a specific organizational unit, activity classification, program and subprogram classification, and/or function of government. Thus, a 16-digit code—for example, 23-07-105-1245-45301—might be used to record a travel expenditure for meals and lodging (1245) of a staff member from the Department of Financial Management (105) under the general government function (23) in conjunction with an audit review project (45301). The code 07 might be used to designate the funding source to which this expenditure will be charged. The project code might also be used to designate the program or subprogram (45xxx) and the activity classification (xx30x). Using such multidigit codes enables accounting entries to be retrieved and sorted to meet a variety of financial management purposes. This capacity to monitor and to "crosswalk" expenditure data for various management purposes will be discussed in further detail in Chapter 3.

Illustrative Budgetary Accounting Transactions

The budgetary accounting equation provides a basis for understanding double-entry fund accounting in government and other nonbusiness organizations. The following illustrations give an overview of the types of double-entry transactions commonly found in governmental funds. These illustrations are not intended to give the reader a complete understanding of the detailed transactions one may encounter in a particular governmental fund. Rather, they are meant to provide a better understanding of the techniques of budgetary accounting.

After appropriate legislative review and public hearings, the following budget was adopted by the city council for the Recreation Department:

Budgeted revenue	$250,000
Budgeted expenditures (appropriations)	240,000
Increase in fund balance	$ 10,000

The entry to record these authorized budgetary amounts would be:

	Debit	*Credit*
Estimated revenue	$250,000	
Appropriations		$240,000
Fund balance—budgetary		10,000

Materials and supplies were ordered at an estimated cost of $66,000. To assure that the appropriation would not be overspent, the order was encumbered against the appropriation in the accounting records. This budgetary entry is:

Encumbrances	$ 66,000	
Reserve for encumbrances		$ 66,000

The ordered materials and supplies were shipped, and an invoice was received in the amount of $63,000. Note that when an actual entry is made, the budgetary entry for the encumbrance is reversed at the original amount estimated for the goods ordered. The current amount is then used to record the actual transaction. The difference between the two amounts (in this case, $3,000) then becomes available for expenditure. These entries would be recorded as follows:

Reserve for encumbrances	$ 66,000	
Encumbrances		$ 66,000
Expenditures: Materials and supplies	$ 63,000	
Accounts payable		$ 63,000

If the goods had been received immediately, there would have been no need for encumbering the order, and the expenditure entry would have been the only one made.

The Recreation Department also ordered a truck estimated to cost $42,000. When received, the truck—which is a fixed asset—will be recorded as an expenditure rather than a capitalized asset. Therefore, it is encumbered upon placing the order, the same as any other operating expenditure:

Encumbrances	$ 42,000	
Reserve for encumbrances		$ 42,000

When the truck is received, the invoice shows that it cost $45,000. Although a long-term asset, the truck is recorded as an expenditure in a governmental fund. A related entry should be made in a separate entity called a fixed asset account group to maintain a permanent record of the truck. When the truck and the invoice are received, the original budget entry is reversed:

Reserve for encumbrances	$ 42,000	
Encumbrances		$ 42,000

To set up the liability for the truck, the entry is:

Expenditure: Equipment delivery	$ 45,000	
Accounts payable		$ 45,000

The fixed asset is recorded as an expenditure—shown as a debit—while the voucher payable, a liability—also an increase—is recorded as a credit. As with the materials and supplies, if the truck had been received immediately, no entry would have been needed for the encumbrance, and only the expenditure entry would have been recorded.

Since uncommitted appropriations/allocations may revert to the general treasury at the end of the fiscal year, orders often are placed to encumber these funds as the closing of the year approaches. A further order was placed by the Recreation Department for materials and supplies estimated to cost $6,000. This entry is:

Encumbrances	$ 6,000	
Reserve for encumbrances		$ 6,000

Budget Adjustments

At times during the fiscal year, the budget may need to be adjusted to reflect additional information concerning estimated revenues and appropriations. Suppose, for example, that the estimated revenue is determined to be $258,000 instead of $250,000. The increase could be reflected in the fund balance account at the end of the year, and the estimated revenue account would not have to be adjusted. However, unless a sufficient amount is available in the fund balance account to meet agency commitments, the estimated revenue account would have to be adjusted before making any additional allocations.

Assume that the Recreation Department is authorized to use a portion of the additional revenue to purchase recreational equipment worth $15,000. Under the original appropriation, only $10,000 was available; therefore, the estimated revenue will have to be increased. This entry would be:

Estimated revenue	$ 8,000	
Fund balance—budgetary		$ 8,000

The entry to increase the amount appropriated would be:

Fund balance—budgetary	$ 15,000	
Appropriation		$ 15,000

Note that the fund balance account now would have only $3,000 left to appropriate ($18,000 minus $15,000).

Any budgetary comparison should be made between the revised budget and actual figures. When the equipment is purchased, the entry to record the purchase would be:

Expenditures: Equipment	$ 15,000	
Accounts payable		$ 15,000

The entry to record payment would be:

Accounts payable	$ 15,000	
Cash		$ 15,000

During the fiscal year, it may become apparent that revenues are falling short of the initial estimates. If the fund balance is insufficient to cover the amount appropriated, it obviously becomes necessary to decrease the appropriation. Assuming that the estimate of the amount of revenue to be collected during the fiscal year is revised from $250,000 to $225,000, it then becomes necessary to revise the appropriation by the same amount. The budget adjustment would be:

Appropriation	$ 25,000	
Estimated revenue		$ 25,000

The amount that can be spent, then, would be only $215,000 instead of the original $240,000.

Closing Entries

Closing entries may be made in one of two ways: (1) by reversing the budget adoption transactions or (2) by closing the actual revenue account to the budget revenue account (estimated revenue) and the actual expenditures account to the appropriation account. Any differences are then closed to the fund balance account.

Assume the following situation with regard to the Recreation Department: (1) Encumbrances do not lapse. (2) The revised budget included an increase of $8,000 in estimated revenue and increased appropriations of $15,000. (3) Actual revenue for the year totaled $260,000. (4) Actual expenditures against the appropriations were $250,000. (5) Appropriations of $6,000 were encumbered at the end of the year for the order of supplies.

Using the first method, the closing entry made by reversing the original budget adoption entry would be:

Appropriation	$255,000	
Fund balance—budgetary	$ 3,000	
Estimated revenue		$258,000

The closing entry related to actual revenue, expenditures, and encumbrances is:

Revenue	$260,000	
Expenditures		$250,000
Encumbrances		$ 6,000
Fund balance		

An alternative approach is to reverse the original encumbrance entry and place the difference in the fund balance account. Then the reserve for encumbrance amount is set up as a reservation of the fund balance. The encumbrance entry is reversed as follows:

Reserve for encumbrances	$ 6,000	
Encumbrances		$ 6,000

Actual accounts are closed:

Revenue	$260,000	
Expenditures		$250,000
Fund balance		10,000

A reservation of the fund balance is set up for the encumbered amount:

Fund balance	$ 10,000	
Reserve for encumbrances		$ 6,000

Using the second method of closing the accounts, revenue is closed to estimated revenue, with the difference going to the fund balance. This entry would be:

Revenue	$260,000	
Estimated revenue		$258,000
Fund balance		2,000

Then the encumbrances, expenditures, and appropriations accounts are closed. The encumbrances account is closed to the appropriations account, leaving the reserve for encumbrances account open as a reservation of the fund balance. This entry is:

Appropriations	$ 6,000	
Encumbrances		$ 6,000

Finally, the expenditures account is closed to the appropriations account:

Appropriations	$250,000	
Expenditures		$250,000

If there were any balance in the appropriations account, it would be closed into the fund balance account.

Use of Subsidiary Ledgers

A running comparison of actual revenue and expenditures with budgeted revenue and expenditures should be maintained in any organization. Therefore, in addition to recording the above journal entries in general ledger accounts, individual amounts would also be recorded in a subsidiary ledger. Accounts would be kept in the subsidiary ledger for the particular budgeted revenue, appropriations, actual revenue, expenditures, and encumbrances accounts.

Records must be kept in much greater detail in the subsidiary ledgers for a breakdown of other classes of revenue and expenditures than those usually shown in the general ledger. In the revenues of local government, for example, licenses and permits may be of several types—automobile licenses, business licenses, dog licenses, building permits, and so on. By using subsidiary accounts and ledgers, it should be possible to provide the detail needed on almost any account. Maintaining this level of detail in the general ledger would be almost impossible, even for a small municipality.

Many line-item expenditures would also be recorded in subsidiary ledgers. It would be almost impossible, for example, to keep track of all the necessary detail on the line-items for functions, subfunctions, and departments without placing these details in subsidiary ledgers.

The Municipal Finance Officers Association, in its *Governmental Accounting, Auditing, and Financial Reporting,* provides an excellent statement concerning the purpose of subsidiary ledger accounts:

The General Fund of most governments has many sources of revenue and, hence, a need for numerous general ledger revenue accounts. A great many expenditure accounts are also normally required. Excessive general ledger accounts are very inconvenient to work with. Most governments, therefore, use general ledger control accounts and subsidiary ledgers.

A subsidiary ledger includes numerous detailed accounts, balances of which in total agree with the balance of a particular general ledger account. A general ledger account supported by a subsidiary ledger is called a general ledger *control* account. Through the use of subsidiary ledgers, a government can maintain a large number of individual accounts without cluttering up its general ledger.[3]

The general fund, for example, might include separate accounts for revenues from taxes, licenses and fees, intergovernmental transfers, and other financing sources. A single expenditure general ledger control account often will be supported by several different expenditure subsidiary ledgers to provide multiple expenditure classifications—by fund, function or program, organizational unit, activity, character, and object code.

Summary

This chapter has provided the basis for understanding the use of budgetary accounting, particularly in accounting for governmental funds. This understanding serves as a foundation for the accounting systems used to produce financial statements and reports that can be audited in accordance with generally accepted accounting principles.

Budgetary and related accounting systems can also be adapted to appropriate managerial accounting systems useful for organizational decision making and control processes in government and other not-for-profit organizations. These adaptations are discussed in Chapter 3.

Endnotes

1. For a comprehensive discussion of the principles and practices of accounting in the public sector, see Leo Herbert, Larry N. Killough, and Alan Walter Steiss, *Accounting and Control for Governmental and Other Nonbusiness Organizations* (New York: McGraw-Hill, 1986).

2. Municipal Finance Officers Association of the United States and Canada, *Statement 1. Governmental Accounting and Financial Reporting Principles* (Chicago: Author, 1979), pp. 5–6.

3. Municipal Finance Officers Association of the United States and Canada, *Governmental Accounting, Auditing, and Financial Reporting* (Chicago: Author, 1981), p. 37.

CHAPTER 3

Managerial Accounting

Financial accounting focuses on the accurate and objective recording of fiscal transactions and the preparation of reports on the fiscal affairs of an organization for external users. *Managerial accounting* provides information to internal users in making decisions about the development of resources and the exploitation of program opportunities. Managerial accounting is involved in the formulation of financial estimates of future performance (the planning and budgeting processes) and, subsequently, in the analysis of actual performance in relation to these estimates (program evaluation and control).

Objectives of Managerial Accounting

Generally accepted accounting principles have not yet been developed to guide (or inhibit) managerial accounting. From a management point of view, any accounting system is desirable as long as it produces incremental benefits that exceed the incremental cost of its maintenance. However, public organizations often must operate under an accounting system developed to satisfy externally imposed legal requirements, rather than to meet their own management needs. A state-funded university, for example, may have to operate under an accounting system that meets the financial reporting needs of the state. Such an accounting system may track revenue and expenditures on a cash basis and require account closeouts at the end of the fiscal year. Externally funded, sponsored research activities within the university, however, do not operate on a cash basis and do not conveniently match the fiscal year cycle anticipated by the state accounting system. These sponsored programs may produce as much as one-third of the total financial resources of the university and may have a multiplicity of reporting requirements not easily served by the state accounting system. Managerial accounting techniques make it possible to "crosswalk" data from the state system to formats more applicable to sponsor requirements.

Underlying Assumptions

The objective of managerial accounting—to improve the effectiveness of both the planning and control functions—is predicated on two basic assumptions. First, plans should be developed on the same information base as the mechanisms of control. Planning depends on the same reporting and control mechanisms that make central oversight possible and decentralized management feasible.[1] Building the mechanism of control on one data base (financial accounting) and the planning process on another (program analysis) places too great a burden on the management system as the intermediary.

The second assumption is that the success of a decentralized management system depends on an understanding at the department level of the rules of the game, as well as the incentives and expectations, governing planning and budgeting. An important task of managerial accounting, then, is to enlarge the circle of those familiar with the processes of planning, budgeting, and control through the communication of pertinent management information as well as financial data.

The significant features of managerial accounting are summarized in Exhibit 3-1. Managerial accounting includes estimates and plans for the future of cost centers and responsibility centers (discussed later in this chapter), as well as information about the past. Although managerial accounting reports contain financial data, much of the information in these reports is nonmonetary—for example, number of employees, number of hours worked, quantities of materials used, purpose of travel, and so forth.

Exhibit 3-1   *Components of Managerial Accounting*

---

1. Information generated for *planning* and *programming* purposes to establish a better balance with the control function of accounting.

2. Emphasis on *cost estimation* for planning or control purposes, rather than on financial reporting.

3. *Performance standards* (workload and unit cost data) added to traditional accounting control mechanisms by which legal compliance and fiscal accountability are evaluated.

4. *Experimentation* and *innovation* encouraged in the types of management information provided.

5. *Cost consciousness* increased among operating units through the identification of cost and responsibility centers and the use of performance standards.

6. *Costs monitored* to determine if they are reasonable for the activities performed.

7. *Cost analyses* facilitate the linkages among management control, program budgeting, and performance auditing.

Timely Information Requirements

Managers need information on a *real-time basis*—that is, as problems occur and opportunities arise. Often they are willing to sacrifice some precision to gain currency of data. Therefore, in managerial accounting, approximations often are as useful as—or even more useful than—numbers calculated to the last penny. In spite of the mystique that often surrounds its data, financial accounting cannot be absolutely precise. Thus, the difference is actually one of degree.

The informational boundaries of managerial accounting are not rigid. There is little point in collecting data unless their value to management exceeds the cost of data collection.[2] Managerial accounting provides a basis for financial interpretations that assist in the formulation of policies and decisions and in the control of current and future operations. Such internal reporting to management often requires the collection and presentation of financial information in a completely different format from that followed for external reporting.[3]

Functions of Managerial Accounting

Managerial accounting is concerned primarily with four basic functions: management planning, cost determination, cost control, and performance evaluation. *Component costs* must be determined before decisions can be made regarding the commitment of resources in support of particular objectives or programs. Costs must be evaluated, both in the immediate future and in the long run, and must be weighed against anticipated benefits. Once commitments have been made, costs must be *monitored and controlled* to ensure that they are appropriate and reasonable for the activities performed. And the overall *performance* of a program, activity, or subunit must be evaluated to improve future decisions regarding resource allocations. The primary focus of this discussion will be on the functions of cost determination and cost control.

Basic Concepts of Cost

Cost can be defined as a release of value required to accomplish some goal, objective, or purpose.[4] Costs should be incurred only if they can be expected to lead to the accomplishment of some predetermined end or serve as a means to an end. Costs are incurred by some organizations for the purpose of generating revenues in excess of the resources consumed. This profit motive is not applicable in most public organizations, where costs are incurred in the provision of some public service. Nonetheless, the test as to whether the cost is appropriate and reasonable is still the same: Did the commitment of resources advance the organization or program toward some agreed-upon goal or objective?

Cost is not a unidimensional concept. A primary objective of managerial accounting is to further define and categorize the basic components of cost that must be incurred in the implementation of the plans and programs of any organization.

Five basic cost components are involved in any activity, operation, project, or program: (1) labor or personal services (salaries, wages, and related employee benefits); (2) contractual services (packages of services purchased from outside sources); (3) materials and supplies (consumables); (4) equipment expenses (sometimes categorized as fixed asset expenses); and (5) overhead.

When applied in the private sector, *overhead* has a fairly specific meaning. Usually it is defined as all costs, other than direct labor and materials, associated with the production process. Used in this context, overhead may involve variable or fixed costs (for instance, supervisory salaries, property taxes, rent, insurance, and depreciation). In the jargon of cost accounting, various direct cost components, such as direct labor and materials, are reclassified as *prime costs,* whereas indirect labor and overhead are reclassified as *conversion costs.*

Decisions must be made in cost accounting as to the distribution of direct and indirect costs. A *direct cost* represents a cost incurred for a specific purpose that is uniquely associated with that purpose. The salary of the manager of a day-care center, for example, would be considered a direct cost of the center. The center might be divided into departments according to different age groups of children, with a part of the manager's salary allocated to each department. Then the salary would be an indirect cost of each department. *Indirect cost* is a cost associated with more than one activity or program that cannot be traced directly to any of the individual activities. In the public sector, the terms *indirect cost* and *overhead* are often used interchangeably.

Costs can be defined by how they change in relation to fluctuations in the quantity of some selected activity—for example, number of hours of labor required to complete some task, dollar volume of sales, number of orders processes, or some other index of volume (see Exhibit 3-2). *Fixed costs* do not change in total as the volume of activity increases, but become progressively smaller on a per unit basis. *Variable costs* are more or less uniform per unit, but their total fluctuates in direct proportion to the total volume of activity. Note that the variable or fixed character of a cost relates to its total dollar amount and not to its per unit amount.

The acquisition of equipment illustrates a fixed cost. As the volume of activity increases, the total cost of the equipment is spread over an increasing number of units. Therefore, the cost per unit becomes less and less. Personnel, on the other hand, illustrate variable costs. Each employee carrying out similar tasks is paid approximately the same amount. As the number of tasks increases, however, the number of employees must also increase (assuming that some level of productivity or efficiency is to be maintained).

Costs may also be *semifixed,* described as a step-function, or *semivariable,* whereby both fixed and variable components are included in the related costs. Salaries of supervisory personnel might be described as semifixed costs; at some level of increased activity, additional supervisory personnel may be required. Maintenance costs often exhibit the characteristics of semivariable costs. A fixed level of cost is required initially, after which maintenance costs increase with the level of activity. Since costs are usually classified as either fixed or variable, the incremental character of these mixed categories is often a determining factor. If the increments between levels of change are large, the costs may be classified as fixed; if the increments are relatively small, the costs are usually defined as variable.

In theory, all costs are controllable by someone within an organization, given a long enough time. For purposes of managerial accounting, however, *controllable costs* are defined as those costs subject to the influence of a given manager of a given program or organizational unit during a given time period. The supervisor of an emergency room in a hospital, for example, might exercise significant control over the costs of supplies, maintenance, assigned nursing staff, and so forth. However,

Exhibit 3-2 *Graphic Illustration of Cost Concepts*

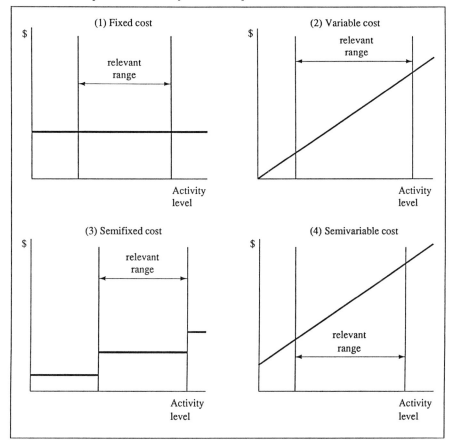

he or she may have little or no control over the cost of doctors working in the emergency room or insurance costs allocated to this aspect of the hospital's operations.

Noncontrollable costs include all costs that do not meet this test of "significant influence" by a given manager. Thus, costs assigned to the manager of any department may contain both controllable and noncontrollable elements. Although clear distinctions are often difficult to make, every effort must be made to separate these cost components for the purpose of performance evaluation.

Other cost categories frequently encountered in managerial accounting are listed and defined in Exhibit 3-3. Many of these cost categories operate in opposing pairs—for example, product and period costs, investment and recurring costs, out-of-pocket and sunk costs.

Cost Approximation Methods

Cost approximation, or cost estimation, involves efforts to find predictable relationships between a dependent variable (cost) and an independent variable (some

Exhibit 3-3   Cost Categories Used in Managerial Accounting

1. *Engineered costs* are any costs that have an explicit, specified physical relationship with a selected measure of activity. Most variable costs fit this classification. Direct labor and direct material costs are prime examples.

2. *Discretionary costs* (also called managed or programmed costs) are fixed costs decided upon by management at the beginning of a budget period as to the maximum amounts to be incurred. Unlike most other costs, discretionary costs are not subject to engineering input–output analysis. Examples include research and development, advertising, employee training programs, and day-care services for employees' children.

3. *Committed costs* typically result from long-term decisions and consist of those fixed costs associated with the physical plant and equipment of the organization. Examples include depreciation, rent, property taxes, and insurance. Salaries of key personnel may also be considered committed costs. Such costs often cannot be reduced without adversely affecting the ability to meet long-range goals.

4. *Product costs* are initially identified as part of the inventory on hand. They become expenses only when the inventory is sold.

5. *Period costs* are deducted as expenses during a given fiscal period without having been previously classified as product costs (for example, general administrative expenses).

6. *Out-of-pocket costs* involve current or upcoming outlays of funds as a result of some decision.

7. *Sunk costs* have already been incurred and, therefore, are irrelevant to the current decision-making process. Allocation of costs based on depreciation and amortization schedules are examples of sunk costs.

8. *Marginal costs* represent the cost of providing one additional unit of service (or product) over some previous level of activity. An example would be the cost of keeping the library open an extra hour each evening.

9. *Differential costs* (or incremental costs) represent the difference in total costs between alternative approaches to providing some product or service.

10. *Opportunity costs* involve the maximum return that might have been realized if resources had been committed to an alternative investment—that is, the impact of having to give up one opportunity to select another.

11. *Associated costs* are incurred by beneficiaries in using programs or services. An example is the cost incurred by individuals in traveling to a public recreational facility.

12. *Investment costs* vary primarily with the size of a particular program or project but not with its duration.

13. *Recurring costs* are operating, maintenance, and repair costs that vary with both the size and the duration of a program. Recurring costs may include salaries and wages, equipment maintenance and repair, and materials and supplies.

14. *Life-cycle costs* are incurred over the useful life of a facility or duration of a program, including investment costs, research and development costs, operating costs, and maintenance and repair costs.

relevant activity), so that costs can be estimated over time based on the behavior of the independent variable. This cost function is often represented by the basic formula $y = a + bx$, where y is the dependent variable (cost), x is the independent variable, and a and b are approximations of true (but unknown) parameters. For example, if the cost of inoculating 20 children is $50 and the cost of inoculating 50 children is $80, then the fixed costs (a) are $30 and the variable costs (b) can be calculated as $1 per child.

In practice, cost approximations typically are based on three major assumptions: (1) linear cost functions can be used to approximate nonlinear situations; (2) all costs can be categorized as either fixed or variable within a relevant range; and (3) the true cost behavior can be sufficiently explained by one independent variable instead of more than one variable. Problems of changing price levels, productivity, and technological changes are also assumed away under this approach. The analytical task is to approximate an appropriate slope coefficient (b)—defined as the amount of increase in y for each unit increase in x—and a constant or intercept (a)—defined as the value of y when x is zero. The analyst may use goodness-of-fit tests, ranging from simple scatter diagrams to full-fledged regression analysis, to ensure that the cost function is plausible and that the relationship is credible.

Four major types of cost functions are suggested by the discussion of fixed and variable costs (see Exhibit 3-2):

1. Total fixed cost does not fluctuate as x changes: $y = a$, because $b = 0$.
2. A proportionately variable cost fluctuates in direct proportion to changes in x: $y = bx$, because $a = 0$.
3. A step-function (or semifixed) cost is nonlinear because of breaks in its behavior pattern: $y' = a'$, $y'' = a''$, $y''' = a'''$, and so forth.
4. A mixed or semivariable cost is a combination of fixed and variable elements; that is, total cost fluctuates as x changes within the relevant range, but not in direct proportion: $y = a + bx$.

The first three of these cost functions are relatively straightforward and simple to resolve. The mixed-cost situation (Exhibit 3-4) is the most common, however, and the most problematic.

The fixed portion of a mixed cost typically is the result of providing some initial capacity. The variable portion is the result of using the capacity, given its availability. A photocopying machine, for example, often has a fixed monthly rental cost plus a variable cost based on the number of copies produced.

Ideally, mixed costs should be subdivided into two accounts—one for the variable portion and the other for the fixed portion. In practice, however, such distinctions are seldom made because of the difficulty of assigning day-to-day cost data to variable and fixed categories. Even if such distinctions were possible, the advantages might not be worth the additional effort and costs.

Several basic methods are available for approximating cost functions. These methods are not mutually exclusive and frequently are used in tandem to provide

Exhibit 3-4 *Graphic Illustration of Mixed Costs*

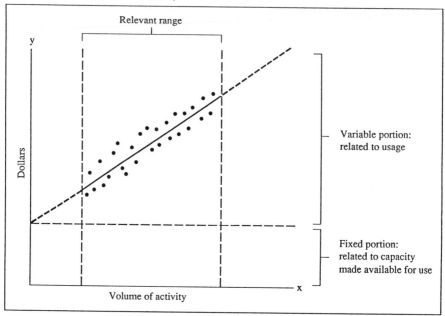

cross-checks on assumptions. The five most commonly applied methods are listed in Exhibit 3-5.

Exhibit 3-5 *Methods for Approximating Cost Functions*

1. *Analytic* or *industrial engineering methods* entail a systematic examination of labor, materials, supplies, support services, and facilities—sometimes using time-and-motion studies—to determine physically observable input–output relationships.

2. *Account analysis* involves a classification of all relevant accounts into variable or fixed cost categories by observing how total costs behave over several fiscal periods.

3. *High–low methods* call for estimations of total costs at two different activity levels, usually at a low point and a high point within the relevant range. The difference in the dependent variable is divided by the difference in the independent variable to estimate the slope of the line represented by *b*.

4. *Visual-fit method* is applied by drawing a straight line through the cost points on a scatter diagram, which consists of a plot of various costs experienced at various levels of activity.

5. *Regression methods* refer to the measurement of the average amount of change in one variable that is associated with unit increases in the amounts of one or more other variables.

The last three of these methods can be illustrated using the data in Exhibit 3-6, which shows the direct labor costs incurred over an eight-month period in providing

Exhibit 3-6 Monthly Labor Costs for Community Health Clinic

Month	Patient Days (x)	Labor Costs (y)	x^2	xy
1	550	$14,400	302,500	7,920,000
2	575	14,700	330,625	8,452,500
3	425	12,300	180,625	5,227,500
4	400	12,150	160,000	4,860,000
5	350	11,250	122,500	3,937,500
6	200	8,400	40,000	1,680,000
7	400	11,700	160,000	4,680,000
8	450	12,750	202,500	5,737,500
Totals	3,350	$97,650	1,498,750	42,495,000

services to patients in a community health clinic. The specific steps in the *high–low method* can be outlined as follows:

1. Select the highest observed value of the independent variable (575 patient days) and the corresponding value of the dependent variable ($14,700).
2. Select the lowest observed value of the independent variable (200 patient days) and the corresponding value of the dependent variable ($8,400).
3. Determine the difference between the selected values of the dependent variable ($14,700 − 8,400 = $6,300).
4. Determine the difference between the selected values of the independent variable (575 − 200 = 375).
5. Divide the difference between the values of the dependent variable by the difference in the values of the independent variable ($6,300 ÷ 375 = $16.80). The result is the estimated slope (b) of the line.
6. Multiply the high- or low-value independent variable by the slope of the line and subtract from the corresponding value of the dependent variable ($14,700 − (575 × 16.80) = $5,040). The remainder represents the y-intercept of the line (a).

The labor cost equation derived through this method is:

$$y = 5,040 + 16.80x$$

A more accurate way of determining the estimated variability rate is to plot all points of observed cost data on a *scatter diagram* (see Exhibit 3-4). The line is fitted so that approximately an equal number of points fall above and below the line. The variability rate can then be calculated by determining the total cost for some point on the line and subtracting the y-intercept value to arrive at total variable costs.

Total cost for 350 days	$11,250
y-intercept value	5,400
Total variable cost	$ 5,850

The variable cost is then divided by the activity level to arrive at the variable cost per unit of activity ($5,850 ÷ 350 = $16.71). The labor cost equation derived by this method is:

$$y = 5,400 + 16.71x$$

Regression analysis (the least squares method) assures the determination of the "best fit" of a straight line drawn between the plots on a scatter diagram. The term *regression analysis* simply identifies a process whereby the average amount of change in a variable associated with changes in one or more other variables is measured. The values of a (the y-intercept) and b (the slope of the line) are determined by solving simultaneously the normal equations of simple regression:

1. $\Sigma y = na + b\Sigma x$
2. $\Sigma xy = a\Sigma x + b\Sigma x^2$

The number of patient days per month is x, the labor costs associated with serving these patients is y, and the number of months is n. The simultaneous equations, as derived from the data in Exhibit 3-6, become:

1. $97,650 = 8a + 3,350b$
2. $42,495,000 = 3,350a + 1,498,750b$

The values of a can be equalized by multiplying (1) by 418.75:

1. $40,890,938 = 3,350a + 1,402,812.5b$
2. $42,495,000 = 3,350a + 1,498,750.0b$

Subtracting (1) from (2) results in:

$$1,604,062 = 0 + 95,937.5b$$
$$b = 16.72$$
$$a = 5,204.75$$

Thus, the labor cost equation derived through regression analysis is:

$$y = 5,204.75 + 16.72x$$

In effect, this equation indicates that there is a fixed labor cost of about $5,205 per month in maintaining the community health clinic and a variable cost of $16.72 per patient served.

Whatever method is used to formulate cost approximations, it is important in managerial accounting to have reasonably accurate and reliable predictions of costs. Such cost estimates usually have an important bearing on a number of operational decisions and can be used for planning, budgeting, and control purposes. The division of costs into fixed and variable components (and into engineered, discretionary, and committed categories) highlights major factors that influence costs. Although cost functions usually represent simplifications of underlying true relationships, the use of these methods depends on how sensitive the manager's decisions are to the errors that may be introduced by these simplifications. In some situations, additional accuracy may make little difference in the decision; in others, it may be very significant. Selection of a cost function is often a decision as to the cost and value of information.[5]

Cost Accounting

Cost accounting is the process of assembling and recording all the elements of expense incurred to attain a purpose, to carry out an activity, operation, or program, to complete a unit of work or a project, or to do a specific job. Cost accounting encompasses a body of concepts and techniques applicable in both financial accounting and managerial accounting. Cost accounting systems can be found in both profit and nonprofit organizations and in both product- and service-oriented entities. Firms providing a service or a product for sale must have a system for accumulating and determining the necessary costs of the service or product. Cost allocation methods, at best, are only as good as the cost data used to provide information for inventory valuation or other purposes. The expense of obtaining cost data, however, must be maintained at a reasonable level, and the distribution of costs should not go beyond the point of practical use.

Classes of Cost Accounts

Several approaches to the measurement of costs may be relevant for the purposes of managerial accounting. *Full costing,* for example, attempts to identify all costs properly associated with some operation or activity. In the governmental and non-profit areas, full costs are often called *program costs.* Patient care costs, for instance, involve hospital room costs, meals, laundry, drugs, surgery, therapy, and other items that are more or less directly attributable to the patient. But what about admission/discharge costs, nursery care, or heat, light, and other utilities? Unless an accrual accounting system has been adopted, several problems may be encountered in considering all the fixed and variable costs associated with particular activities.

One of the more controversial aspects of the full costing approach is the method of assigning overhead or indirect costs to operating departments. *Overhead* includes the cost of various items that cannot conveniently be charged directly to those jobs or operations that are benefited. General administrative expenses are included in this concept of overhead. It can be argued, for example, that the cost of a personnel department, an accounting department, and other service or auxiliary units should be assigned in some fashion to the operating departments of an organization. By the same logic, utility costs, building maintenance costs, depreciation, and so forth can also be assigned to specific operating units. These indirect costs are often distributed (prorated) on a formula basis, as determined by labor hours, labor costs, or total direct costs of each job or operation.

Many indirect costs, however, are clearly beyond the control of the managers of operating departments. In recognition of this fact, *responsibility costing* assigns to an operating department only those costs that its managers can control, or at least influence. Many argue that this approach is the only proper measure of the financial stewardship of an operating manager. Responsibility costing will be discussed further in a subsequent section of this chapter.

A useful approach to cost accounting is to consider only the variable or *incremental costs* of a particular operation. For example, a city manager might want to know how much extra it would cost to keep the public swimming pools open evenings, or how much it would cost to increase the frequency of trash collection from two to three times a week. The same questions might be raised by the management of any organization that delivers a service on some regularly scheduled basis. This approach, called *direct costing,* is relatively easy to associate with an organization's budget. Direct costing can be very helpful for incremental decision making.

Partial costs are often used to gauge the cost impact associated with a particular approach to service delivery—for example, the costs that result from treating patients through a specific rehabilitation program. Such costs would not be incurred by the hospital if the program or the patients did not exist.

Job order costing, as the name implies, is frequently used in the private sector by companies whose products are readily identifiable by individual units or batches. Industries that commonly use job order costing include construction, printing, furniture manufacturing, machinery manufacturing, and so forth. The essential feature of the job costing method is the attempt to apply cost to specific jobs, which may consist of a single physical unit (for example, a custom sofa) or a few like units in a distinct batch or job lot (for example, a dozen end tables).

Process costing is most often found in such industries as chemicals, oil refining, meat packing, mining, glass, and cement. These industries are characterized by the mass production of like units, which usually pass in continuous fashion through a series of uniform production steps called *operations* or *processes.* Costs are accumulated by departments (often identified by operations or processes), with attention focused on total department costs for a given period in relation to the number of units processed. Average unit costs may be determined by dividing accumulated department costs by the quantities produced during the period. Unit costs for various operations can then be multiplied by the number of units transferred to obtain total costs applicable to those units. This method cannot be used to determine cost differences in individual products, however.

Process costing creates relatively few accounting problems when applied to various types of service organizations, including public agencies. *Unit costs* can be calculated for many activities simply by dividing total program costs for a given period by the number of persons served (or tons of trash collected, number of inspections made, miles of road patrolled, or some other applicable measure of the volume of activity during some period). A job order costing approach is necessary, however, when it is important to determine costs in greater detail by individual projects or tasks.

In public programs, unit costs are often determined simply by dividing the current budget allocation for a given activity by the number of performance units. If the annual budget of the welfare department is $2 million and the case load is 2,500, then the "unit cost" is $800 per case. This approach may produce rather misleading results, however. Budgetary appropriations may not be a good measure of current expenses, since encumbrances for items not yet received may be included. At the same time, expenditures to cover outstanding encumbrances from the preceding fiscal period may be excluded. Even if costs are limited to expenditures, current unit costs may be overstated if new capital equipment is included in the expenditures or if there is a large increase in inventories. Conversely, unit costs may be understated in many organizations because of a failure to account for the drawing down of inventories or for depreciation (or user costs) of equipment.

Cost Allocation

Cost allocation (sometimes called cost absorption) is necessary whenever the full cost of a service or product must be determined. In cost allocation, the variable, fixed, direct, and indirect components of cost, in particular, must be considered. Examples of this requirement in the public sector include the costing of governmental grants and contracts, the establishment of equitable public utility rates, the setting of user rates for internal services expected to operate on a "break-even" basis (that is, recover full costs), and the determination of fees (such as for inspections).

Variable costs directly associated with a given service or activity do not present an allocation problem. Such costs can usually be measured and assigned to appropriate activities or programs using methods outlined in the previous section.

A given organizational unit may also experience direct fixed costs, such as rent. Such costs should be allocated to specific services or projects. Since these direct costs do not vary with the activities being measured, they might be allocated by assuming some level of operation, such as number of persons to be served. Then the total annual cost can be divided by the estimated level of activity to arrive at a unit rate. In other instances, direct fixed costs may have to be allocated on the basis of some arbitrary physical measure, such as floor space occupied. In either case, it is important that full accrued costs are allocated to avoid the problem of encumbrances.

For the purpose of determining full unit costs, costs identified as direct to the total organization must be allocated to various departments or programs. This represents a major allocation problem. The salaries of various administrative and support personnel in a hospital, for example, are direct costs to the hospital as a whole. When allocated to various separate departments or service functions—such as the intensive care unit, nursery, surgery, cafeteria, laboratories, and other components of the hospital—these salaries become indirect costs to these units. Although often arbitrary, the basis for such allocations should be reasonable and based on services provided to these related units.

As noted previously, some *overhead* items can be identified directly with specific programs or departments (that is, they are direct costs of these organizational units). Others have to be allocated arbitrarily because they cannot be traced directly to the individual organizational units (they are indirect costs). Therefore, overhead is often divided into two categories. *Actual* overhead costs incurred by an organizational unit typically are recorded by means of an overhead clearing account and some type of subsidiary record, such as a departmental expense analysis or overhead cost sheet. *Allocated* or *applied* overhead (indirect costs) is distributed through the use of predetermined rates.

One approach to the allocation of indirect costs involves the identification of a number of *indirect cost pools*. Each pool represents the full costs associated with some specific administrative or support function (which cannot be allocated directly to individual projects or activities)—for example, operation and maintenance of the physical plant (including utility costs); central stores, motor pool, computing center, or other internal service units; general building and equipment usage; and central administration. Note that with internal service units, some part of operating costs can often be assigned directly as organizational units use these services. Indirect costs often represent the "fixed" costs of these service units (the basic cost of having the services available).

Once these indirect cost pools have been identified, they can be arrayed from the most general to the most specific with regard to the particular programs or activities for which indirect cost rates are to be established. Costs from the more general pools are allocated (or stepped down) to the more specific pools and, finally, to the primary functions or activities of the organization.

An example of an indirect cost rate determined through the step-down method is shown in Exhibit 3-7. Building and equipment use allowances (depreciation) are common to all functions and activities of the organization (in this case, a research university), and therefore, these indirect costs (shown in percentage terms in Exhibit 3-7) are distributed "across the board." Central administrative functions incur space and utility costs, and these indirect costs must be allocated to the administrative (G&A) pool before it can be allocated, in turn, to other functions. The same procedure is followed to distribute the costs of the library, student services, departmental administration, and the administrative services provided to each of the primary functions of the university—research, public service, and instruction. Finally, the indirect cost rate is determined by dividing the total direct costs associated with a given program or activity into the total indirect costs allocated to that function. Through this method, it is possible to determine the impact of changes in these indirect costs on the full costs of individual programs, projects, or activities.

Under- or overapplication of overhead may develop when predetermined rates are used, and significant differences may arise from month to month. However, if the cost approximation methods have produced reliable estimates, these accumulated differences should become relatively insignificant by the end of the fiscal year.

Posting to Cost Accounts

The procedural steps for summarizing and posting data to cost accounts are outlined in Exhibit 3-8. The primary record of work performed and expenses incurred is provided through field reports. The particular design and maintenance of such reports often depend on local circumstances. A job ordering system, for example, may be installed to monitor and record street maintenance costs. A crew foreman or project

Exhibit 3-7 *Step-Down Method for Determining Indirect Cost Rate (shown as percentages)*

Indirect Cost Pool	O&M	University G&A	Library	Student Services	Dept. Admin.	Research Admin.	Public Service	Instruct. Admin.	Auxiliary Enterprises	Research	Public Service	Instruction	Total
Building use allowance	0.08	0.09	0.26	—	—	—	—	—	1.32	0.53	0.06	0.93	
Equipment use allowance	0.40	0.15	0.08	—	—	—	—	—	0.24	2.10	0.34	1.40	
State central service charge	0.14	0.06	0.06	0.04	0.15	0.03	0.01	0.05	0.20	0.55	0.40	0.48	
SUBTOTAL: Use charges	0.62	0.30	0.40	0.04	0.15	0.03	0.01	0.05	1.76	3.18	0.80	2.81	8.55
Operations and maintenance	22.33 →	1.35	2.27	—	—	—	—	—	1.45	6.64	1.02	10.22	19.33
General and administrative		9.45 →	0.42	0.28	1.07	0.24	0.11	0.33	1.36	2.34	1.65	3.30	8.65
Library			10.00 →	—	—	—	—	—	1.11*	0.68	0.24	11.06	13.09
Student services				6.67 →	—	—	—	—	—	0.32	0.02	6.65	6.99
Departmental administration					25.40 →	—	—	—	—	7.72	6.84	12.06	26.62
Research administration						5.63 →	—	—	—	5.90	—	—	5.90
Public service administration							2.50 →	—	—	—	2.62	—	2.62
Instructional administration								7.87 →	—	—	—	8.25	8.25
TOTAL	22.95	11.10	13.09	6.99	26.62	5.90	2.62	8.25	5.68*	26.78	13.19	54.35	100.00

*Includes 1.11% from the library indirect cost pool assigned to general public utilization.

Exhibit 3-8 *Posting Data to Cost Accounts*

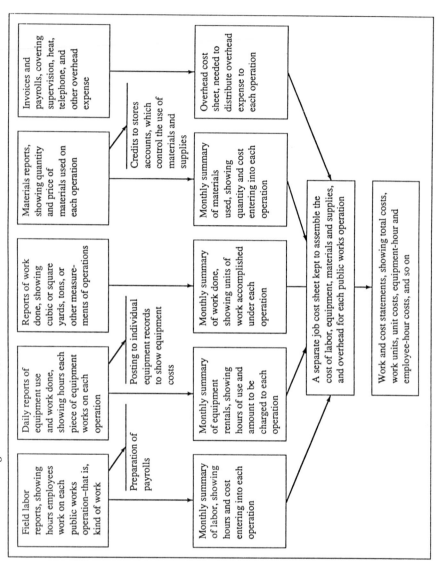

Field labor reports, showing hours employees work on each public works operation—that is, kind of work

Daily reports of equipment use and work done, showing hours each piece of equipment works on each operation

Reports of work done, showing cubic or square yards, tons, or other measurements of operations

Materials reports, showing quantity and price of materials used on each operation

Invoices and payrolls, covering supervision, heat, telephone, and other overhead expense

Preparation of payrolls

Posting to individual equipment records to show equipment costs

Credits to stores accounts, which control the use of materials and supplies

Monthly summary of labor, showing hours and cost entering into each operation

Monthly summary of equipment rentals, showing hours of use and amount to be charged to each operation

Monthly summary of work done, showing units of work accomplished under each operation

Monthly summary of materials used, showing quantity and cost entering into each operation

Overhead cost sheet, needed to distribute overhead expense to each operation

A separate job cost sheet kept to assemble the cost of labor, equipment, materials and supplies, and overhead for each public works operation

Work and cost statements, showing total costs, work units, unit costs, equipment-hour and employee-hour costs, and so on supervisor may prepare the field report. Or it may be desirable to have each employee prepare a daily or weekly "time-and-effort report," indicating specific work assignments and the time spent on each operation. Separate bills of materials used and statements of equipment used for each job or operation would have to be provided by supervisory personnel. Field reports should be summarized before posting to job cost sheets or work and cost ledgers.

The information gathered through these reports can serve several purposes. Field labor reports, used to determine the cost of labor entering into each operation or job, can also provide a basis for payroll preparation (a general accounting function). Daily reports of equipment operators provide summaries of the prorated costs (equipment rental charges) to be distributed to the various jobs on the cost ledger. These reports can also be used to post individual equipment records (showing, for each piece of equipment, the expenses for labor, gasoline, oil, and other supplies, repair costs, overhead, and depreciation). Materials and supplies reports indicate stores withdrawn from stockrooms, providing credit to stores accounts as well as charges to operating costs accounts.

Many indirect costs can be reported in substantially the same manner as direct costs—from time reports, store records, and so forth. Certain indirect costs can also be determined from invoices on such items as travel expenses, utility services, and general office expenses. These indirect costs are initially posted to an overhead cost sheet and then allocated to jobs and activities on some predetermined prorated basis.

The job cost sheet is the final assemblage of the information with respect to all work performed and all costs incurred. Accounts in the work and cost ledger are generally posted monthly and closed upon completion of a specific job or at the end of the regular accounting period, when unit costs on an activity or program are recorded.

Monthly summary statements of work completed, expenses, units costs, and employee-hour production can be compiled readily from information on the job cost sheets. Other statements may be prepared periodically, according to management needs, on such subjects as total labor costs, employee productivity, equipment rental costs, analysis of noneffective time and idle equipment, and loss of supplies through waste or spoilage.

Standard Costs and Variance Analysis

Standard costs relate the cost of production to some predetermined indexes of operational efficiency. If actual costs vary from these standards, management must determine the reasons for the deviation and whether the costs are controllable or noncontrollable with respect to the responsible unit. Misdirected efforts, inadequate equipment, defective materials, or any one of a number of other factors can be identified and eliminated through a standard cost system. In short, standard costs provide a means of cost control through the application of variance analysis.

Although standard cost systems have been widely used in the private sector, government and other not-for-profit applications have been very limited. Nevertheless, such standards have relevance in a number of organizational environments.

In setting up standards, optimal or desired (planned) unit costs and related workload measures are established for each job or activity. Workload measures usually focus on time-and-effort indices, such as number of persons served per hour, yards of dirt moved per day, or more generally, volume of activity per unit of time. After these measures have been established, total variances can be determined by comparing actual results with planned performance. Price, rate, or spending variances should then be determined for differences between standard and actual costs. Quantity or efficiency variances can be developed for measured differences between the anticipated and actual volume of activity. Knowledge of differences in terms of cost (price) and volume (efficiency) enables the manager to identify more clearly the cause and responsibility for significant deviations from planned performance.

If, for example, the anticipated volume of a city bus system is 625,000 riders at a fare of $0.50, but only 525,000 riders actually use the service, then the bus system's *volume variance* is $50,000 (100,000 riders times $0.50). If the actual fare charged is $0.55 instead of $0.50, the *total variance* is only $23,750 [(625,000 × $0.50) − (525,000 × $0.55)]. The volume variance is still $50,000. However, there is a favorable *price variance* of $26,250 [(525,000 × $0.55) − (525,000 × $0.50)]. If different routes call for different fares, and the actual mix of routes used is different from that anticipated (and budgeted), then a *mix variance* would result.

There are no hard-and-fast methods for establishing cost standards. However, workload and unit cost data from previous years serve as a logical starting point. More detailed studies may be required to determine the quantity and cost of personal services, materials, equipment, and overhead associated with particular kinds of effort or volumes of activity. Unit costs can be estimated for each of these cost elements by adjusting trend data for expected changes during the next fiscal period. Standards should be established for each of the cost elements entering into a given job or operation. These standards can then be combined to establish an overall cost standard for the particular type of work, activity category, or program element.

Standard costs should be systematically reviewed and revised when found to be out of line with prevailing cost conditions. Changes in these standards may be required when new methods are introduced, policies are changed, wage rates or material costs increase, or significant changes occur in the efficiency of operations. Furthermore, standard costs are "local" in their application. Such standards often differ from organization to organization, reflecting different labor conditions, wage rates, service delivery problems, and operation methods.

Responsibility Accounting and Performance Evaluation

The concept of *responsibility accounting* has emerged to accommodate the need for management information at a more specific level of detail than can be provided by financial accounting procedures. Responsibility accounting attempts to report results (actual performance) in such a way that (1) significant variances from planned performance can be identified, (2) reasons for the variances can be determined, (3) responsibility can be fixed, and (4) timely action can be taken to correct problems.

Responsibility and Cost Centers

Under this approach, pertinent costs and revenues are assigned to various organizational units—departments, bureaus, programs—designated as *responsibility centers.* In municipal government, for example, the chief of police might receive separate reports on the cost of operations of the traffic control division, the vice squad, the detective division, the forensic laboratory, and so forth, so that each unit can be held accountable for its respective area of responsibility.

In the private sector, responsibility centers may take several forms:

1. A *cost center* is the smallest segment of activity or area of responsibility for which costs are accumulated.
2. A *profit center* is a segment of a business, often called a division, that is responsible for both revenue and expenses.
3. An *investment center,* like a profit center, is responsible for both revenue and expenses, but also for related investments of capital.

Outside of relatively large corporations, the cost center is the most common building block for responsibility accounting. In fact, the terms *cost center* and *responsibility center* are often used interchangeably.

Costs charged to responsibility centers should be separated between direct and indirect costs. Not all direct costs are controllable at the responsibility center level. Therefore, direct expenses should be further broken down between those that are controllable and those that are noncontrollable at the responsibility center level. A distinction is sometimes made between a cost center, which is fully burdened with indirect costs, and a *service center,* which may be assigned only the direct portion of overhead.

The ability to control costs is a matter of degree. A *controllable cost* has been defined as any cost that is subject to the influence of a given manager during a given period of time. Responsibility accounting focuses on human responsibility, placing emphasis on specific costs in relation to well-defined areas of responsibility. Managers often inherit the effects of their predecessors' decisions. The long-term effects of such costs as depreciation, long-term lease arrangements, and the like, seldom qualify as controllable costs on the performance report of a specific responsibility center manager.

To illustrate this point, consider the costs of nursing services in a hospital. The extent to which these costs are controllable at the responsibility or cost center level depends on the policies of top management regarding intensive care, the lead time available for planning the number of nurses in relation to patient load, the availability of short-term or part-time help, and so on. Some nursing managers may have relatively little control over such cost-influencing factors. These factors should be taken into account when judging performance. Clearly, an item such as depreciation on the hospital building is outside the realm of controllable costs at the responsibility center level.

Performance Reports

Most models that measure performance in the private sector are tied to profits—for example, profit percentage (profit divided by sales), return on investment (profit divided by initial investment), or residual income (profit minus a deduction for capital costs). Profits are not a viable measure, however, at the cost center level. Rather, performance most often is measured by comparing actual costs against a budget. A *variance* can thus be defined as the difference between the amount budgeted for a particular activity and the actual cost of carrying out that activity during a given period. Variances may be positive (under budget) or negative (over budget).

Detailed expenditure categories may be monitored within a given cost center (for example, as various objects of expenditure or line-items). These categories may then be aggregated into a single comparison for reporting to the next management level. Such comparisons are often made in terms of the actual costs of personal services (salaries, wages, and employee benefits) and of operations (all other direct costs) versus the amounts budgeted for these broad categories. Specific items may be broken out from operations (for example, travel, computing, rental charges), depending on the nature of the cost center's activities and the information needs of management. This aggregation/selective reporting supports the concept of *management by exception*: at each level in the organizational hierarchy, the manager's attention can be concentrated on the variance from the budget items deemed to be most important.

Performance data can be developed for management purposes independent of the budget and control accounts. In fact, this kind of performance reporting has been used in many organizations for some time, particularly in the justification of resource requests. It has also been used as a management control mechanism for assessing cost and work progress where activities are fairly routine and repetitive.

Under this approach, units of work are identified, and changes in quantity (and, on occasion, quality) of such units are measured as a basis for analyzing financial requirements. The impact of various levels of service can be tested, and an assessment can be made of changes in the size of the client groups to be served. This approach is built on the assumption that certain fixed costs remain fairly constant regardless of the level of service provided and that certain variable costs change with the level of service or the size of the clientele served. *Marginal costs* for each additional increment of service provided can be determined through such an approach. With the application of appropriate budgetary guidelines, these costs then can be converted into total cost estimates.

Responsibility Versus Blame

Variances, budgeted results, and other techniques of responsibility accounting are relatively neutral devices. When viewed positively, they can provide managers with significant means of improving future decisions. They can also assist in the delegation of decision responsibility to lower levels within an organization. These techniques, however, are frequently misused as negative management tools—as means of finding fault or placing blame. This negative use stems, in large part, from a misunderstanding of the rationale of responsibility accounting.

Responsibility accounting seeks to assign accountability to those individuals who have the greatest potential influence, on a day-to-day basis, over the costs in question. It seeks to determine which individuals in an organization are in the best position to explain why a specific outcome has occurred. It is the reporting responsibility of these individuals to explain the outcome regardless of the degree of their control or influence over the results.[6]

Passing the buck is an all-too-pervasive tendency in any large organization. When responsibility is firmly fixed, this tendency is supposedly minimized. Nevertheless, a delicate balance must be maintained between the careful delineation of responsibility, on the one hand, and a too rigid separation of responsibility, on the other. When responsibility is overly prescribed, many activities may fall between the cracks. This problem is particularly evident when two or more activities are interdependent. Under such circumstances, responsibility cannot be delegated too far down in the organization but must be maintained at a level that will ensure cooperation among the units that must interact if the activities are to be carried out successfully.

Multipurpose Accounting System

As discussed in Chapter 2, the object-of-expenditure classification—with its more detailed enumeration of object and subobject codes—offers two distinct advantages over other classification systems: (1) *accountability*—a pattern of accounts is established that can be controlled and audited; and (2) *personnel management information*—the control of personnel requirements can be used to control the entire budget. These two characteristics have sustained the object-of-expenditure format for more than sixty-five years. Recent efforts to develop financial information that is more responsive to the needs of management have found these features somewhat intransigent to other objectives, however.

Data Crosswalks

A multipurpose accounting system can be built upon the two basic characteristics of an object-of-expenditure classification. The departmental budget and expenditures for a city's Financial Management Department, shown in Exhibit 3-9, serve to illustrate this process. The department consists of five agencies: the City Treasurer's Office, the Budget Division, the Division of Accounts, the Data Processing Section, and the Purchasing Office. The City Treasurer's Office is responsible for cash disbursements, maintenance of the city's cash position, administration of tax collections, and management of investments. The Budget Division supervises the formulation and administration of the city's operating and capital budgets. The Division of Accounts directs the general accounting and payroll activities and co-ordinates the debt administration programs of the city. The Data Processing Section provides management information to assist officials in their management and

Exhibit 3-9 Line-Item Budget Commitments

FUND General	DEPARTMENT Financial Management	FUNCTION General Government	
Object Classifications		Current Budget	Actual Expenditures
Personal Services			
1100 Salaries		$378,020	$363,760
1120 Wages		0	10,500
1130 Special Payments		0	0
1140 Overtime Payments		5,250	7,990
Subtotal: Personal Services		$383,270	$382,250
Employee Benefits			
1610 Retirement and Pension Benefits		$ 12,780	$ 11,495
1620 Social Security Contributions		10,229	10,768
1630 Federal Old-Age Insurance		2,168	1,529
1640 Group Insurance		1,724	945
1650 Medical/Hospital Insurance		10,899	11,643
Subtotal: Employee Benefits		$ 37,800	$ 36,380
Contractual Services			
1210 General Repairs		$ 700	$ 755
1220 Utility Services		3,600	3,900
1230 Motor Vehicle Repairs		500	540
1240 Travel		2,100	2,270
1250 Professional Services		5,725	6,185
1260 Communications		6,780	7,320
1270 Printing		1,000	1,080
1280 Computing Services		84,725	80,900
1290 Other Contract Services		3,000	3,240
Subtotal: Contractual Services		$108,130	$106,190
Supplies and Materials			
1310 Office Supplies		$ 29,440	$ 32,200
1320 Fuel Supplies		0	0
1330 Operating Supplies		1,000	1,060
1340 Maintenance Supplies		900	955
1350 Drugs and Chemicals		0	0
1360 Food Supplies		0	0
1370 Clothing and Linens		0	0
1380 Education and Recreation Supplies		0	0
1390 Other Supplies		1,500	1,590
Subtotal: Supplies and Materials		$ 32,840	$ 34,805

Equipment		
1410 Office Equipment	$ 700	$ 845
1420 Electrical Equipment	250	270
1430 Motor Vehicles	0	0
1440 Highway Equipment	0	0
1450 Medical and Lab Equipment	0	0
1480 Data Processing Equipment	15,000	12,000
1490 Other Equipment	0	0
Subtotal: Equipment	$ 16,020	$ 13,115
Current Obligations		
1510 Payments to Sinking Funds	0	0
1520 Interest on Temporary Loans	0	0
1530 Rental Charges	0	0
1540 Insurance	300	350
1550 Dues and Subscriptions	5,000	5,300
1560 Electrostatic Reproduction	1,640	1,740
1590 Other Obligations	0	0
Subtotal: Current Obligations	$ 6,940	$ 7,390
TOTALS	$585,000	$580,130

decision-making responsibilities. The Purchasing Office acts as the central procurement agency for the city.

A program budget has been adopted on an experimental basis as part of the city's efforts to develop improved financial management and accounting procedures. Four major programs have been identified for the Financial Management Department: Cash and Debt Management, Program Budgeting and Service Level Analysis, Financial Managerial Accounting, and Procurement and Inventory Maintenance. To some extent, these programs cut across the organizational lines of the five agencies. Therefore, the expenditure data must be "crosswalked" to provide an accounting summary on a *program* basis. The term *crosswalk* refers to any data conversion that involves a change in classification systems (for example, from objects of expenditure to programs, or vice versa).

The first step is to distribute the line-item expenditures by agency. In all likelihood, an initial distribution was accomplished in the budget-building phase and is reflected in the administration of the budget in terms of allocations and allotments. Line-item expenditures across the five agencies of the Financial Management Department are summarized in Exhibit 3-10.

The next step is to prepare a parallel distribution, or crosswalk, of the line-item expenditures by the four programs that have been identified for the department's operations during the current fiscal year. This crosswalk is shown in Exhibit 3-11. As noted in Chapter 2, multidigit account codes facilitate the assignment of expenditures in such a crosswalk of accounting data.

Program costs are summarized by the five agencies of the Financial Management Department in Exhibit 3-12. A major task in the assignment is to distribute the operating costs of the Data Processing Section, since this section serves all four

Exhibit 3-10 *Line-Item Expenditures by Agencies*

Line-Items	Agencies					
	CT	BUD	ACC	DP	PUR	Totals
Personal Services	53,768	90,518	77,869	111,389	48,706	382,250
Benefits	5,262	8,810	7,620	9,922	4,766	36,380
Contractual Services	3,655	6,120	5,300	87,800	3,315	106,190
Supplies and Materials	5,035	8,425	7,295	9,490	4,560	34,805
Equipment	—	—	1,115	12,000	—	13,115
Current Obligations	1,370	1,705	1,475	1,920	920	7,390
Totals	69,090	115,578	100,674	232,521	62,267	580,130

CT = City Treasurer's Office
BUD = Budget Division
ACC = Division of Accounts
DP = Data Processing Section
PUR = Purchasing Office

Exhibit 3-11 *Line-Item Expenditures by Programs*

Line-Items	Programs				
	A	B	C	D	Totals
Personal Services	87,078	122,750	100,177	72,245	382,250
Benefits	8,265	11,755	9,545	6,815	36,380
Contractual Services	34,480	29,885	27,070	14,755	106,190
Supplies and Materials	7,195	11,490	9,785	6,335	34,805
Equipment	3,250	4,210	4,090	1,565	13,115
Current Obligations	1,765	2,757	1,825	1,043	7,390
Totals	142,033	182,847	152,492	102,758	580,130

A = Cash and Debt Management
B = Program Budgeting and Service Level Analysis
C = Financial and Managerial Accounting
D = Procurement and Inventory Maintenance

programs. A crosswalk back to a line-item budget, as shown in Exhibit 3-13, can assist in this effort.

Costs Versus Expenditures

In order to determine where the costs come from, it is necessary to know the amount of costs from each department or agency that goes into each program. These *cost allocations* are illustrated in Exhibit 3-14. In this context, the program entities represent cost centers or responsibility centers.

Exhibit 3-12 *Agency Operating Costs by Programs*

Agencies	A	B	C	D	Totals
CT	62,639	—	—	6,451	69,090
BUD	2,008	109,554	2,008	2,008	115,578
ACC	8,000	—	92,674	—	100,674
DP	69,386	73,293	57,810	32,032	232,521
PUR	—	—	—	62,267	62,267
Totals	142,033	182,847	152,492	102,758	580,130

Exhibit 3-13 *Line-Item Expenditures by Programs: Data Processing Section*

Line-Items	A	B	C	D	Totals
Personal Services	29,945	38,095	27,640	15,709	111,389
Benefits	2,686	3,483	2,460	1,293	9,922
Contractual Services	30,825	23,765	21,770	11,440	87,800
Supplies and Materials	2,160	3,065	2,490	1,775	9,490
Equipment	3,250	4,210	2,975	1,565	12,000
Current Obligations	520	675	475	250	1,920
Totals	69,386	73,293	57,810	32,032	232,521

Exhibit 3-14   *Operating and Capital Costs by Programs*

Agencies	Programs				Totals
	A	*B*	*C*	*D*	
CT	67,639	—	—	6,451	74,090
BUD	2,008	119,554	2,008	2,008	125,578
ACC	8,000	—	92,674	—	100,674
DP	89,386	93,293	77,810	52,032	312,521
PUR	—	—	—	67,267	67,267
Totals	167,033	212,847	172,492	127,758	680,130

It is important to note that total costs exceed recorded expenditures by $100,000. From the discussion of the basis of accounting (Chapter 2), it may be recalled that expenditures represent costs measured by the amount of actual cash paid out during a given fiscal period. On an accrued cost basis, however, adjustments must be made for inventories, depreciation of fixed assets, and other accounts. Such adjustments are critical in answering the question: how much does a program actually cost?

The distribution of accrued costs by programs is shown in Exhibit 3-14. The major adjustment occurs in capital outlay ($80,000), assigned to the Data Processing Section and distributed equally across all four programs. Other adjustments are evident in supplies ($5,000) under Purchasing; travel ($5,000) incurred by the City Treasurer under Program A; and contractual services ($10,000) incurred by the Budget Division under Program B.

From an accounting standpoint, perhaps the most valuable type of program crosswalk is one that brings together the types of costs by cost center or department for each program. Therefore, in order to compare program costs with the overall effectiveness of program activities, it is essential that a program budget be based on costs rather than expenditures.

Summary: Future-Oriented Accounting Information

The primary concern of financial accounting is the accurate and objective recording of past events (financial transactions). The basic objective of managerial accounting is the provision of information for improved financial management decisions.

This chapter has focused on two basic functions of managerial accounting—cost determination and cost control—and on the more specific techniques of cost accounting and responsibility accounting that support these basic functions. The five basic cost components involved in any activity or program are: (1) labor (personnel), (2) contractual services, (3) materials and supplies, (4) equipment expenses, and (5) overhead, or indirect costs. The first step in controlling these costs is to determine how they function under various conditions. This process is called *cost approximation* or *cost estimation*. It involves efforts to find predictable relationships (cost functions) between a dependent variable (cost) and one or more independent variables (organizational activities). Several methods for approximating cost functions were discussed in this chapter, the regression method being the most reliable.

Whenever the full cost of a service or product must be determined, costs must be allocated according to their variable, fixed, direct, and indirect components. Fixed costs of any project remain constant as the volume of activity increases; on a per unit basis, these costs become progressively smaller. Variable costs are more or less uniform per unit, but the total of these costs increases as the volume of activity increases. A direct cost is incurred in support of a specific, identifiable purpose. An indirect cost is associated with more than one activity or program and cannot be traced directly to any individual activity.

Various accounting mechanisms must be used to ensure the proper recording of cost flow. These mechanisms, for the most part, are embodied in the procedures of cost accounting.

Responsibility accounting seeks to assign accountability to those sectors of an organization (cost centers and responsibility centers) in which day-to-day influence can be exercised over the costs in question. The concept of controllable costs—that is, any cost that can be influenced by a given cost center manager during a given period—is a key to responsibility accounting. The emphasis on controllable costs and budgeted results makes responsibility accounting a good supporting component of the financial management process.

Endnotes

1. Robert Zemsky, Randall Porter, and Laura P. Oedel, "Decentralized Planning: To Share Responsibility," *Educational Record* 59 (Summer 1978): 244.

2. Robert N. Anthony and James S. Reese, *Management Accounting: Text and Cases* (Homewood, IL: Richard D. Irwin, 1975), p. 422.

3. James H. Rossell and William W. Frasure, *Managerial Accounting* (Columbus, OH: Charles E. Merrill, 1972), p. 4.

4. Leo Herbert, Larry N. Killough, and Alan Walter Steiss, *Governmental Accounting and Control* (Pacific Grove, CA: Brooks/Cole, 1984), p. 212.

5. Charles T. Horngren, *Introduction to Management Accounting* (Englewood Cliffs, NJ: Prentice-Hall, 1978), p. 225.

6. Horngren, *Introduction to Management Accounting*, p. 252.

CHAPTER 4

Cash Management

Problems of cash management are not widely discussed in the literature of public financial administration. Even less attention has been given to the constraints that may impede efforts to maximize returns on the investment of temporarily idle public funds. Local governments and other public organizations stand to realize considerable financial benefits if they manage their resources efficiently. However, few public organizations have established specific policy guidelines with regard to the management of cash.

Maximizing Returns on Cash Flows

Most local governments must continuously seek additional funds to provide an increasing array of services for their citizens. At the same time, many jurisdictions may be losing significant revenue through a lack of understanding of the techniques of maximizing returns on their cash flows. Local financial administrators frequently encounter numerous constraints in their efforts to maximize the benefits from these idle funds.

Two Types of Decision Costs

When cash is committed to future use, the holder must forfeit income that could be earned through the investment of the cash in marketable securities. The amount of cash to be held can be determined by balancing two kinds of decision costs:

1. The opportunity cost of not investing, which increases as the size of the cash balance increases.
2. The costs of reviewing information and making the decisions required to invest, disinvest, borrow, or repay loans. These costs decrease as the amount of cash balance increases.

The basic problem in the management of cash is how to balance these two types of conflicting costs. The objective is to incur minimum costs, while at the same time holding a critical minimum cash balance. This minimum cash balance should be just large enough to reduce the risk of running out of cash (and thereby incurring additional costs) to an acceptable level. Beyond that minimum, temporary idle cash is expensive. When the short-term market rate of interest is 8 percent per annum, for example, the opportunity cost of an idle cash balance of $1 million is about $219 a day, or $80,000 a year.

In the private sector, rising interest rates and the profit incentive have spurred vigorous activity to maximize the utilization of cash resources. Businesses have recognized the potential earnings that can accrue from the short-term investment of idle cash. Many private organizations have several employees whose sole responsibility is to manage the organization's cash position.

The opportunity to minimize interest costs should motivate public organizations to initiate more efficient cash management practices. Public funds should be managed no less prudently than private funds.

Emerging Interest in Cash Management in the Public Sector

Interest in cash management in the public sector has emerged only in the past twenty years, spurred by increasing costs of providing services amid decreasing tax resources, high unemployment rates, and inflation. The primary concern of public financial officers in the past had been to hold sufficient amounts of cash to satisfy the financial obligations of their organizations. This attitude began to change, however, in the face of increasing costs of borrowing, increasing yields of marketable securities, and the rapid expansion of activities that require large amounts of working capital. Many public organizations gradually realized the importance of minimizing cash holdings, accelerating cash inflows, and controlling cash outflows.

Although cash management originally developed out of a custodial function, its role today has expanded and become more sophisticated. Nevertheless, safeguarding of funds remains a key responsibility.[1] Thus, the main objectives of a cash management system are (1) to provide for the adequate availability and safekeeping of funds under varied economic conditions and (2) to achieve an organization's financial objective of an adequate return on investments. These objectives may seem to be contradictory: cash that must be available to meet daily financial obligations cannot at the same time be invested in interest-yielding securities.

The ability of local governments to achieve the goals of cash management is often limited by constraints imposed by state constitutions, local ordinances and by-laws, and even federal laws or regulations. The financial management practices of local government are restricted by laws that establish procedures for the collection of monies and payment of obligations and regulate the deposit of funds and the purchase of securities.

Elements of Cash Management

Cash management is made up of four elements: forecasting, mobilizing and managing the cash flow, maintaining banking relations, and investing surplus cash (see Exhibit 4-1). Each of these elements must be actively pursued to achieve an effective

Exhibit 4-1 *Elements of Cash Management*

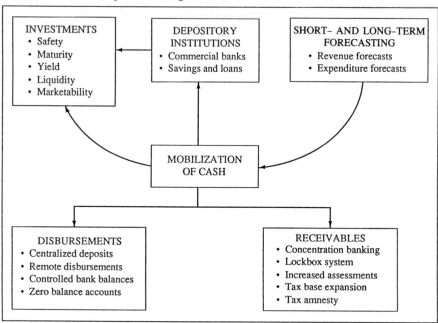

cash management system. Following an overview of these four elements, the balance of this chapter will focus on cash flow forecasting and cash mobilization techniques.

Forecasting

As applied to cash management practices, *forecasting* can be defined as the ability to calculate, predict, or plan future events or conditions using current or historical data. In general, forecasts that cover periods of one year or less are considered *short-term,* and those that extend beyond one year are considered *long-term.* These forecasts form the basis for a *cash budget.*

A cash budget monitors how much money will be available for investment, when it will become available, and for how long. Thus, a successful investment strategy for any organization depends on the accuracy and timeliness of its cash budget. A number of constraints, however, may make it difficult to construct efficient cash budgets for governmental and other public organizations.

Revenues and expenditures in public organizations are not always well coordinated. A significant time lag often occurs between the receipt of funds and their disbursement. Owing to the large inflow of revenue just prior to the penalty dates on the tax calendar, there are periods during which idle cash balances accumulate. Intergovernmental transfers—local government entitlements from federal and state sources—are also disbursed on a periodic basis and in relatively large amounts. Bonds issued for capital construction normally are sold before the commencement of the project to ensure complete financing in advance. These funds are then disbursed as costs are incurred throughout the period of construction, leaving a cash balance for investment.

There usually is some variance between forecasts and actual cash flow, because all necessary information and variables cannot be incorporated into the forecast model. This variance may increase or decrease depending on what management does or does not do. The ability of management to make decisions and take actions compatible with sound forecasting techniques is a constraint that affects the cash budget. As Hartley has observed, specific management action will be constrained by "circumstances ruling at the time the decision is taken," including "the nature and size of the cash problem, the financial standing of the local government, the economic environment and the ongoing market rate of interest."[2]

Managing the Cash Flow

Cash management involves three basic operations: collection, deposits, and disbursements. The techniques used to assemble funds and make them readily available for investment are known as *cash mobilization*. Organizations must:

1. Develop policies and procedures to guide each major source of income/ revenue.
2. Establish deposit procedures to handle major revenue processing problems (such as the semiannual collection of property taxes in local governments).
3. Establish deposit procedures for each type of revenue and collection location.
4. Adopt and maintain policies and procedures for each type of expenditure or category of vendor.

An area with great potential for providing additional usable cash is the reduction of time delays in *collecting receivables*. The collection of local property taxes and the penalties that may be assessed on delinquent accounts are strictly prescribed by state statutes. Although the law requires people to pay their taxes within a predetermined time span, some people deliberately delay payments, particularly if they will not be penalized for doing so. Efforts to mobilize cash will be futile unless taxpayers make prompt payments. This same caveat applies to prompt payments by clients of other public organizations.

Since many receipts and expenditures are predictable, the cash budget should provide a workable schedule of cash flows for a given period of time. The cash flow problem is essentially that of having sufficient resources in current bank deposits to meet cash obligations. All receipts, checks, money orders, and cash should be deposited as soon as possible. Although this may seem obvious, Smith has noted that it is the practice of many organizations to collect these items for a week or more before depositing them.[3] Idle funds, such as checks sitting in safes, cash registers, or desk drawers over the weekend or even overnight, could be earning income for the organization. Techniques that have been developed and successfully applied to accelerate collections and deposits are summarized in Exhibit 4-2.

In spite of the overwhelming evidence regarding the efficiency and effectiveness of electronic transfers, some local governments prohibit their treasurers from using

Exhibit 4-2   *Techniques to Accelerate Collections and Deposits*

- *Lockbox systems* involve the use of special post office boxes to intercept payments of accounts receivable and accelerate deposits for cash utilization.

- *Electronic transfers* provide a quicker, less costly, and more secure means of moving funds than checks or other instruments that have to move through the postal system.

- *Area concentration banking* refers to a network of depository accounts in local banks into which receivables are paid. The accumulated payments are then transferred to a number of regional banks that serve as collection centers.

- *Disbursement procedures* focus on methods, policies, and procedures that an organization can employ in paying its bills.

such transfers to perform investment transactions.[4] This constraint may severely restrict investment opportunities in a rapidly changing money market.

In recent years, keeping a tight rein on bank balances has become one of the most highly touted principles of cash management. Money not needed for operating costs or compensating balances (discussed in the following section) is money unemployed. Hill contends that "cash can be conserved by employing a sound payables system that centralizes the payment of large bills. This allows for careful timing of disbursements, the ability to take offered discounts, and the possible use of drafts rather than cheques."[5] Organizations have developed several ways of controlling their cash balances to avoid the buildup of idle cash. These techniques will be discussed in further detail in a subsequent section.

Banking Relations

Maintenance of good relations with the financial community—banks, savings and loan associations, investment bankers, commercial paper dealers, and security analysts—is an important part of cash management. Local governments are creatures of the states and, as such, are frequently constrained by state laws in the formation of relations with depository institutions. State laws may determine, for example, the bank or banks with which a local jurisdiction may do business. Banks licensed to operate in the state are preferred, and localities may be further restricted to banks operating in their particular city or county. Total deposits by the local government in each local bank may be legally restricted, based on the bank's capital. Finally, local politics may influence financial management practices in selecting depository institutions and making investments.

Although the idea of "spreading the wealth around" makes good political sense, it makes bad economic sense. From a cash management perspective, the use of too many local banks makes it difficult to determine how much cash is available on any given day for investment purposes. On the other hand, if a jurisdiction "puts all its eggs in one basket," it is likely to receive lower yields on its investments than if it had "shopped around." The choice of one bank for deposit of the majority of local government funds may be based on tradition or on politics.

Shifting business among three or four local banks on an annual or biannual basis is a good political strategy that also simplifies cash management by minimizing the number of open bank accounts. However, competition is limited, and local banks may not be motivated to offer additional services to the local government or to improve existing ones.

Whenever possible, the banks with which a government or other public organization does business should be selected through a *competitive bid* process. The bidding process involves four steps. First, an evaluation must be made of the financial environment to determine the basic requirements of the organization and what it is willing to pay for these services. Next, a request for proposals should be prepared and circulated to competing banks. Third, the proposals submitted should be reviewed in an open manner, making the criteria for selection public. Finally, local officials should select and enter into contractual agreement with the bank or banks that best meet the established criteria. The benefits to be derived from competitive bidding are listed in Exhibit 4-3.

Exhibit 4-3 *Benefits of Competitive Bidding for Banking Services*

- Additional interest earnings from improved yield, resulting in overall increase in amounts available for investment.
- Additional services provided for the same amount of bank charges.
- Reductions in bank service charges or compensating balances.
- Overall increase in efficiency of cash management operations.

Bankers prefer *compensating balances* to fee payments because deposits are the main source of a bank's loanable funds. The compensating balance is a constraint on the ability of a local government to maximize earnings, however, because banks require a minimum average rather than an absolute minimum balance.[6] This issue is critical, since the average cash balance determines interest revenue, a key factor in cash management profitability.

Compensating balances generally are negotiated and mutually agreed upon by the local jurisdiction and its banks. Prior to these negotiations, local financial executives must come to definite decisions on a number of issues: (1) how much money should be kept in the bank to cover the jurisdiction's operating needs; (2) what types of services are expected from the bank; and (3) how much the locality is willing to pay for these services. As Sanders and Kirk point out, compensating balances represent "potential lost revenue that may exceed the amount the jurisdiction might have paid if fees for each service had been levied by the bank."[7]

Banks should provide an analysis of compensating balances periodically. If the jurisdiction determines that its banks' demands for compensating balances have been excessive, it should take appropriate action to renegotiate them downward. On the other hand, if the analysis indicates that the banks are being undercompensated, the jurisdiction should be prepared to rectify the situation by leaving larger amounts on balance to support the established quality of services.

Investment of Excess Funds

Cash on hand to meet future financial obligations should be invested in short-term securities. A cash budget should provide an estimate of the organization's cash requirements for disbursement by months, weeks, or days. Such an estimate should enable the financial manager to determine what part of the cash balances can be invested. Different investments can be timed to mature when the funds are needed. When the timing is uncertain, funds can be held in securities that can be quickly converted into cash. Longer investment periods offer higher yields but less liquidity.

Since local governments and other public organizations are not profit-oriented, they are often encouraged to hold short-term securities that have high liquidity and can be easily converted into cash, either through the market or through maturity. The most attractive instruments are securities supported by the full faith and credit of the federal government. Other relatively risk-free securities are time deposits, time certificates of deposit, commercial paper, banker's acceptances, and repurchase agreements.[8]

Investors should be aware of seven characteristics of securities: (1) yield, (2) maturity, (3) marketability or liquidity, (4) risk, (5) call provisions, (6) the availability of denominations, and (7) taxability. In most cases, however, the decision to purchase a specific security will be guided by considerations of yield, liquidity, and maturity. Risk is a relatively minor factor in local government because of restrictions by state and federal laws on the financial officer's ability to engage aggressively in the money market.

Cash Flow Forecasting

A forecast indicates the most likely outcome of a future event based on what is currently known about the circumstances that will influence that event. As Hartley has observed,

> a forecast is no more than someone's belief in the future based upon certain assumptions that have been made regarding future events. If the assumptions subsequently prove to be wrong, then the forecast will not prove to be right either. For this reason, it is necessary to set down formally the key assumptions on which major parts of the forecast are based.[9]

In the context of cash management, the ultimate objective of a forecast is to guide appropriate and timely management action toward improved control of the organization's cash flow. Thus, a forecast that turns out to be incorrect is not necessarily a "bad" forecast. By the same token, a forecast that turns out to be right is not always a "good" forecast. Rather, a good forecast is one that provides a sound basis for management action as the future unfolds and as events begin to diverge from the forecast. A good forecast provides alternative scenarios and strategies that can be adopted as environmental conditions and organizational needs change.

Forecasting in the Budget Process

The primary objective of cash management is to ensure that sufficient funds are available to meet organizational needs at a minimum cost, including the opportunity cost associated with uninvested funds. This objective calls for:

1. An accurate cash flow forecast to eliminate the need for (or to minimize the cost of) short-term borrowing.
2. The efficient collection of receivables, from the point of receipt to the place where funds can be invested or spent.
3. A scheduling of reimbursements to ensure that obligations are paid on time, but not ahead of payment deadlines.

Forecasting must be an integral part of an organization's overall budgeting process. Without a cash budget, a manager cannot obtain a long-term view of cash flow patterns and, therefore, cannot effectively plan future cash requirements and optimal investments.

Actions That Affect the Movement of Cash

Cash flows as a result of management actions regarding receivables and disbursements. Management decisions that elicit the flow of cash can be summarized under the following categories: (1) operating decisions, (2) capital expenditure decisions, (3) credit decisions, (4) investment decisions, and (5) financing decisions.

Operating decisions stem from the policies of the organization, such as the creation or elimination of a service unit or department, increases in the charges for services or in the tax rate in the case of local government, changes in the salaries and fringe benefits extended to staff, and so forth. The implementation of such policies will result in adjustments in the inflow and outflow of cash.

Capital expenditure decisions that affect the infrastructure of the organization give rise to the outward flow of cash. An organization's infrastructure involves the construction, repair, and maintenance of fixed, physical assets. Local governments must provide the necessary infrastructure for social and economic development. In this context, Holland defines *public infrastructure* as "all government capital investment including social investment such as education and health care."[10]

Credit decisions involve the length of time an organization takes to make payments to its vendors for goods and services provided, as well as the length of time a client/customer may take to make payment to the organization without penalty. An increase in supplier credit time is like providing the organization with an interest-free loan. The organization can invest the amount owed in short-term financial assets and earn interest prior to the payment deadline. An increase in the credit period granted to customers/clients, on the other hand, delays the flow of cash into the organization's treasury.

Investment and financing decisions set the flow of funds in motion. *Investment decisions* result in the use of inactive cash to purchase financial assets or the liberation of funds by the sale of such assets. *Financing decisions* involve the acquisition of new money by selling bonds, borrowing, or increasing revenues (as by raising user charges, prices, or taxes).

It is obvious that cash does not flow of its own accord. Its flow is precipitated by any number of organizational decisions. Managers are responsible for initiating the flow of cash and must also be able to monitor and control the direction of the flows to ensure that their organizations will not encounter cash flow problems.

Rationale for Forecasting

Forecasting can serve a number of objectives, including:

1. Avoidance of bankruptcy.
2. Avoidance of costly mistakes.
3. Assistance in management control.
4. Increased lender confidence in the organization.
5. Improved utilization of capital.[11]

The prospect of going bankrupt is the most serious threat to the life of any organization. Organizations do not go bankrupt because they have had to liquidate their financial assets. Rather, they go bankrupt because they have cash flow problems. The avoidance of bankruptcy should be adequate justification for cash forecasts.

Ill-conceived and premature ventures usually result in serious financial consequences. Systematic forecasts of an organization's cash position, however, should reveal the potential impact on cash flow of such expenditures. This advance warning provides an opportunity to reconsider the expenditures and/or their timing. A cash budget reveals the movement of cash into and out of the treasury. An astute manager uses a cash budget to identify early signs of an impending cash problem and to indicate appropriate steps to avert the problem. In this way, a cash budget facilitates management control.

The preparation of a cash budget on a regular and systematic basis increases the confidence of lending institutions in the organization and those who manage it. Any financier or lender would like to know when an organization will need additional funding, for how long, and in what amounts. Answers to these questions, coupled with the availability of relevant data and charts to support the answers, enhance the ability of an organization to raise funds when required.

The cash budget also enables improved use of capital. Forecasting not only spots cash deficiencies but also indicates if and when cash surpluses are likely to occur and the expected amount of the surplus or deficit. Surpluses can be invested in interest-yielding securities. Conversely, when deficits occur, short-term borrowing can be arranged or maturing assets redeemed.

Timing is an important element in cash forecasting. Even if all quantities of future cash flows can be estimated correctly, an organization may still be in considerable financial difficulty if the timing of the forecast is flawed. Thus, accurate timing of receipts and expenditures will enhance the capacity of the cash budget to serve the objectives enumerated above.

Types of Forecasts

Broadly speaking, there are two types of forecasts, each serving a distinct purpose. *Short-term forecasts* usually cover a period of less than one year. If appropriately designed and regularly revised, a short-term forecast can assist in the day-to-day operations of an organization because it is based on a detailed statement of all the accounts that either generate or absorb cash. A short-term forecast highlights the peaks and troughs resulting from the daily, weekly, or monthly operations of the organization.

Long-term forecasts evaluate the financial position of an organization over an extended period of time—two, three, or even five years into the future. Unlike highly detailed short-term forecasts, a long-term forecast attempts to provide only a rough sketch of an organization's more distant financing requirements. Private firms use long-term forecasts to gauge the impact of proposed acquisitions, mergers, or new product developments on the cash flow position a number of years into the future. Such forecasts may also be used in determining the future cash needs of the organization, especially its working capital requirements. If, for example, an organization is experiencing a serious cash outflow without a corresponding cash inflow, the cash forecast should give a good indication of the rate and duration of this occurrence and why it is happening.

The long-term forecast also facilitates the appraisal of proposed capital projects. It shows "not only how much cash the organization will generate to support these projects, it also shows how much financing, if any, will be required to complete them."[12] Thus, the extended cash forecast assists in deciding which proposed projects related to the expansion of the organization should be approved, deferred, or abandoned.

The Decision Environment of Government

In the private sector, the corporate hierarchy determines objectives and adopts the strategic plan, which is updated from time to time to reflect changing conditions both inside and outside the organization. In the public sector, however, the plan, or budget, that ultimately emerges is a reflection of a consensus reached and deals struck in extended negotiations among various participating parties. In other words, the discipline evident in private-sector expenditure patterns is often lacking in the public sector, making forecasting very difficult.

The mood of the voters, as interpreted by elected and appointed officials, determines the direction of expenditures (and also receipts). Major expenditure decisions are made by the county board of supervisors or city council. Disbursement authority over major expenditures may also reside with the board or council. Thus, the finance officer has little or no control over the timing of the disbursements that must be made. Any attempt to forecast revenues and expenditures can be seriously undermined by the uncertainties and irregularities of the timing of major commitments.

The major argument of those who believe that forecasting serves only limited objectives is that the world is not static and that the assumptions under which a cash budget is developed can change even before the exercise is completed. Revenues are forecast on the assumption that all the variables taken into consideration—such as the general economic climate, legislation, and prevailing prices—will remain as they were. They almost certainly will not. Opponents of forecasting argue that the knowledge and theoretical basis to predict what the economy will do in the next five years do not exist. They further argue that a forecast, the stability of which cannot be guaranteed, cannot form the basis for future financial planning.

This negative perspective misses a basic premise of forecasting. A forecast is an approximation of what will likely occur in the foreseeable future. The objective of forecasting is not to be accurate, but to provide a basis on which to measure the differences between actual events and the plan. In this way, the nature and extent of corrective actions can be more clearly defined. As Smith points out, a forecast is "used to measure the gap between what will probably happen, leaving things alone, and what we want to happen. It gives a measure of the difference, which then forms the basis for developing different strategies . . . to eliminate the difference."[13] Once this point is understood and accepted, the utility of forecasting as a tool of cash management can be more fully appreciated.

The notion that revenue forecasting is impossible in the public sector is furthermost from the truth. A recent survey of county governments indicated that 60 percent of the responding jurisdictions regularly attempted some form of forecast of their revenues and used these forecasts as the basis for financial decision making.[14] Forecasting in the public sector seems relatively easy because governmental cash requirements are based on budgeted expenditures, which are finite and known in advance. Government revenues are tax-based and, therefore, estimable.

Wildavsky asserts that the best predictor of next year's budget is this year's budget. "Those in government operate in a world they never made, which is only partially subject to their ministrations. Commitments of the past make up the largest part of the budget, and it is either legally or politically impossible to alter them drastically."[15]

In order to estimate revenues, the manager should be knowledgeable about the specific historical characteristics and collection patterns of each revenue source. The development of a three-year "historical detail profile" is necessary to obtain a trend about the behavior of the various revenue sources.[16] This profile should include when revenue was received, the amounts received at those times, significant deviations in collection patterns, and relevant explanatory information.

The development of a historical profile may not be necessary for some revenue sources—for example, intergovernmental transfers and other revenues that are received according to established contracts and agreements. Revenues such as property taxes and user fees are received according to well-established patterns, but the amounts collected during each specific time period may vary significantly from year to year. Consequently, a historical detail profile would facilitate more accurate projections of these revenues. Thus, although the environments of public institutions are different from those of private firms, these differences do not preclude the application of cash management models in government and other public organizations.

Summary

The inability of local governments to develop and install efficient cash budgeting systems is a major constraint, limiting their capacity to maximize the returns on the investment of otherwise inactive cash. Unless local governments can develop reliable estimates of their cash flow positions, enabling them to identify how much cash will become available, they will not be in a position to take full advantage of the securities market. Consequently, they will not be able to maximize the returns on whatever financial assets they are able to purchase.

Cash Mobilization

A cash budget focuses on the productivity of various revenue sources, the timing of surpluses, and the amounts likely to be available. Management must develop policies to tap and mobilize these resources to meet organizational needs. Cash mobilization falls into two functional areas: (1) acceleration of receivables and (2) control of disbursements. *Receivables* are funds that come into the organization's treasury; *disbursements* are funds that must be paid out to vendors and others who provide services at a fee to the organization. Disbursements also include salaries and wages for the organizational staff.

Various approaches have been developed for increasing control of cash receipts and disbursements. Private firms and corporations have provided the major impetus behind the development of these techniques. The subsequent growth of interest in cash management has precipitated the exchange of information and ideas among private firms and banking and other financial institutions.

Fisher suggests that "companies that have exemplary cash management programs invariably place great emphasis on three objectives in overseeing their day-to-day money transactions. These are (1) speeding up collections, (2) controlling payables, and (3) controlling bank balances."[17]

Accelerating Collections

From the standpoint of fund availability and borrowing costs, the most effective collection system is one that minimizes the lapse between the time money is due to be received by the organization and the time the money is available for disbursement. The optimum system would be immediate wire transfer from the payee to the organization when payment is due. Given the different types of payments and necessary documentation that must be part of each payment, however, such a system is not feasible.

The flow and availability of cash to the organization can be expedited by collection systems that provide for advance billing and payment on or before receipt of goods and services. Such systems should include provision for the processing of payments separate from accounting documentation. The aggregate benefit of sound collection procedures is an increase in the productivity of cash as a working asset.

Systems that bill and subsequently process documents and remittances together before deposit retard the availability of funds to the organization.

Accelerated collection of money owed reduces an organization's borrowing costs and enhances its ability to earn additional income. Since the 1950s, when this principle gained widespread acceptance, banks and other private firms have conscientiously developed techniques to aid corporations in collecting and processing receivables and in making funds available quickly. The techniques used to accelerate receipts include lockbox services, preauthorized checks, and concentration banking.

Lockbox services involve the use of special post office boxes to intercept payments and accelerate deposits. A bank is authorized to collect mail directly from such boxes.

Lockbox processing was initiated in 1947 by Bankers Trust of New York and First National Bank of Chicago. The major impetus for development of these techniques, however, was provided in the mid-fifties by the Radio Corporation of America, which was seeking new approaches to speed up collections while at the same time reducing paperwork.

As applied in the public sector, the lockbox system consists of a post office box, rented in the name of the jurisdiction, to which taxpayers mail their property taxes, utility bill payments, and other remittances. The services usually provided by a lockbox system are detailed in Exhibit 4-4. The necessary accounting documentation is completed following receipt of payment, using deposit information from the bank. Meanwhile, the funds received have been invested with minimal delay. An additional advantage of the lockbox system is the reduction of local government staff time devoted to the collection process. It can also lead to significant reductions in staff required for manual processing of receivables. These advantages, however, should be weighed against the charges that the bank makes for these services.

Exhibit 4-4   *Lockbox Services*

- The box is emptied at least daily.
- The mail is opened, and original bills are matched with payments.
- Same-day deposits are made of the payments.
- The local government is provided with all bills or other paperwork indicating that payments have been made.
- Any checks that do not have adequate documentation regarding what is being paid and by whom are returned to the local government.

A *preauthorized check* (PAC) is a signatureless demand instrument used to accelerate the collection of fixed-payment types of obligations. Under this collection technique, the customer signs an authorization agreement that allows checks to be drawn against his or her account at specified, agreed-upon intervals. The company typically signs and sends an indemnification agreement to the customer's bank to notify it that signatureless checks are issued against some of the bank's accounts. Following completion of the authorization and indemnification agreements, the company or its PAC service bank produces the preauthorized checks on the specified payment dates. The advantages accruing from the use of this system are listed in Exhibit 4-5.[18]

Exhibit 4-5 *Advantages of Preauthorized Check Systems*

- Increased predictability of cash inflow: the dollar amounts generated each day are known in advance, facilitating daily cash flow forecasting.

- Elimination of billing costs: no repetitive notice to the customer is necessary, thus saving postage, clerical, and invoice production expenses.

- Reduction of collection float: checks are produced and deposited by banks, and no cost for receipts is involved.

- Elimination of collection problems associated with late payments or forgotten remittances: PAC assures payments as long as funds are available in the customer's account.

The primary purpose of *concentration banking* is to mobilize funds from decentralized receiving locations into a central cash pool. The cash manager can then monitor only a few cash pools, thereby facilitating better cash control.

Under this approach, a firm's sales offices make collections and deposit daily receipts in local banks. From this point, the money is moved either by bank wire or by depository transfer checks to designated regional banks, which serve as territorial collection centers. From there, the funds are wired directly to the firm's major bank.

Under a concentration banking system in the public sector, a number of local banks may serve as depositories for the payment of property taxes, utility bills, and other periodic receipts. From these banks, the money can be moved quickly by wire to a depository bank, which serves as a central collection center.

Lockbox services, preauthorized checks, and concentration banking are all aimed at speeding up receipts and reducing the time that remittances stay in transit. The number of days saved in transit time are days that the funds can be invested in interest-yielding securities.

Controlling Disbursements

Disbursements represent the outflow of funds in the form of checks issued and cash payments made. Delaying cash outflows enables an organization to optimize earnings on available funds. Good cash management practices generally dictate that disbursements be made only when due. The timing of disbursements is a very important decision that has implications for the liquidity position of the organization.

In large organizations, the potential for great variability in the quality and form of disbursement decisions often presents a considerable challenge to the cash manager. Two approaches have been devised for meeting this challenge:

1. Centralize, to the extent practical, the management of an organization's payables, particularly those involving large dollar amounts.
2. Establish administrative limits on the amount of disbursements particular organizational units are authorized to make within specified time periods.

The first objective is achieved through the use of a *central depository account.* The second objective, which is designed to control subsidiary working funds, is achieved through a *zero balance account.*

Many local governments maintain so many bank accounts to cater to the jurisdiction's various obligations that it is sometimes difficult to know how much cash is available for investment. Financial management experts have noted the advantages of consolidating various local government accounts into one central depository account. All deposits from such sources as general funds, general revenue sharing, federal and state grants, and other funds can be concentrated into this single account, thus reducing compensating balances and increasing surplus cash. The consolidation of accounts provides better control over the timing of payments, increases the effective use of excess cash, and permits the streamlining of banking relations. As Sanders and Kirk point out, the concentration of accounts

> provides readily available information on the total cash balances available for investment, permits the easy determination of how much cash to maintain in a checking account in order to pay the bank for its services, facilitates the pooling of cash from the various funds to invest in higher yielding securities, prevents overdrafts and avoids the problem of "forgotten accounts" that are not utilized for extended periods.[19]

Consolidation of accounts enables management to control and schedule the disbursement process. Decisions can then be made and carried out on the basis of sound and uniformly applied economic considerations that are in the best interest of the local jurisdiction.

Administrative limits on obligations are maintained through the effective use of *zero balance accounts*—concentration accounts that are maintained with a zero balance at the end of each banking day, thus affording the opportunity to maximize earnings on the float. *Float* is the time between when a check is written and when it clears the payer's and payee's banks. There are two kinds of float: deposit float and disbursement float.

Deposit float is the period between collection and the time funds are available for the payee's use or investment. Deposit float consists of mail time, processing procedures, and the time it takes for the payment to clear the sender's bank.

Disbursement float is the dollar difference between the balance on the organization's books and the amount actually in the bank. In other words, a time lag occurs after an organization writes a check: delivery time, processing time at the recipient's bank, and processing time at the organization's bank. The time lags of the disbursement float can be diagramed and monitored. For example, if an organization writes a check on Friday, the check may not clear the organization's account until the middle of the following week. If the treasurer moves money to the checking account from either an interest-bearing account or another investment on the same day the check is written, the organization will lose interest on those funds. However, if the fund transfer is made on the day the check clears the organization's bank, those funds can remain invested, earning additional interest. Although the potential lost revenue may be insignificant for one check, the losses for a full year can be quite considerable.

A concentration account with a zero balance is perhaps the most useful tool in sound deposits management. An organization maintains a single central account, or concentration account, in addition to separate bank accounts for each major functional category. Deposits are credited to each of the accounts for record-keeping purposes. These accounts are automatically debited for the amount deposited to maintain a current balance of zero, with the receipts being credited to the concentration account. As checks drawn on these functional accounts are presented for settlement, the exact amounts are automatically transferred from the concentration account to make the necessary payments. Thereafter, the accounts revert to zero balances.

Zero balance accounts eliminate the need to maintain excess amounts in disbursement accounts. They relieve the cash manager of the burden of estimating when checks will be presented for payment and deciding when to transfer money from one account to the other. Finally, such accounts permit the pooling of resources for investment purposes.

Controlling Bank Balances

Keeping a tight rein on bank balances has become increasingly popular as a principle of cash management. Organizations have come to realize that money not needed to meet operating costs or for compensating balances should be invested in interest-yielding securities. Consequently, organizations seek to avoid the accumulation of inactive cash in their accounts by (1) using daily cash reports and/or (2) making payments through drafts.

Daily cash reports provide daily contact with the bank to monitor changes in the organization's accounts. Banks are required to submit daily summaries of collections and disbursements handled on behalf of the organization. On the basis of these reports, the treasurer decides what to do with the balances in the accounts.

Using *drafts* enables the float to be managed without running the risk of overdrafts or inadvertently using uncollected funds. Additionally, any legal problems involving insufficient funds are circumvented, since the drafts are not "obligations" against the issuer until they are presented for payment. Drafts differ from checks in that they are drawn not on a bank but on the issuer, and are payable by the issuer. Banks act only as agents in the clearing process, presenting the draft to the issuer for redemption. Although drafts have found wide acceptance in the financial community, a serious deterrent to their expanding use is that banks take no responsibility for the final payment of drafts once they are presented.

Constraints on Cash Mobilization

Local jurisdictions may find some of these techniques for cash acceleration and disbursement unacceptable. A jurisdiction must evaluate the possible effects on its taxpayers and clients of aggressive collection practices as well as disbursement techniques that delay payments and maximize float. The objectives of cash management must be artfully blended with the need to maintain good public relations with the vendors that serve the jurisdiction.

The use of lockbox systems and preauthorized checks reduces the time required for a locality to handle receivables and deposit checks for collection. However, the speed with which these checks clear an individual's account has made citizens angry and has stiffened their opposition to electronic transfers.

The objective of the zero balance account is to maximize float, earning a return on funds even though technically they have been committed for the settlement of an already issued check. In some states, however, it is illegal to write a check on any account unless sufficient funds are present in that account to cover the obligation.

State laws often place other constraints on local financial management procedures. Historically, states have imposed special legal restraints and controls on local borrowing, including limits on outstanding debts and requirements for local referenda prior to the issuance of bonds. State laws may also specify the purposes for which debt may be incurred and the characteristics of debt instruments, including maturities, interest rates, and methods of sale. (For further discussion of this topic see Chapter 9.)

State intervention in cash management procedures and processes affects the ability of local governments to mobilize cash to meet their obligations and for investment purposes. The state usually prescribes local revenue sources, limiting the legal authority of localities to exploit other potential revenue sources.

Local governments must rely largely on property taxes as the revenue source directly under their control. However, state governments control property tax collection procedures, the assessment function, and procedures for determining the penalties that may be added to delinquent accounts. These state controls are designed to facilitate uniformity in the assessment of property values and in the application of legal requirements as these relate to property taxation.

Plausible as these requirements may be, local officials complain that such regulations deny them essential control over their most vital revenue source. Because tax increases are politically dangerous, elected officials often prefer to reduce the existing level of services rather than raise taxes. However, if local authorities had responsibility over the assessment function, property could be assessed at an inflated value and then taxed at a lower rate.

Local jurisdictions also have only limited control over the collection and deposit of transfers from the state and federal governments. State-administered taxes, such as general sales, gasoline, and liquor taxes, are collected by the state and then returned on a proportional basis to localities monthly or quarterly. Many federal grants are also disbursed to localities at the discretion of the state. State authorities may be insensitive to the cash needs of jurisdictions in determining disbursement schedules. If state officials decide to disburse the proceeds from sales taxes on a quarterly basis, local governments can do little to expedite the receipt of funds. They not only must forego the interest that such funds would have earned, but often must borrow funds on a short-term basis to meet the obligations that these state transfers are intended to cover.

Adequate credit must be available if any organization or local government is to survive in the short term. Lines of credit are committed by banks to make loans available, subject to certain mutually agreed-upon conditions. A *revolving line of credit* legally obligates the bank to lend funds up to a specified limit. A *standby line of credit* only indicates that a bank will lend money if funds are available. Lines of credit are important as a hedge against unanticipated contingencies, such as temporary financing needs and short-term cash flow shortages. The cost of maintaining a line of credit, however, ranges from three-eighths of a percent to one percent.[20] Consequently, lines of credit should not be maintained unless they are used with some frequency. Otherwise, the jurisdiction or organization will be paying for the privilege of having a line of credit that may be underutilized or unnecessary.

Strategies for Coping With Constraints

More frequent collection of property taxes may reduce the delinquency rate and improve public perception of the property tax as an acceptable form of taxation by reducing the burden of lump-sum payments. More frequent collection can also reduce administrative costs. Most states have established property tax payment periods, and taxpayers tend to wait until a few days before the deadline to mail their checks. The volume of checks to be processed during a relatively short time period usually necessitates hiring temporary workers or moving some clerical staff from other departments to the treasurer's office to process checks. At times, the costs associated with this can be prohibitive.

The status of delinquent accounts should be reviewed and stiffer penalties imposed for continued nonpayment. More important, however, the procedures for follow-up contacts and collections should be improved.

Although localities may add interest charges to unpaid taxes until the account is settled, the allowable rate of interest, as determined by the state, is often below prevailing market rates. In that case, the threat or actual imposition of interest charges may not be sufficient to bring about compliance with the law. For penalties to be meaningful and effective, they must be at least equal to the prevailing rate of interest.

Bills for property taxes, as well as for licenses, permits, and other services that localities provide on a fee basis, should be sent out promptly. The jurisdiction should specify on the face of the bill that beyond a certain date, late charges will be levied. At the same time, localities might offer discounts as an incentive for prompt payment of bills. The provision of self-addressed, postage-paid envelopes further encourages prompt payment of accounts. These strategies are advisable, however, only to the extent that the dollar return on the investment of early payments can be shown to equal or exceed the cost of the discount, envelopes, and postage.

Administrative rearrangements may accelerate receipt of other revenues. The local cash manager should be familiar with the disbursement schedules and funding rules for locally shared state taxes and should apply promptly for reimbursement. Since large sums of money are usually involved, one individual should be assigned the responsibility of coordinating these activities with state government agencies. The collection and deposit of such funds is automatic, well-documented, and secure because it is effectuated through wire transfers.

Smaller amounts, often paid in cash, are frequently handled by localities. By minimizing the number of collection points—consistent with the public's desire for convenience—the jurisdiction can ensure that fewer people handle receipts and that receipts are deposited promptly in the banks. During heavy property tax collection time, bank deposits may be made on an hourly basis to ensure that resources are not left idle. Caution should be exercised, however, in bringing in personnel or extending work hours. If the yield is low, the cost of overtime may exceed the return on investment. Therefore, local jurisdictions should undertake a cost–benefit analysis to determine if these measures should be adopted.

Revenue Enhancement Initiatives

The public's natural antipathy to increases in property taxes has limited the capacity of local governments to respond to changing fiscal requirements. This problem was compounded in 1986 when Congress eliminated a key source of local government revenue—general revenue-sharing grants. Therefore, the need to diversify local revenue sources has become increasingly urgent.

Tax Base Expansion

Expanding the tax base is difficult for local governments because, in most cases, it is not within their authority to determine their sources of revenue. The only avenue open to local governments, therefore, is to seek ways to make existing revenue sources more productive. This can be accomplished through efforts to stimulate economic growth, through more aggressive collection practices, or by increasing the tax rate.

Local governments today resist the idea of increasing taxes because of changed political priorities that emphasize "level spending." Persistent fiscal restraints at all levels of government have resulted in statewide referenda, such as Proposition 13 in California and Proposition 2½ in Massachusetts.

The most reliable source of local revenues is the property tax, and a primary way of enhancing this source is to improve the assessment function. Montgomery County, Maryland, has instituted a *recapture tax*. Its purpose is to recapture, at the time of sale or transfer of real property, revenues that would have been collected in prior years if the assessment had reflected the actual market value of the property, as demonstrated by the selling price. The formula for the recapture tax excludes minor underassessments (under $8,000). In its first six years, the recapture tax netted Montgomery County more than $10 million in additional revenue.

Tax Amnesty Programs

In some localities, delinquent tax bills may go unpaid and unpenalized year after year. According to a recent survey, about 16 percent of local governments in the United States have a tax delinquency rate in excess of 10 percent. Tax evaders are not only individuals; firms and corporations are also guilty of tax evasion.

While the federal government is still debating what to do about tax evasion, some states and localities have implemented programs that have yielded impressive results. These programs, known as tax amnesty programs, have been initiated in Massachusetts, Arizona, Missouri, North Dakota, Philadelphia, and New York City.

The Massachusetts state legislature made tax evasion a felony, punishable by up to five years in jail and/or fines up to $100,000 for individuals and $500,000 for corporations. A period of tax amnesty was then proclaimed, from October 17, 1983, to January 17, 1984. During this period, taxpayers could settle outstanding state tax obligations without any penalty charges and without criminal prosecution for past violations. All tax returns and payments that were due before October 17, 1983, were eligible for amnesty relief.

The program gained national prominence in February 1984, when state tax officials reported that the three-month program had netted more than $58 million in additional revenues from 40,000 to 50,000 delinquent taxpayers. Arizona's two-month amnesty in 1983 produced $6 million from 10,000 tax delinquents; Missouri's program yielded an additional $853,000; and North Dakota estimates that its program brought in approximately $150,000. The Taxpayer Automated Compliance System in New York City persuaded more than 55,000 individuals and companies to pay more than $43 million in delinquent taxes in 1983–1984. The city of Philadelphia reported collecting more than $30 million in delinquent taxes.[21] Other states and localities are working on similar programs.

Given the sluggish economy in the late 1970s and early 1980s, it is not surprising that tax delinquency rates in most localities have been so high. In the mid-1980s, with the economy on the mend and personal and corporate incomes rising, amnesty programs for delinquent taxes, coupled with enforcement of stiffer penalties for tax evasion in some cases, were enacted to provide inducements for the recovery of these back taxes. The argument that amnesty programs tend to encourage delinquency (since people may assume that further amnesties will be granted) does not seem to be well founded.

Tax Administration

Another means of increasing revenue is through improved tax administration procedures. One approach is reciprocity, involving a mutual exchange of enforcement and/or collection responsibilities between jurisdictions. The District of Columbia and the neighboring states of Virginia and Maryland, for example, have an agreement whereby outstanding tickets issued for traffic-related offenses in the three jurisdictions must be paid before an individual can renew his or her automobile registration. The District of Columbia estimates that 45 percent of its outstanding parking violations are issued to residents of Virginia and Maryland, representing more than $4 million in potential additional revenue to the city.[22]

Tax-Exempt Property

Local jurisdictions often include a number of tax-exempt properties owned by state and federal governments. Compensatory payment programs are designed to reimburse local governments both for the revenues lost because of the tax-exempt provisions attached to these properties and for the cost of providing services. Like other property, federal lands appreciate in value. By reassessing these properties to reflect actual market values, local governments may have a basis for seeking more equitable payments in lieu of taxes to reflect this appreciation.

Curtailing Mandated Expenditures

Local governments can press for fewer mandated expenditures as a way of conserving local resources. Mandated expenditures are obligations that must be met irrespective of annual budgetary decisions. These expenditures include social security payments and retirement benefits for employees, mandated educational standards, environmental impact analyses, and many other programs required to meet federal or state guidelines. Local governments often are compelled to devote significant resources to the fulfillment of long-standing obligations in these areas.

Local government officials should make state and federal lawmakers aware of how much these mandates cost localities by seeking *fiscal note legislation,* which calls for independent cost estimates of a bill's fiscal impact. In some states, local governments have achieved partial reimbursement of state-mandated costs. In other states, full responsibility for some traditional local functions have been assumed by state government. In this way, local resources that would have been devoted to these functions are freed up, thus enabling them to be devoted to other priorities, including investment in interest-yielding securities.

Changing Mood of Taxpayers

The so-called "taxpayers revolt," which gained national attention in 1978 with California's Proposition 13, seems to have stalled after the November 1984 elections. The Voter's Choice initiative in Michigan was defeated. This initiative would have rolled back a 1983 state income tax increase, required a referendum for any future tax hikes, and forced government bodies to muster a four-fifths majority to raise licensing fees. Nevada's Question 12, calling for a two-thirds vote of state or local lawmakers and a majority of the voting public on any new state or local taxes, also was defeated. Jarvis IV—named after Howard Jarvis, the author of Proposition 13—called for state property tax rollbacks in California to 1979 levels and would have forced state and local governments to rebate roughly $13 billion in tax revenues. This proposition also would have forbidden the imposition of user fees to generate revenues beyond the actual costs of the services included under the fee. Jarvis IV was also defeated.

Several reasons can be offered for the changing mood of the taxpaying public. First, the public in many localities has come to recognize the cause-and-effect relationship between the overall vitality of the local economy and the public services provided. They are reluctant to take actions that might adversely affect economic growth. Second, many people blame the 1981 tax cuts as being largely responsible for the ballooning federal deficits. They feel that there have already been plenty of tax cuts at the federal level and that lower levels of government cannot sustain the same kinds of cuts. These developments notwithstanding, the basic need remains for continued improvement and enhancement of cash management practices.

Endnotes

1. Roger W. Hill, Jr., *Cash Management Techniques* (New York: American Management Association, 1970), p. 23.

2. W. C. F. Hartley, *Cash: Planning, Forecasting and Control* (London: Business Books, 1977), p. 74.

3. J. E. Smith, *Cash Flow Management* (London: Woodhead Faulkner, 1975).

4. Rhett D. Harrell and Lisa A. Cole, *Banking Relations: A Guide for Local Government* (Chicago: Government Finance Research Center, Municipal Finance Officers Association, 1982), p. 44.

5. Hill, *Cash Management Techniques,* p. 31.

6. John Wiley, "A Perspective on Public Cash Management in the 80's," *Governmental Finance* 10 (December 1981): 6.

7. Kenneth Sanders and James E. Kirk, *Local Government Cash Management and Investments* (Columbia, SC: University of South Carolina, Bureau of Government Research and Services, 1981), p. 11.

8. Joseph Van Fenstermaker, *Cash Management: Managing the Cash Flow, Bank Balances, and Short-Term Investment of Non-Profit Institutions* (Kent, OH: Kent State University Press, 1966), p. 35.

9. Hartley, *Cash: Planning, Forecasting and Control,* pp. 56–57.

10. Stuart Holland, *The State as Entrepreneur* (London: Weidenfeld and Nicolson, 1972), p. 214.

11. Hartley, *Cash: Planning, Forecasting and Control,* pp. 30–34.

12. David I. Fisher, *Cash Management* (New York: Conference Board, 1973), p. 14.

13. Smith, *Cash Flow Management,* p. 13.

14. Chukwuemeka O'Cyprian Nwagwu, *Cash Management in Local Government* (Blacksburg, VA: Center for Public Administration and Policy, 1985).

15. Aaron Wildavsky, *The Politics of the Budgetary Process* (Boston: Little, Brown, 1979), p. viii.

16. For a further discussion of the cash budget, see Sanders and Kirk, *Local Government Cash Management and Investments,* pp. 55–58.

17. Fisher, *Cash Management,* p. 25.

18. These issues are discussed in greater detail in Paul Beehler, *Contemporary Cash Management: Principles, Practices and Perspective* (New York: Wiley, 1978), p. 44.

19. Sanders and Kirk, *Local Government Cash Management and Investments,* p. 21.

20. Harrell and Cole, *Banking Relations: A Guide for Local Government,* p. 34.

21. Government Finance Research Center, "Improved Tax Collection Strategies Bolster States' and Cities' Revenues." *Resources in Review* 2, no. 6 (March 1984): 14.

22. Municipal Finance Officers Association, *Elements of Financial Management,* Financial Management Series, vol. 6. (Chicago: Municipal Finance Officers Association, 1980).

CHAPTER 5

Investment Strategies

The focus of cash management is on maintaining sufficient funds on hand to satisfy legal obligations while providing opportunities to invest any excess cash in interest-yielding securities. The primary objective in adopting improved forecasting and cash mobilization techniques should be the development of sound investment strategies.

Cash Management Model

The various elements of cash management, diagramed in Exhibit 4-1, can be integrated into a general model, as shown in Exhibit 5-1. Central to this model is a management information system that provides data and analyses regarding available resources, such as taxes, fees, and intergovernmental transfers, as well as historical data and other information necessary to develop short- and long-term forecasts of revenues and expenditures.

Mobilization of Cash

As discussed in the previous chapter, receipt of expected revenues can be accelerated by using available technologies, such as lockbox systems and area concentration banking. Other sources of revenue can be exploited by improving property tax assessments, expanding the tax base, and minimizing delinquent taxes (as by levying penalties and/or granting a tax amnesty). At the same time, the productivity of available cash can be maximized by controlling disbursements. Techniques include centralized deposits, zero balance accounts, controlled bank balances, and remote disbursements (writing checks on remotely located banks).

Receivables are deposited in banks and other financial institutions for safekeeping and/or investment. Localities may authorize their banks to invest amounts in excess of their operating requirements or can hire cash managers or investment brokers to take charge of their investments.

Exhibit 5-1 Cash Management Model

```
┌──────────────────────────────────────────────────────────────────────────┐
│  ┌─────────────────────────────────────┐                                   │
│  │      EXOGENOUS FACTORS              │                                    │
│  │  • Interest rates                   │                                    │
│  │  • Minimum investment requirements  │                                    │
│  │  • Maturation dates                 │                                    │
│  └─────────────────────────────────────┘                                   │
│                                                                            │
│                      ┌──────────────────┐                                  │
│                      │   MANAGEMENT     │                                   │
│                      │   INFORMATION    │                                   │
│                      │    SYSTEMS       │                                   │
│                      └──────────────────┘                                  │
│                                                                            │
│              ┌──────────────┐   ┌──────────────┐                           │
│              │ Taxes, fees, │   │  Historical  │                           │
│              │  transfers   │   │     data     │                           │
│              └──────────────┘   └──────────────┘                           │
│                                                                            │
│  ┌────────────────┐   ┌──────────────────┐   ┌──────────────────────────┐  │
│  │ INVESTMENTS    │   │   DEPOSITORY     │   │  SHORT- AND LONG-TERM    │  │
│  │ • Safety       │   │  INSTITUTIONS    │   │      FORECASTING         │  │
│  │ • Maturity     │   │ • Commercial     │   │  • Revenue forecasts     │  │
│  │ • Yield        │   │   banks          │   │  • Expenditure forecasts │  │
│  │ • Liquidity    │   │ • Savings and    │   │                          │  │
│  │ • Marketability│   │   loans          │   │                          │  │
│  └────────────────┘   └──────────────────┘   └──────────────────────────┘  │
│                                                                            │
│                      ┌──────────────────┐                                  │
│                      │   MOBILIZATION   │                                   │
│                      │     OF CASH      │                                   │
│                      └──────────────────┘                                  │
│                                                                            │
│  ┌──────────────────────────┐       ┌──────────────────────────┐          │
│  │ DISBURSEMENTS            │       │   RECEIVABLES            │          │
│  │ • Centralized deposits   │       │ • Concentration banking  │          │
│  │ • Remote disbursements   │       │ • Lockbox system         │          │
│  │ • Controlled bank        │       │ • Increased assessments  │          │
│  │   balances               │       │ • Tax base expansion     │          │
│  │ • Zero balance accounts  │       │ • Tax amnesty            │          │
│  └──────────────────────────┘       └──────────────────────────┘          │
└──────────────────────────────────────────────────────────────────────────┘
```

Investment Characteristics and Exogenous Factors

It has been said that the ideal investment is one that yields a high return at no risk, offers promise of substantial growth, and is instantly convertible into cash if money is needed for other purposes. This ideal specimen, of course, does not exist in reality. Each form of investment has its own special virtues and shortcomings. In a market economy, *yield* is the ultimate measure of a successful cash management program. Several exogenous considerations influence the yield on an investment. These factors include interest rates, minimum investment requirements, and the maturation dates of investments.

Information flows from banks and other financial institutions to the management information system (MIS). This information is used to maintain the fiscal cycle on its existing course or to modify it. Information generated at each level of the model feeds into and facilitates the achievement of objectives at the next level. In this way, a cycle is created, proceeding from the MIS to forecasting, cash mobilization, banking, investments, and back to the MIS. With appropriate cash management, the cycle is continuously repeated.

Excess Balances

Local governments accumulate cash balances for a number of reasons. A large inflow of revenues occurs, for example, immediately prior to penalty dates on the tax calendar. Intergovernmental transfers tend to be made in lump sums as a consequence of statutory regulations and administrative practices governing such payments. Bonds for capital improvements are usually issued before a project begins, whereas disbursement of these funds occurs only as bills are paid throughout the construction period.

As a consequence of these factors, a jurisdiction often is able to meet current obligations and, at the same time, have some noncommitted cash left over to invest in interest-yielding securities.

> Investment of idle funds is one of the tools of sound fiscal management being used more frequently by all levels of government. . . . It offers a source of additional revenue without increasing taxation, through the use of funds which would otherwise be temporarily unproductive.[1]

Upward trends in interest rates in recent years have been a contributing factor to the increased interest among local governments in the investment of idle cash balances.

Criteria for Selecting Investments

Good cash management programs can accelerate receipts, delay disbursements, and minimize idle balances. The real measure of the overall effectiveness of a cash management program, however, is the investment practices adopted by the program. The principal factors to be considered in selecting a specific security in which to invest public funds are: (1) safety/risk, (2) price stability, (3) liquidity/marketability, (4) maturity, and (5) yield.

Safety/Risk

Public officials generally follow a set of investment principles whereby safety is accorded the highest priority, followed by liquidity and yield. Public officials are very much aware that government funds must be employed to achieve expressed objectives. Local finance officers are likely to lose their jobs if a portion of these public funds is lost as a consequence of risky investment practices.

As a result, local governments tend to invest in securities with relatively low rates of return. Treasurers often take this conservative approach because they are concerned that a bad investment may jeopardize their position. Many localities, however, are large enough and strong enough to take limited risks without serious damage. If the risk is only slightly higher, an investment in a higher-yielding security may be appropriate.

Many state legislatures restrict local government investments to securities that are *collateralized* or backed by the U.S. government. Nevertheless, even these investments—for example, long-term government bonds—"fluctuate in value and thus present some risk if they must be sold prior to maturity in an unfavorable market."[2] The risk characteristics of different securities should be understood before decisions are made about which specific instruments to purchase.

Price Stability

Investments should not be viewed only as income-producing assets. They also constitute *cash reserves.* In the event of an unexpected cash shortage, the first reaction often is to convert some of a local government's financial assets into cash. The desire to avoid financial loss in such circumstances explains the concern for the price stability of investments.

Generally speaking, U.S. Treasury bills (T-bills) are the most stable of all money market instruments, principally because they are backed by the full faith and credit of the federal government. In addition, T-bills are usually issued on a short-term basis, maturing before new market conditions alter the assumptions on which the investment was based. Other investment instruments characterized by price stability are short-term obligations of the U.S. Treasury, federal agency issues, and certificates of deposit.

Liquidity/Marketability

The concept of liquidity involves managing investments so that cash will be available when needed. The fundamental question is: Can the security be sold quickly and easily when the need arises? Marketability varies among money market instruments, depending not only on the price stability of the instrument, but more important, on the extent of the secondary trading market available to it. Treasury bills, for example, are practically riskless and are actively traded. As Harrell and Cole observe, "the sheer volume of Treasury bill issues and their tradeability in the secondary market establish the bills as the nearest equivalent to pure cash in the market."[3] Federal agency issues and certificates of deposit also have excellent liquidity.

Maturity

One way around the liquidity problem is to time placements so that the investments mature at times when the locality expects to need cash. Part of the investment portfolio may be earmarked for capital projects, and part for anticipated operating expenses. In managing the portfolio, the maturity dates of holdings should be synchronized with the dates when these funds will be needed. It should be relatively easy to align these dates, because securities are usually classified according to their maturity periods, such as thirty days, ninety days, one year, or five years.

The sale or redemption of a security prior to the agreed-upon maturity date usually results, at the very least, in the loss of accrued interest. This predicament can be avoided by buying a mix of securities with scattered maturity dates. In this way, any time cash is needed, some asset is maturing, and losses from premature sales can be avoided. The maturities of the various securities and how these would affect the portfolio mix must be understood before a cash manager decides to invest in them.

Yield/Return on Investment

In general, securities with little risk, high liquidity, and short maturities also have low yields. For a security to provide a high yield, one or more of the other relevant criteria must be compromised.

In spite of the constraints imposed by safety and liquidity, local governments are becoming increasingly interested in yield. As a first step, many financial executives have increased their efforts to monitor account balances to ensure that excess cash is invested immediately. In addition, some localities are backing away from state and local government obligations, which characteristically have low yields, in favor of high-yield, high-grade corporate bonds. At the same time, however, many local officials still rank yield as the least important of all the criteria in selecting an investment instrument.

Characteristics of Investment Securities

The majority of states allow municipalities to use a variety of investment instruments, including U.S. Treasury bills, commercial bank certificates of deposit (CDs), savings and loan deposits, federal agency securities, and repurchase agreements. However, the majority of states prohibit local governments from investing in banker's acceptances and commercial paper (which generally earn higher rates of return than the approved securities).

U.S. government obligations are practically riskless, as they are backed by the full faith and credit of the federal government. Other securities carry varying degrees of risk and, therefore, must offer higher interest to make them attractive. Exhibit 5-2 arrays the money market instruments most widely used by local governments against the characteristics described above. Understanding the unique features of each type of security available to local governments is critical to the formulation of prudent investment strategies.

Treasury Bills

The U.S. Treasury bill (T-bill) is the most important money market instrument available for local government investment. A Treasury bill is an obligation of the United States government to pay a fixed sum of money after a specified period of

Exhibit 5-2 Money Market Instruments Used by Local Governments

Investment Instrument	Obligation Issuer	Denomination	Maturities	Marketability	Yield Basis	Comments/Restrictions
U.S. Treasury bills	U.S. government obligations	$10,000 to $1 million	3, 6, 9, and 12 months	Excellent secondary market	Discounted on 365-day basis. Also offered as tax anticipation bills through special auctions.	Popular investment. Can be purchased in secondary market for varying maturities.
Repurchase agreements	Commercial banks	$100,000 minimum	Overnight minimum; 1–21 days common	No secondary market	Established as part of purchase agreement. Yield generally close to prevailing federal rates.	Open: can liquidate at any time. Fixed: maturity set for specific period.
Negotiable certificates of deposit	Commercial banks	$500,000 to $1 million	Unlimited; 30-day minimum	Active secondary market	Interest maturity on 360-day basis.	Backed by credit of the issuing bank.
Nonnegotiable certificates of deposit	Commercial banks and savings and loan assoc.	$1,000 minimum (usually $100,000)	30-day minimum	Limited secondary market	Interest maturity on 365-day basis.	Lower interest rates for amounts under $100,000. 90-day interest penalty for early withdrawal.
Commercial paper	Promissory notes of finance companies	$100,000 to $5 million	5–270 days	No secondary market	Either discounted or interest-bearing on a 360-day basis.	Dealers will often negotiate "buy-back" agreements at a lower rate prior to maturity.
Banker's acceptances	Commercial banks	$25,000 to $1 million	Up to 6 months	Good secondary market	Discounted on a 360-day basis.	Backed by credit of issuing bank with specific collateral.
U.S. agency securities	Various federal agencies	$1,000 to $25,000	30 days; 270 days; 1 year	Good secondary market	Discounted on a 360-day basis.	Not legal obligation of or guaranteed by the federal government.

time from date of issue. Thus, T-bills have virtually no default risk and are the most liquid of money market instruments. The Treasury auctions three-month and six-month bills on a weekly basis and one-year bills each month. T-bills are discount instruments and, as such, carry no coupon payments. The difference between the selling price and the face value represents interest income. The minimum denomination is $10,000, with additional amounts in increments of $5,000.

An attractive feature of Treasury bills is the ready market for resale. If the holder has a sudden need for funds, T-bills can be sold quickly for relatively predictable prices on the so-called secondary market. This characteristic has earned T-bills the label of "near money."

Certificates of Deposit

The popularity of certificates of deposits (CDs) has increased dramatically among governmental subdivisions in the past several years. A certificate of deposit is a receipt for funds that have been deposited in a commercial bank for an agreed-upon period of time. The owner of the CD receives both principal and interest on the maturity date. There are two types of CDs: (1) *negotiable,* which the original investor can sell to another party on the secondary market; and (2) *nonnegotiable,* which must be retained by the original investor until maturity.

CDs may be purchased for various amounts, but those under $100,000 usually carry a significantly lower interest rate. CDs are sold according to specified maturity periods, ranging from 14 to 180 days. Some banks may allow purchases for periods of more than 180 days, up to one year.

A characteristic that makes CDs attractive to investors is that most can be sold in a resale market prior to maturity if the funds are needed, giving CDs the liquidity necessary to make them competitive in the money market. Emergency liquidation of a CD prior to maturity can result in a loss of interest, however. Although a CD may have been purchased for only thirty or sixty days, in some cases the bank may require a penalty of ninety days' interest for early withdrawal.

Federal Agency Securities

Federal agency securities include Federal Farm Credit bonds, Federal Home Loan Bank bonds and discount notes, and Federal National Mortgage Association bonds. These securities are issued by privately owned, government-sponsored agencies that have been established to implement various federal policies. Although these securities are not backed by the full faith and credit of the United States government, each agency guarantees its own issued securities. Thus, the risk factor is considered to be very low.

Federal agency securities are excellent investment instruments for local governments and are often characterized as close substitutes for Treasury bills. Because the market for agency paper is smaller than for T-bills, however, these agency securities have less liquidity. Agency securities trade at a yield premium over T-bills, but the earnings from some agency securities are subject to state and local taxes.

Repurchase Agreements

A repurchase agreement is a contract between two parties whereby one party sells an instrument (such as a T-bill) to the other and agrees to buy it back at a later date (often the next day) at a specified higher price. Repurchase agreements are most often entered into for very short periods of time, usually from one to twenty-one days. The minimum amount is usually $100,000, with increments of $5,000 above the minimum. Lower minimums can sometimes be negotiated, however.

Two types of repurchase agreements are available: (1) *fixed,* wherein the specific interest rate and maturity period for the amount invested are established at the outset; and (2) *open,* meaning that the agreement may be liquidated at any time, with the interest rate dependent on the duration of the transaction. A fixed repurchase agreement might be set for $100,000, with a 12.5 percent annual interest rate for six days. If the agreement is liquidated prior to maturity, the bank has the option of levying a penalty. The interest rate for an open agreement may be slightly lower than for a fixed agreement.

Repurchase agreements are the most flexible investment instruments available because they allow the locality to negotiate both yield and maturity. There is little risk involved in such agreements because the principal is guaranteed and the return is fixed. However, no secondary market exists for repurchase agreements. They can be used most effectively to invest unexpected windfall revenues on a very short-term basis while alternative investments are being considered.

Banker's Acceptances

Banker's acceptances, usually created in conjunction with foreign trade transactions, are time drafts negotiated by commercial banks to finance the export, import, shipment or storage of goods.[4] The bank guarantees to honor the draft on the due date by stamping "accepted" on the draft. In making such a guarantee, a well-known bank can significantly enhance the marketability of obligations of less well-known companies.

After accepting the draft, the bank sells it at a discount to an importer. On the due date (typically ninety days after issue), the bank honors the draft for the full face value and debits the account of the issuing company. Banker's acceptances are sold in denominations ranging from $25,000 to $1 million. The default risk is very low, and the secondary market is correspondingly good.

Commercial Paper

Commercial paper includes promissory notes of finance corporations or industrial firms. Commercial paper offers higher yields than T-bills because such investments have higher default risks. As a result, many states have restrictions against investment by local governments in commercial paper. Maturities of commercial paper range from 5 to 270 days. Liquidity is generally low, as no secondary trading market exists for commercial paper. Denominations start at $100,000 and may go as high as $5 million.

All of the securities described above are excellent, safe investment alternatives for local jurisdictions. The specific yield–liquidity–safety configuration of each should be considered when making investment decisions. A locality usually purchases a mix of investments with varying yield–liquidity–safety arrangements, depending on which considerations public officials wish to emphasize in the overall investment program.

Portfolio Management

The balances held in demand deposit accounts at commercial banks traditionally have earned no interest. Record high interest rates have provided compelling incentives to reduce these cash balances and to maximize investment returns within the constraints imposed by local, state, and federal laws. The investment portfolio of most local governments, however, is managed to avoid losses, with little regard for the resulting opportunity costs—that is, potential investment returns that remain unrealized.

Maximize Yield/Minimize Risk

The fundamental cash management goal is to maximize yield and minimize risk. To this end, public officials need to formulate an investment strategy that reflects the investment objectives of the community. This strategy should then govern the actions taken on a day-to-day basis.

The first step is to determine available funds. Cash flow projections should accurately reflect the impact of various economic conditions on the overall availability of funds for investment. An intervening credit crunch and high interest rates, for example, may cause suppliers to shorten their credit terms and to press for more prompt payment of invoices. Conversely, cheap credit and lower interest rates may ease supplier terms. Information on these broader conditions should enable the financial manager to arrive at reasonable predictions as to *how much* money will be available to invest, and for *how long*.

The next step is to formulate a policy on investments. As suggested earlier, many public officials tend to overemphasize safety and, as a result, to invest in securities with relatively low rates of return. In formulating an investment policy, the financial manager should investigate the investment instruments available in the market, determine their relative yields for the maturities required, and evaluate the differences in risk associated with them. On the basis of this evaluation, a policy should be developed and submitted to a *finance committee* for review and approval. In this way, the financial manager can attain broader counsel on the implementation of an appropriate investment policy.

Building an Investment Structure

In general, the longer the maturity of an investment, the higher the yield. For this reason, it is important to design an investment pattern whereby each security will mature close to the time that the money invested will be needed to cover operational needs. For example, a locality may determine through its forecasts that a given amount of money will be available for a ninety-day period. This amount may be invested in, say, ninety-day commercial paper. Another sum, available for only thirty days, might be invested in a certificate of deposit. In some cases, funds may be available only for a day or a week at a time. These funds might be invested in repurchase agreements or other securities that can be held for indeterminate periods.

Large local governments may have millions of dollars to invest and may have several employees whose primary responsibility is handling these investments. Smaller jurisdictions may be unable to afford an investments manager because of the relatively small amounts to be invested, often for only a few days at a time. Such localities may authorize their banks to invest automatically any surplus funds in certificates of deposits or other short-term securities.

The inadequacy of resources is a major constraint on the maximization of investment returns. A locality cannot invest in the money market unless it can raise enough revenue to satisfy current obligations and accumulate a surplus. Whereas some local governments are relatively affluent and have large tax bases, others often are hard-pressed to maintain needed services to their citizens. Thus, central to the issue of optimal return on investment is the question of resources: (1) the availability of surpluses to invest and (2) the technical expertise necessary to manage a portfolio of investments.

Restricted Securities

Investment activities of local governments are governed by state statutes that reflect public policy. Some of these regulations restrict the investment opportunities available to localities, thereby depriving the public of the benefits of efficient investment funds.

Such regulations were once necessary to control the imprudence of some local officials in the management of public funds. However, more recent developments have tended to render the typical state investment law obsolete.

> First, the money markets themselves have become increasingly sophisticated and competitive, with a myriad of financial institutions seeking investment capital through new securities and instruments. Thus, the options available to investment officers have increased dramatically.[5]

Securities are now available with varying levels of risk, investment return, and maturities. Whatever the financial objectives of a locality, a range of appropriate investments are available.

> Secondly, the sophistication of state and local government investment officials has grown in the past decade. . . . With increasing specialization and professionalism common

throughout the state and local government sector, these public money managers increasingly rival their private sector counterparts in their understanding of investment securities and relative risks and rewards.[6]

At the same time, some local jurisdictions have self-imposed additional restrictions and limitations on their investment policies. The overriding objective is to identify proper eligibility standards, investment limits, and safekeeping requirements. The goal remains to maximize investment income and minimize the risk of loss.

Localities have tried to mitigate risk by setting up a variety of investment criteria designed to diversify investment holdings and avoid investments in weak financial institutions. Even smaller jurisdictions, located in remote areas with minimal funds available for investment, have minimized risk by joining state-managed investment pools. These pools resemble money market mutual funds in their portfolio composition. They provide professional management, diversification, and money market rates of return on liquid assets. State investment pools provide competition and often superior yields to local depository institutions.

Collateralization of Public Funds

Many experts have questioned the need for banks to pledge securities as collateral to secure public deposits and investments. *Collateralization* imposes excessive costs on the financial institution—costs that are usually passed on to the public entity in the form of reduced rates of return. Experts argue that in the event of widespread failures in the banking system, many of the securities used for collateral pledges could prove equally worthless.

There are positive benefits associated with collateralization of public funds, however, particularly when a public organization deals with a single financial institution. These benefits become most obvious should the institution default because of poor management or other microeconomic factors. A case in point is the 1982 collapse of Penn Square Bank, in which collateralization provisions protected the assets of the state and its political subdivisions. Collateralization is akin to an insurance policy aimed at protecting the safety of public deposits.

Exogenous Factors

Exogenous factors may be more imporant in determining investment yields than the characteristics of the investment instruments themselves or the ability of the local government to accumulate resources for investment. These factors include (1) maturity dates of investments, (2) minimum dollar requirements for each investment, (3) interest rates, and (4) staff capabilities.

Maturity dates are an important determinant in choosing investments. Suppose, for example, that an investment officer determines that about $500,000 will be available for investment from May 1 to June 10. After taking bids from several banks and brokers, a list of maturity dates and yields is developed, as follows:

Issue	Maturity Date	Yield
T-bills	June 11	12.50
Certificate of deposit	June 8	11.59
Banker's acceptances	June 13	13.50
Repurchase agreements	June 15	14.37

Although the banker's acceptances and repurchase agreements offer the highest yields, their maturity dates occur after June 10, when the principal must be available for other uses. The CD has the lowest yield, but may be considered the best alternative because it matures prior to the June 10 date. The T-bills mature on June 11, and depending on the possibility of a one-day leeway in the need for these invested funds, these may be the best choice. Although the amount available for investment is substantial, the primary consideration may be the maturity date of the investment, despite a smaller yield than might be considered optimal.

High-yield issues often require a *minimum investment* of $100,000 or more. In smaller jurisdictions, this amount may represent a sizable portion of the total budget. Therefore, such investments may not be feasible without seriously jeopardizing the ability to deliver necessary services to their citizens. One way around the minimum investment requirement is the state investment pool. Through this means, a locality can earn a substantially higher yield on the relatively small amount available for investment.

Wide fluctuations in *interest rates* have occurred over the past several years. It is important for a cash manager to understand how these fluctuations can affect investment decisions. The cash manager should endeavor to predict the interest rate cycle and use those predictions in managing the jurisdiction's investments.

A cash manager may determine, for example, that $125,000 is available for investment during a 179-day period, after which the principal and interest will be applied to finance a capital improvements project. After taking bids from several investment firms and banks, the manager decides to invest the funds at 10.3 percent. No consideration is given to the possibility that interest rates could be rising, and the investment is "locked in" at 10.3 percent. The expected yield on this investment is:

$$\$125.000 \times 0.103 \times 179/360 = \$6,402$$

Instead of locking in the investment for the full 179 days, the cash manager could have decided to purchase a short-term CD and to reevaluate the movement of interest rates at its maturity. The rate bid for a 30-day CD is 10.15 percent; therefore, the expected yield for the 30 days is $1,057. At the end of 30 days, bids are again sought and the following quotations received:

14–29 days	10.90%
30–59 days	11.75%
60–89 days	11.90%

A new CD might be purchased for another 30 days at 11.75 percent, with the expectation of a further evaluation of the interest rate situation at the end of that time. The expected yield for this 30-day period on $126,057 ($125,000 + $1,057 interest) is $1,234. Assume that at the end of the second 30-day period, interest rates have peaked. At that time, the cash manager decides to "lock into" the current rate of 13.15 percent for the remaining 119 days. The expected interest yield on $127,291 ($126,057 + $1,234) is $5,533. Thus, the total interest earned under this managed approach would be $1,057 + $1,234 + $5,533, or $7,824—$1,422 more than under the initial approach. This second approach also creates a measure of liquidity to respond to unexpected cash flow problems.

Staff capability may limit the time spent in searching out the best type of investment. A small, overworked department often does not have the time or skills to keep up with current developments in the money market, nor can it determine which investments are best under various circumstances that may confront the organization or jurisdiction.

An Investment Matrix

An investment matrix for local government is presented in Exhibit 5-3. Each political subdivision has its own economic and fiscal environment. *Characteristics* refer to broad sets of circumstances that reflect the economic and fiscal environment of a given jurisdiction. *Emphasis* suggests the element or elements to which cash managers may attach the greatest importance, given the stated characteristics. *Investment options* identify the types of investments that best "fit" the characteristics and emphasis used to describe a particular jurisdiction.

Emphasis on Safety

It is important that the yield–liquidity–safety mix be considered in every investment decision. The degree of emphasis placed on any particular element is a function of the fiscal and economic circumstances confronting the locality. When the resources of a jurisdiction are very limited, for example, yield cannot serve as the primary objective because high-yield securities usually have correspondingly higher risks attached to them. A resource-poor community must be more concerned with the safety of its investments and its ability to convert these investments to cash on short notice. The investment options available under such circumstances are determined by the safety–liquidity considerations. The locality accepts a level of yield that is not optimal as a trade-off for the safety of its investment, while at the same time retaining the leverage to convert its investments easily to cash if the need arises.

The failure of several investment companies specializing in government securities in the 1980s has led to renewed emphasis on the safety of local government investments. These firms dealt largely with savings and loan associations, engaging primarily in repurchase agreements. Such agreements allow institutions to

Exhibit 5-3 *Investment Matrix for Local Government*

Characteristics	Yield	Liquidity	Safety	Investment Options
	Emphasis			
Limited resources; low tax base; minimal cash balance		X	X	• Investment of cash balances at guaranteed rates through local banks and other depository institutions • Treasury bills • Agency securities • State investment pools
High income; high tax base; large cash balances; expanding economy	X			• Certificates of deposit • Commercial paper • Repurchase agreements • State investment pools
Minimum training in financial management	X		X	• Contracts with banks to invest excess balances • Treasury bills • State investment pools
Elected treasurer			X	• Funds left uninvested • Certificates of deposit • Treasury bills • Agency securities • State investment pools
Cash investment manager	X	X	X	• Treasury bills • Agency securities • Certificates of deposit • State investment pools
High rate of tax delinquency		X	X	• Treasury bills • State investment pools
Low rate of tax delinquency	X		X	• Certificates of deposit • Treasury bills • State investment pools
Upward trend in interest rates	X	X		• Certificates of deposit (purchased on a short-term basis) • Treasury bills
Downward trend in interest rates			X	• Certificates of deposit (locked in at prevailing high rate of interest) • Commercial paper
Capital expenditure needs		X	X	• Treasury bills • Certificates of deposit • Repurchase agreements

borrow or lend funds by selling or buying government securities and agreeing to repurchase, or sell them back, at specified prices. Under these arrangements, the investment companies bought securities from savings and loans seeking to raise cash temporarily, then sold them to local governments with idle cash to invest.

The local governments that lost money in these incidents neglected a cardinal rule of government securities trading: get possession of the securities. They allowed the dealers to retain control of the securities, and these dealers, in turn, pledged the same securities to different investors. State laws guiding public investments generally require localities to take physical possession of investment securities as well as collateral. Much of the blame for the losses incurred by local governments must fall on the financial naivete of the savings and loan associations and municipalities involved and cannot be attributed to inadequate legal protection.

Rate of Return on Investment

A 1985 survey of county governments in the northern Virginia and Maryland area provides further data in support of this investment matrix.[7] This survey showed that the rate of return on investment was a direct function of the fiscal and economic characteristics of the jurisdiction. A small, rural jurisdiction with limited resources

> cannot afford the luxury of losing any part of its principal investment. As a result of its concerns for security, its investment options are limited to securities with rapid convertibility to cash so that the ability of the jurisdiction to undertake major capital expenditures is not handicapped by funds being tied up in non-maturing financial assets.[8]

The investments of such localities, of necessity, are concentrated in low-risk, low-yield securities, such as T-bills, agency securities, and state investment pools.

A second group of counties was characterized as having appreciably larger annual budgets (averaging around $36 million), larger population bases (15,000 to 20,000 people), and professional management staffs. With sizable amounts of resources at their disposal, these counties were found to be more aggressive in the money market. "Their investment strategies pay adequate attention to safety, liquidity, and yield. However, the yield of investments is pursued with greater intensity."[9] Rates of return on investments of these counties were calculated in the 9 to 11 percent range, in contrast to the returns of the smaller, more rural counties, which were in the 5 to 9 percent range.

A third category was comprised of counties

> that have an enormous amount of expendable and investable resources, relative to other jurisdictions in this study. The annual budgets of the jurisdictions in this category are beyond the billion dollar mark; their daily cash balances and investable amounts run into several millions; and their investments realize rates of return between 11 and 12.99 percent.[10]

Investment models had been adopted in these localities to predict the movement of interest rates over time, thus enabling investment managers to ride the interest rate curve with their investments. These counties were not threatened by cash flow problems but had a steady inflow of revenue through taxes, fees, and transfers. As a consequence, financial assets could be structured to emphasize high-yield, long-term securities.

The characteristics of the counties included in this study and the investment options they pursued tend to reinforce the general assumptions of the investment matrix. Only those counties with substantial financial resources were able to include in their investment portfolios securities such as repurchase agreements and commercial paper, which are relatively risky but offer compensating high yields.

Other Constraints on Optimal Investment Strategies

Safety and liquidity considerations preclude many local governments from investing in high-risk securities. The only avenue open to these localities is to invest in low-yield, risk-free instruments, such as T-bills, other government obligations, and certificates of deposits. Many jurisdictions may not be in a position to follow this strategy, however, because they do not have the funds necessary to operate aggressively in the money market. Shortcomings in other phases of financial management, such as the collection of delinquent taxes, may severely limit a jurisdiction's options.

Competence in all aspects of financial management affects the jurisdiction's relations with banks and other financial institutions. These relations help determine the size of the compensating balances that banks require, which, in turn, can influence the types of instruments in which funds are invested.

The structure of many local governments is not consistent with the maximization of returns in cash management. Some local government officials do not see the utility of "gambling" with the taxpayers' money and prefer to leave excess funds secured on deposit in the banks. To the extent that these funds are not invested, returns cannot be optimized.

Many of the securities approved for local government investment carry very low interest rates. In addition, several procedural requirements are often attached to cash management in local government, including:

1. A requirement that cash managers obtain prior approval before an investment security is bought or sold.
2. A requirement that written quotations be obtained for all investment purchases.
3. Prohibitions on the use of wire transfers for investment transactions.
4. Restrictions that narrow the range of potential money market instruments.

Legal constraints influence the formation of banking relations, the level of bank compensating balances, and the safety–liquidity requirements of the securities in which a local government may invest. Local governments cannot achieve optimal returns on their investments because they are not at liberty to use their discretion in investing in securities that meet their individual needs.

Political constraints are evident in several forms, including prohibitions against using nonlocal banks or investing outside the local area and the practice of sharing deposits among all banks in the community. The primary argument in support of these prohibitions is the notion of "keeping the money at home." As long as investments are limited to local options, however, local governments may be foregoing higher interest rates available in other markets.

Summary and Conclusions

Safety of principal is an important component of any investment strategy. Concerns about safety have been diminished, however, by the adoption of state laws that offer adequate protection to public funds by (1) limiting banks with which local governments can do business, (2) determining, in most instances, the amounts that can be left on deposit in each bank, and (3) requiring collateral for uninsured funds. In addition, public funds on deposit in commercial banks and savings and loan associations are protected under the Federal Deposit Insurance Corporation and the Federal Savings and Loan Insurance Corporation. Under these circumstances, safety cannot be used as the only measure of an investment strategy. Nonetheless, investment options open to local governments have been prescribed by state laws and by self-imposed local statutes, and local financial managers must operate within these parameters or be in violation of the law.

Liquidity is an important investment consideration, especially when a need for funds occurs unexpectedly. Careful planning and structuring of the portfolio mix, however, will ensure that liquidity is built into the investment strategy. Since various securities mature in 30, 90, 180, or 270 days, one year, or even longer, a locality can structure its assets in such a way that securities will mature at the time the funds are needed for other commitments.

Yield, or return on investment, is the paramount criterion for measuring the success or failure of an investment strategy. In the face of continuing demands to provide expanded and improved services, local governments confront (1) the need to expand revenues if these demands are to be met, (2) already heavily burdened taxpayers, and (3) narrow restrictions on their ability to borrow to finance public expenditures. Under these circumstances, local governments can be expected to respond enthusiastically to any source of additional revenue that does not involve increased taxation or additional debt. The financial asset portfolio is such a source, and the net return on investments can be an especially important source of revenue.

Thus, in evaluating the effectiveness of investment strategies, safety of principal and liquidity must be balanced against yield. The primary benefits of an investment strategy must be measured in terms of the increased interest earned through the investment of temporarily idle cash.

Endnotes

1. Public Affairs Research Council of Louisiana, *Investment of Idle State Funds* (Baton Rogue, LA: Public Affairs Research Council, 1956), p.iii.

2. Municipal Finance Officers Association, *A Treasury Management Handbook for Small Cities and Other Governmental Units* (Chicago: Municipal Finance Officers Association, 1979), p. 41.

3. Rhett D. Harrell and Lisa A. Cole, *Banking Relations: A Guide for Local Government* (Chicago: Municipal Finance Officers Association, 1982), p. 27.

4. Frank Pataucci and Michael Lichtenstein, *Improving Cash Management in Local Government: A Comprehensive Approach* (Chicago: Municipal Finance Officers Association, 1977), p. 59.

5. Committee on Cash Management, *Model Investment Legislation for State and Local Governments* (Chicago: Government Finance Officers Association, 1984), p. 6.

6. Ibid., p. 6.

7. Chukwuemeka O'Cyprian Nwagwu, *Cash Management in Local Governments: An Evaluation of Local Government Money Management Policies and Practices, and the Constraints on the Maximization of Investment Returns,* unpublished doctoral dissertation, Virginia Polytechnic Institute and State University, Blacksburg, VA, May 1985.

8. Ibid., p. 203.

9. Ibid., pp. 203–204.

10. Ibid., p. 204.

CHAPTER 6

Financial Planning and Cost Analysis

The common denominator among the various resources of any organization is the cost involved in their utilization. Therefore, the focus of management is usually on the most effective deployment of financial resources. The consequences of past decisions form the basis for much of the financial and cost analysis in complex organizations. Resource management, however, demands analytical techniques that can accommodate the risk and uncertainty inevitably associated with future decisions.

Analysis of Financial Data

Accounting data can be useful in assessing the internal strengths and weaknesses of an organization. Numbers connote precision, and precision is often assumed to have its own virtue. It is important to bear in mind, however, that the numbers provided in balance sheets and income statements are condensed from many detailed accounting records and reports. Therefore, any further analyses based on these data must be undertaken with full awareness of the abstractions that have already been made. Accounting data merely reflect the financial dimensions of an organization. Other important factors that may impinge on the overall performance of the organization must also be considered.

Financial Ratio Analysis

Various indicators have been used for many years in the private sector to measure the well-being of a business with respect to liquidity, leverage, profitability, and the utilization of assets. Three approaches can be applied to evaluate organizational performance with respect to these financial indicators:

1. *Organizational comparisons:* Comparative data should encompass organizations of similar size, serving the same or similar clientele with similar products or services.
2. *Time series analysis:* Ratios can be plotted for several periods to determine whether significant changes have occurred and, on this basis, to project the future financial performance of the organization.

3. *Absolute standards:* Minimum requirements can be established appropriate to the expectations of a given organization.

Liquidity is essential for the survival of an organization and, therefore, is often given priority in financial analysis. Liquidity measures are based on the fundamental notion that a sufficient amount of cash and other short-term assets must be available when needed by an organization to pay its bills. On the other hand, most short-term assets do not produce any significant returns. Therefore, management must try to keep the liquidity of the organization low, while ensuring that short-term obligations can be met.

A *current ratio,* determined by dividing current assets by current liabilities, indicates the extent to which the claims of short-term creditors can be covered by short-term assets. Consider the financial data in Exhibit 6-1. The current ratio for the XYZ Company is $550,000 divided by $400,000, or 1.375. The higher the ratio, the greater the presumed ability of the organization to meet its current obligations. Stable organizations with predictable financial demands generally require smaller current ratios; more volatile organizations need higher ratios.

Exhibit 6-1   *Financial Data for the XYZ Company*

Current assets		$550,000
Inventory	$100,000	
Current liabilities		$400,000
Accounts payable	$200,000	
Short-term debt	200,000	
Owner's equity		$150,000
Long-term debt		$300,000

Quick ratios indicate an organization's ability to pay off short-term obligations without having to sell current inventory. Inventories are subtracted because they are the least liquid of current assets. In a forced sale, inventories may be worth very little. A ratio of 3.0 or higher suggests a cash-rich organization; substantial deviations below 1.0 may indicate a cash crisis. The quick ratio for the XYZ Company is 1.125 ($550,000 − $100,000 = $450,000, divided by $400,000).

The extent to which the working capital of an organization is tied up in inventory can be calculated by subtracting current liabilities from current assets and dividing the result into the value of inventory. The ratio of inventory to net working capital for the XYZ Company is 0.67 ($550,000 − $400,000 = $150,000, divided into $100,000). A ratio approaching 1.0 indicates that the organization may be carrying too much inventory; that is, too much of its working capital is tied up in relatively unproductive supplies and materials.

Debt management ratios (sometimes called *leverage ratios*) show how the operations of an organization are financed. *Positive leveraging* occurs when an organization has the opportunity to borrow at a low rate of interest and to invest this borrowed money at higher rates of return. Negative leveraging occurs when an organization is forced to borrow at interest rates higher than the anticipated rate of return on the investment. The use of debt financing implies both opportunity and risk. Too much equity often means that management is not taking advantage of the leverage associated with long-term debt. On the other hand, as the debt-to-equity ratio increases, outside financing becomes more expensive. Thus, leverage must be viewed in relation to profitability and the volatility of activities in which the organization is engaged.

Three principal measures of leverage are used:

1. *Debt-to-assets ratio* measures the extent to which borrowed funds are used to finance the organization's operations. The higher the ratio, the greater the leveraging. ($500,000 ÷ $550,000 = 0.91)
2. *Debt-to-equity ratio* is the ratio of funds from creditors (long- and short-term debt) to funds from stockholders. ($500,000 ÷ $150,000 = 3.33)
3. *Long-term-debt-to-equity ratio* measures the balance between long-term borrowing and equity. ($300,000 ÷ $150,000 = 2.0)

The debt management ratios for the XYZ Company are shown in parentheses.

Profits are limited by the cost of production, on the one hand, and by the marketability of the product or service, on the other. Therefore, profit maximization entails the most efficient allocation of resources by management. There are two categories of *profit ratios. Margin ratios,* relating profits to sales, are derived from the income statement. These margin ratios measure the performance of cost controls. *Return ratios* measure profit against resources committed to the organization.

The following profit ratios are those used most often:

1. *Gross profit margin* is the total margin available to cover operating expenses and yield a profit. This ratio is calculated by subtracting the cost of goods sold from total sales and dividing the result (gross profit) by total sales.
2. *Net profit margin* is the return on sales, determined by dividing profits after taxes by total sales.
3. *Return on assets* represents the return on the total investment from both stockholders and creditors. This ratio is calculated by dividing earnings before interest and taxes by total assets.
4. *Return on equity* is the rate of return on stockholders' investment in the firm, calculated by dividing profits after taxes by total equity. This ratio will be most affected by positive or negative leveraging.

It is often difficult to apply these measures to not-for-profit and nonprofit organizations, since the basic objective of such organizations is to "break even."

Asset utilization ratios measure the productivity and efficiency of an organization. A *fixed asset turnover ratio,* for example, can be compared to industry averages to show how well a company is using its productive capacity. Similarly, an *inventory turnover ratio* can indicate whether the company is producing too much inventory in generating sales or carrying too much obsolete inventory. Asset utilization ratios can be tailored to the needs of nonprofit and not-for-profit organizations. Such measures usually entail some measure of volume of activity or work load (such as cases per caseworker) divided by some measure of cost or time.

Strategic Funds Programming

A second type of financial analysis considers the sources, flow, and uses of organizational resources in an effort to identify discretionary funds that might be used to implement new programs and strategies. This technique provides a future-oriented perspective on financial requirements and potential sources to meet those needs. As such, it can be applied to organizations in both the private and public sectors.

Introducing a new program or strategy is something like attempting to rebuild a ship while at sea. The current organization must be kept afloat and operating properly at the same time as programs are introduced to move the organization into new areas. Managers may become so enamored of the potential opportunities of a new strategy that they fail to provide sufficient support to current operations.[1] In identifying appropriate sources of funds to implement the new strategy, therefore, management must also weigh the financial needs of the current organization.

The first step is to determine how current financial resources are allocated from period to period. This *cash flow analysis* can help identify sources of discretionary funds and show where potential adjustments must be made. Generally speaking, an organization can generate new funds from three sources:

1. Regular operations and other internal sources (such as profits after taxes, depreciation, disposition of excess inventory or unused facilities, increased revenue through adjusted tax levies).
2. Expansion of short-term debt consistent with the financial structure of the organization (for example, having banks provide extended lines of credit, leasing rather than buying equipment, factoring accounts receivable).
3. Changes in the financial structure of the organization to permit the addition of new long-term debt or equity funds.

Funds accumulated from these sources generally comprise the total funds available for managing the organization's operations. These funds, in turn, fall into two categories: baseline funds and strategic funds.

Baseline funds support the current, ongoing operations of the organization. They are used to pay current operating expenses, provide adequate working capital, and maintain current plant and equipment. Baseline funds are used to maintain (a) the same level of production or services, (b) the organization's "market share," or (c) a specified, ongoing rate of growth.

Strategic funds are invested in the new programs required to meet the organization's goals and objectives. They are used to purchase new assets, such as equipment, facilities, and inventory; to increase working capital; and to support direct expenses for research and development, marketing, advertising, and promotions. Strategic funds are also used in the private sector for mergers, acquisitions, and market development. A market penetration strategy, for example, may call for a more intensive investment of funds in the current business. A market expansion strategy usually requires aggressive use of strategic funds for advertising and promotion. A company must use strategic funds to produce more diverse products or services and to develop new markets for them.

The programming of strategic funds begins with the identification of basic organizational units (program or budget units) and the formulation of goals and objectives for these units. The total amount of strategic funds available to the organization can be determined by subtracting baseline funds from total assets (revenue or appropriations). Strategies must be formulated to carry out the goals and objectives of each unit. Once estimates have been made as to the funds required for each strategy, the strategies can be ranked according to their potential contribution to the achievement of the identified goals and objectives. In undertaking this ranking, the kinds of strategic funds available and the level of risk involved must be taken into account. Procedures for dealing with risk will be described in greater detail in a subsequent section of this chapter.

The available strategic funds should be allocated to each program in priority order. Key decision points concerning risk and return are encountered (1) when funds available from internal sources have been fully consumed and (2) when readily available credit sources have been exhausted. At this point, proposed strategies must be evaluated in terms of the changes required in the financial structure of the organization. The final step is to establish a management control system to monitor the generation and application of funds to achieve the desired results.

The programming of strategic funds simply identifies *feasible options* under different financial assumptions. A further assessment of risk and return on investment must be made before the final option is chosen. This approach is discussed in further detail in Chapter 7, under the heading of Service Level Analysis.

Computer-Assisted Financial Planning

In recent years, computer-based methods of analysis have become a significant tool for financial planning. Interactive financial planning software allows the nonprogrammer to use the computer as an on-line, real-time decision support system (DSS) to test assumptions on which a plan is based, to consider the risk associated with different available alternatives, and to explore a range of possible decision scenarios. Traditional methods of financial analysis often can only explain from hindsight why things went right or wrong under a particular plan of action. Computer-assisted methods of financial planning, however, provide a basis for the continuous fine tuning of a plan so as to anticipate things to come (and adjust to unanticipated events that may arise as the plan is implemented).

In early approaches to interactive financial planning, a fixed structure was used to provide the capacity to pose "what if" questions about certain input variables. These programs usually display the results as pro forma balance sheets or income statements. Simultaneous equations are used to project the organization's financial performance. Sales revenues are often the driving force in these models: alternative income and balance sheet projections can be made by using different sales forecasts.

The balance sheets show expected changes in assets and liabilities based on various scenarios with regard to sales.

Obviously the results of such analyses are only as valid as the forecasts made by the planners. However, running through different financial scenarios increases management's awareness of potential problems and its preparedness to deal with them when they occur.

Individuals lacking experience in computer programming often were unable to use these early models, however, for two reasons: (1) the need to learn a new, unfamiliar computer language that was often difficult to communicate; and (2) the inflexibility associated with procedural languages, which force the user to make input statements in a sequence different from the structure of the actual problem. Software packages designed to eliminate these problems are now available. Such software is, in the jargon, "user friendly": menus and submenus are written in English and allow users with very little programming experience to select the analytical steps appropriate to their needs. These packaged programs use a nonprocedural approach in which there is no "correct" or predetermined sequence of statements required to describe the problem. Thus, they offer a great deal of flexibility in terms of both model design and subsequent modifications that may be necessary.

Modern interactive packages for financial planning provide a number of important options in addition to generating automatic reports for various "what if" questions. Models applicable to the particular conditions confronting an organization can be developed and used (1) to project financial statements, (2) to analyze cash flow requirements, (3) to optimize financial leverage, (4) to compare lease versus purchase options for different depreciation schedules, and (5) to evaluate the impact of proposed mergers or acquisitions. Models can often be consolidated or combined so that managers in different functional areas of the organization can use the same financial planning package (and assumptions) to design models to meet their particular needs. By combining these models, it may be possible to attain an overall "metamodel" for the whole organization.

Goal-seeking procedures can also be applied in such models. Certain targets (goals) are set by management, and the computer works back from these targets to determine the conditions that will have to prevail to achieve the specified goals. Goals can be viewed as constraints to problem solving; in some instances, it may be necessary to relax some of the constraints (lower the targets) in order to arrive at a feasible solution.

Available software packages also make it possible to perform *sensitivity analyses* to determine how an optimal solution might change if some of the key variables in the model should change. Models often respond to key assumptions, while the majority of variables may have little effect on the results. Thus, management has a means of selecting those variables that require more detailed analysis. This selection is the first step in performing a *risk analysis.*

In the application of *deterministic models,* it is assumed that a single estimate can be specified for each of the input variables. Behind any precise calculation, however, are often data that may not be precise. Taken together, these combined uncertainties could result in an overall uncertainty of major proportions. Many computer-based systems for financial planning, however, have the capacity to introduce and analyze risk and uncertainty, as outlined below.

Risk and Uncertainty

Financial management is often concerned with events in the distant future—events that are inevitably characterized by uncertainty. This important aspect of strategic decision problems must be recognized and treated explicitly from the outset. Strategic decisions must involve an assessment of risk and uncertainty based on available estimates of alternative payoffs or gains. A risk is taken no matter what the decision. Even the decision to do nothing involves the risk of lost opportunity. An effective financial manager, whether in the public or private sector, must be aware of how opportunity, innovation, and risk are interrelated and must be willing to take risks appropriate to his or her level of responsibility.

Converting Uncertainty to Risk

One manager's uncertainty may be another's acceptable risk. What one manager may interpret as an uncertain situation to be avoided, another may see as an opportunity, albeit involving some risk. Although the two terms often are mistakenly used interchangeably, the distinction between *uncertainty* and *risk* is important in financial management.

Certainty can be defined as a state of knowledge in which the specific and invariable outcomes of each alternative course of action are known in advance. The key to certainty is the presence of only one state of nature (although under some circumstances, numerous strategies may achieve that state). This condition enables the manager to predict the outcome of a decision with 100 percent probability.

Uncertainty can be defined as a state of knowledge in which one or more courses of action *may* result in a set of possible specific outcomes. The probabilities of these outcomes, however, are neither known nor meaningful. As Archer has observed, uncertainty involves a range of conditions in which probability distributions vary from a condition of relative confidence, based on *objective probabilities,* to a condition of extreme uncertainty, with little or no information as to the probable relative frequency of particular events.[2]

If the financial manager is willing to assign objective or subjective probabilities to the outcome of uncertain events, then such events may be said to involve risk. *Risk* is a state of knowledge in which each alternative leads to one of a set of specific outcomes, each outcome occurring with a probability that is known to the decision maker. More succinctly, risk is reassurable uncertainty. Risk is measurable when decision expectations or outcomes can be based on statistical probabilities. The event of drawing a red card from a well-shuffled deck is an example of a risky outcome with a probability of 50 percent. The event of a Republican or Democratic victory in any given election is an uncertain outcome.

Uncertainty, Risk, and Probability Functions

Financial managers must face risk and uncertainty from two primary sources: (1) statistical uncertainty and (2) uncertainty about the state of the real world in the future. The first type of uncertainty is usually less troublesome to handle. It arises from chance elements in the real world and would exist even if the second type of uncertainty were zero. When encountered, statistical uncertainty can be dealt with using Monte Carlo and related probability techniques.[3]

Establishing a probability function can bring problems within more manageable bounds by reducing uncertainty to some level of risk that may be tolerable, depending on the risk threshold of the manager or organization. Probabilities can be established either *a posteriori* (by induction or empirical measurement) or *a priori* (by deduction or statistical inference).

The basic conditions necessary to establish a posteriori probability are: (1) the number of cases or observations must be sufficiently large to exhibit statistical stability; (2) the observations must be repeated in the appropriate population or universe; and (3) the observations must be made on a random basis. The inductive approach offers the maximum opportunity for applied decision theory, because the number and range of situations in which such objective probabilities can be used are increasing significantly.

Under the deductive, or a priori, approach, a probability statement is not intended to predict a particular outcome for a given event. Rather, it asserts that in a large number of situations with certain common characteristics, a particular outcome is likely to occur. In short, a statistical inference is made regarding the probable outcome of an uncertain event or series of events.

Uncertainty and Cost Sensitivity

The second type of uncertainty—uncertainty about the future state of the real world—is more troublesome for financial management. In such cases, the use of sophisticated statistical techniques may be little more than expensive window dressing. When the environment is uncertain, an *expected value* approach often must be applied. Expected value is determined by multiplying the value products across all possible outcomes. In mathematical terms, expected value (*EV*) can be expressed as:

$$EV = P_1\$_1 + P_2\$_2 + \ldots P_n\$_n$$

where P stands for probability, $\$$ stands for the value of an outcome, and

$$P_1 + P_2 + \ldots P_n = 1$$

Several techniques utilizing the concept of expected value have been developed to analyze uncertainty about the future state of events. These techniques include (1) sensitivity analysis, (2) contingency analysis, and (3) a fortiori analysis. Each of these techniques is applicable under varying circumstances. The purpose here is not to present a how-to approach, but rather to identify the conceptual framework underlying these methods.

Sensitivity analysis is designed to measure (often quite crudely) the possible effects that variations in uncertain elements (for example, costs) may have on the alternatives under analysis. In most strategic decisions, a few key parameters exhibit considerable uncertainty. The analyst must determine a set of *expected values* for these parameters (as well as other parameters). Recognizing that these expected values may be, at best, "guesstimations," the analyst may use several values (optimistic, pessimistic, and most likely) in an attempt to ascertain how sensitive the results might be to variations in the uncertain parameters.

Exhibit 6-2 illustrates how sensitivity analysis can be used to determine the variations in rankings among several alternatives, based on anticipated costs. First, the analyst sets the expected values for all costs that are certain (for which some reliable basis exists for establishing an estimated cost). Three values for the uncertain costs are then determined. The optimistic cost represents an assessment of cost based on the assumption that everything goes right with the project—that all of the uncertainty is resolved favorably. The pessimistic cost represents the opposite assumption. The most likely cost figure falls somewhere in between these two extremes.

Exhibit 6-2 *Illustration of Sensitivity Analysis*

Cost Levels	Alternative A	Alternative B	Alternative C
Expected values of certain costs	$ 90,000	$ 80,000	$100,000
Optimistic expected values of uncertain costs	$ 10,000	$ 30,000	$ 20,000
Expected values of all costs	$100,000	$110,000	$120,000
Rankings	1	2	3
Pessimistic expected values	$110,000	$115,000	$ 90,000
Expected values of all costs	$200,000	$195,000	$190,000
Rankings	3	2	1
Most likely expected values	$ 60,000	$ 40,000	$ 20,000
Expected values of all costs	$150,000	$120,000	$170,000
Rankings	2	1	3

Two related points concerning uncertainty are illustrated in Exhibit 6-2. First, the range of uncertainty may vary from alternative to alternative (for alternative A, the uncertain range is $10,000 to $110,000; for alternative B, $30,000 to $115,000; and for alternative C, $20,000 to $90,000). Second, uncertain costs may not always be the critical factor in determining the "best" alternative. For example, although uncertain costs for alternative C vary over the narrowest range, this alternative still ranks third except under conditions of high, or pessimistic, uncertain costs.

Probability theory can be applied in connection with sensitivity analysis. Assume, for example, that the probability of the most likely costs being realized is 50 percent; the most pessimistic costs, 30 percent; and the most optimistic costs, 20 percent. The composite expected values for all costs would then be:

Alternative A = [.50(150,000) + .30(200,000) + .20(100,000)] = $155,000

Alternative B = [.50(120,000) + .30(195,000) + .20(110,000)] = $140,500

Alternative C = [.50(170,000) + .30(190,000) + .20(120,000)] = $166,000

Given these probability assumptions, alternative B is clearly the preferred alternative.

Contingency analysis is designed to examine the effects on alternative choices when a relevant change is postulated in the evaluation criteria. This approach can also be used to determine the effects of a major change in the general decision environment, or "ground rules," within which the problem situation exists. In short, contingency analysis is a "with and without" approach. In the field of public health, for example, alternative approaches to environmental health might be evaluated with and without a major new code enforcement program. In a more local context, a public service organization might evaluate various sites for the location of its headquarters under existing conditions of client distribution and access routes. Additional evaluations might then be made, assuming different client distributions and other route configurations.

A fortiori analysis (from the Latin, meaning "with stronger reason") is a method of deliberately "stacking the deck" in favor of one alternative to determine how it might stand up in comparison to other approaches. Suppose that, prior to analysis, the governing board strongly favors alternative C. In performing the analysis on C in comparison to the other feasible alternatives, a deliberate choice is made to resolve any major uncertainties in favor of C. The analyst would then determine how each of the other alternatives compared under these circumstances. If some alternative other than C looks good (that is, if C does not show up to be the best alternative), there may be a very strong case for dismissing the initial intuitive judgment in favor of C. This type of analysis can be carried out in a series of trials, with each alternative, in turn, being favored in terms of the major uncertainties.

These three techniques for dealing with uncertainty may be useful not only in a direct analytical sense; they may also contribute indirectly to the resolution of problem situations. Through sensitivity and contingency analyses, for example, it may be possible to gain a better understanding of the really critical uncertainties of a given strategic problem. With this knowledge, a new alternative might be formulated that would provide a reasonably good hedge against a range of more significant uncertainties. This is often difficult to do. When it can be accomplished, however, it may offer one of the best ways to offset the uncertainties of a problem situation.

Uncertainty, Risk, and Expected Utility

The assumption that people actually behave rationally in the manner suggested by the mathematical notion of *expected value* is often contradicted by observable behavior in risky situations. People are willing to buy insurance, for example, even though they know that the insurance company makes a profit. People are willing to buy lottery tickets even though the chances of winning are minimal. Consideration of the problem of insurance and the so-called "St. Petersburg paradox" led Daniel Bernoulli, an eighteenth-century mathematician, to propose that these apparent contradictions could be resolved by assuming that people act so as to maximize their *expected utility* rather than expected value.[4] Thus, people buy insurance because the consequences against which they are insured are significant in view of the costs, including the profit made by the insurance company. People are willing to invest a small amount of money in a lottery ticket, even though the probability outcome is highly uncertain, because the payoff is so high relative to their expected utility.

Extensive research has been performed in the area of risk and uncertainty because the behavior of decision makers often appears to violate commonly accepted axioms of rational behavior. Although no exact probabilities may exist for the success or failure of a particular event, Kassouf has observed that an individual with "clear-cut, consistent preferences over a specified set of strategies . . . will act as if he has assigned probabilities to various outcomes."[5] The values for the probabilities will be unique for each individual and not unlike the values of utility that might be assigned to an individual through a study of his or her *social preferences.* The obverse of social preferences, of course, is *risk aversion,* a subject on which opinions vary.[6]

As most economists will now admit, utility theory alone cannot resolve the disputes over social preference and/or aversion to risk. There are numerous situations in which financial managers will have to obtain a more careful reading of the various utility functions or preferences of their clientele and the organization as a whole. As Stokey and Zeckhauser explain, strategic choice under uncertainty is a threefold process.[7]

1. Alternatives must be assessed to determine what probabilities and payoffs are implied for individual members of the organization and its clientele.
2. Attitudes toward risk of these individuals must be evaluated to determine the certainty equivalents of these probabilities and payoffs.
3. Having estimated the equivalent benefits that each alternative offers to different members of the organization/clientele, the decision maker must select the preferred outcome.

Although this process may sound simple, it often is very complex in application. Some basic tools have been developed to aid in unraveling these complexities. *Dynamic equilibrium analysis* is designed to identify relative aversion to risk. *Markov chains,* a modeling technique that assumes a system can be described in terms of discrete states, trace probabilities for various states of the system over time. *Distribution analysis* provides for calculation of the level of divergence from an equal distribution of policy payoffs.[8]

These relatively mechanical techniques can be brought into play only after the manager has a fairly good understanding of organizational and/or clientele preferences. Once the groundwork for approximating utility has been laid, the financial manager will be better prepared to address uncertainties in a more systematic fashion.

A basic objective of financial management is to reduce uncertainty by bringing to light information that will clarify relationships among elements in the decision process. This reduction of uncertainty may cause the risk associated with a particular choice: (1) to remain unchanged; (2) to decrease (as in the case where a reduction in uncertainty permits the assessment of more definitive probabilities); or even (3) to increase (as happens when the additional information reveals risk factors previously unknown). Thus, although risk and uncertainty are interrelated, they must be treated independently in many situations.

Cost Analysis

Factors that influence future costs must be examined as part of the financial planning process. Often the tendency is to consider costs strictly in terms of dollar inputs—the financial resources required to support personnel, equipment, materials, and so forth. Future costs that cannot be conveniently measured in dollar terms all too often are dismissed as noncost considerations. Such costs, however, may have important implications beyond their measurable monetary value.

Factors Influencing Future Costs

No program decision is free of cost, whether or not the decision leads to the actual commitment of organizational resources. And certainly, the choices among alternative strategies for the accomplishment of goals and objectives are likely to involve many costs. Such choices include not only the expenditure of money but also the consumption of physical resources, the employment of human resources, and the use of time—all critical commodities in any organization.

The financial manager must be cognizant of the following factors that influence future costs:

1. Scope and quality of the services or products to be delivered.
2. Volume of activity required to deliver these services or products.
3. Methods, facilities, and organizational structure required to perform these activities.
4. Qualities and types of labor, materials, equipment, and other cost elements required by these programs.
5. Price levels of the various cost elements.

These factors must be analyzed as they relate to the various programs, activities, and operations to be performed. Cost factors should be considered (1) in the development of plans and programs; (2) in the preparation of budget requests; and (3) after commitments have been authorized, as programs or projects enter the implementation phase.

Many organizational activities can be measured in terms of *units of production* (workload measures). Current records of personnel activities may provide sufficiently accurate and reliable data to determine workloads. In some cases, however, it may be necessary to undertake more extensive, descriptive analyses of the nature and scope of the activities involved. Further refinements are possible where cost accounting procedures have been adopted.

Having established the volume of work required to perform certain activities under existing organization and methods, it may be appropriate to examine *alternative approaches* to determine if greater efficiency and effectiveness can be attained. The analysis of alternatives should precede the formulation of a financial plan. The analysis should also continue after the actual allocation of resources, to ensure that the approach adopted fits the resources available. Work methods should be analyzed to establish the appropriate mix of personnel, equipment, supplies, and other operating requirements to do the job with the least effort and at the least cost. Particular attention should be given to possible increases in productivity through simplified procedures and the use of labor-saving equipment.

Personnel (labor) is the most critical cost element for most organizational operations. Therefore, performance measures expressed in terms of personnel-hours required to carry out an activity or program are most useful to program managers. *Unit cost standards* may be established for activities that are of a type and importance to justify cost accounting procedures. For nonroutine (nonrepetitive) activities, however, workload and unit cost measures may not adequately represent the cost elements involved. In such cases, management may have to rely on more subjective measures to provide an adequate basis for strategic decisions.

Personnel costs are subject to management control in two important areas: salary rates and job classifications. Periodic reviews should be made to see that each employee has the proper work assignment in view of his or her pay rate. All too often, skilled employees with higher pay classifications are assigned tasks that lower-rated persons should perform. Eliminating positions at the lower end of the pay scale may result in serious false economies if higher-paid personnel eventually have to do the work previously assigned to these positions.

Changes in salary plans should be made only after a thorough study of such factors as trends in the cost of living, rates paid by comparable organizations, and fringe benefits, including sick leave, vacations, extra holidays, and security of tenure. Often, improved fringe benefits can provide a bigger "payoff" to employees than increases in salaries or wages, which are likely to be subject to a larger "tax bite." Sound personnel and pay policies will yield economic benefits to the organization in the long run.

Prices for materials and equipment can be controlled to some extent by scheduling purchases to take advantage of the lowest price consistent with necessary quality. Price trends of frequently used commodities should be analyzed continuously, and appropriate inventories should be maintained of items subject to price fluctuations. At the same time, the cost of maintaining inventory (space requirements, shelf life, anticipated price changes, and so forth) must also be considered.

Monetary Costs and Economic Costs

Monetary costs are those commonly reflected in financial accounts. They include research and development costs, investment costs, and the costs of operations, maintenance, and replacement. At times, it may be appropriate in financial planning to look beyond these monetary costs to what economists call *opportunity costs, associated costs,* and *social costs.*

Research and development involve "front-end" costs that may or may not figure into the actual expenses of a given project or program. R&D costs incurred explicitly for a given project should be included as a project expense. However, general R&D costs that eventually benefit more than one project or program must be considered as *sunk costs.* Such costs should not be included in the direct cost estimate for a specific project or program.

Investment costs are expenses incurred to obtain future benefits. Such investments may be classified as sunk costs or actual project outlays, depending on their timing. Consider the decision to build a public health clinic on land that was purchased some years earlier for another public purpose. Only those additional investment costs required to prepare the site for the clinic should be considered as project outlays. The previous investment for the land purchase is a sunk cost.

Sunk costs can become an *inheritable asset* if previous investments can be used to the particular advantage of one alternative over another. The decision as to the site of the health clinic should not be based solely on the past investment, however. If that location would be an inferior alternative in view of identified client needs, this decision would simply result in throwing good money after bad.

Investment costs vary with the size of a particular program or project, but not with its duration. *Recurring costs,* on the other hand, include operating and maintenance costs that vary with both the size and duration of the program. Such recurring costs include salaries and wages, employee benefits, maintenance and repair of equipment, miscellaneous materials and supplies, transfer payments, insurance, and direct overhead costs. These recurring, or operating, costs do not add to the stock of capital. Rather, they are incurred to maintain the value of the existing stock. In preparing cost estimates, it is important that these recurring costs be considered over the life of the project or program, not just in the initial fiscal period.

As these distinctions suggest, some program costs are *fixed*; that is, they are the same regardless of the size or duration of the program. Other costs are *variable*; that is, they may change significantly as the scope of the project or program is increased. Some uncertainty may exist regarding these costs, particularly if the project has a relatively long duration. It is important, therefore, to consider the marginal, or incremental, costs of increasing the size or scope of a program or project.

Suppose, for example, that the decision is whether to build one or two public health clinics. It may be possible to get quantity discounts on materials and equipment that would reduce the cost of a second clinic. As a result, suppose the cost of building one clinic is $1,000,000, and the cost of building two clinics is $1,700,000.

The average cost of each clinic would be $850,000, but the *marginal cost* of the second clinic would be only $700,000.

If resources are committed to one program, the opportunity has been preempted to use these resources elsewhere. The concept of *opportunity costs* can be illustrated by returning to the health clinic example. Having determined the monetary cost of the proposed facility, it may be appropriate to describe some of the alternative uses of these resources. For example, to what other purpose could the land be put? What other use could be made of the required staff salaries? If bonds are to be issued, what other uses might be made of the funds required for interest and principal payments?

If these alternative uses are sufficiently important, an attempt should be made to estimate their value. This evaluation would consider the benefits that must be given up if the decision is made to go ahead with the proposed clinic. Keep in mind that a basic purpose of cost analysis is to estimate the value of alternatives foregone. Opportunity costs may be extremely important in making decisions among alternative program strategies.

Associated costs are "any costs involved in utilizing project services in the process of converting them into a form suitable for use or sale at the stage benefits are evaluated."[9] Associated costs are often incurred by the beneficiaries of public programs and services. The incremental costs of travel, food, lodging, and so forth represent the associated costs that must be borne by users of public recreational facilities, for example. If access to a facility is improved, so that the users' travel costs are reduced, then these savings in associated costs can be considered benefits arising from improved access.

Social costs can be defined as the subsidies that would have to be paid to compensate persons adversely affected by a project or program for their suffering, or "disbenefits." Rarely is such compensation actually made (except perhaps when affected individuals enter into litigation and are awarded damages). Thus, social costs represent an analytical concept.

In making a cost analysis, social costs can be handled in one of two ways.[10] They may be treated as external costs and subtracted from the market value of the output of the project to obtain a *net social value*. Alternatively, they may be treated as opportunity costs by examining the *potential benefits* to those who are likely to be adversely affected if the project resources were spent on some other program. For example, the location of a sewage treatment facility may result in reduced property values in adjacent residential areas. These losses may be treated as "negative benefits" and subtracted from the overall benefits of the project to the larger community. Alternatively, planners may calculate the benefits that would accrue to these property owners from an alternative use of project funds (for example, development of a park site). The project with the larger "yield" would represent the better use of these resources.

Unfortunately, social costs, if included at all in a cost analysis, are seldom treated fairly. Such cost considerations are either underplayed by proponents of a project or overplayed by its opponents. Social costs often carry significant emotional overtones and, therefore, may be difficult to evaluate. Nevertheless, such an evaluation may be a very important factor in the overall strategic decision.

Elements of Cost–Benefit Analysis

It has been suggested that "one can view cost–benefit analysis as anything from an infallible means of reaching the new Utopia to a waste of resources in attempting to measure the unmeasurable."[11] Many criticisms of cost–benefit analysis are equally applicable to other analytical techniques. All too often, the assertion is made that, since analysis is difficult, costly, and troublesome, more intuitive approaches should be applied. This is not a valid argument, however, for abandoning efforts to improve analytical techniques.

Basic Components

A comprehensive cost–benefit analysis requires that estimates be made of both direct and indirect costs and tangible and intangible benefits of a program or project. Costs and benefits must then be translated into a common measure, usually (but not necessarily) a monetary unit. The costs and benefits are then compared by computing (1) a benefit-to-cost ratio (benefits divided by costs), (2) net benefits (benefits minus costs), or (3) some other value (such as internal rate of return) summarizing the results of the analysis. Given adequate estimates, cost–benefit analysis offers a relatively straightforward assessment of economic efficiency, providing information on which to base effective resource allocations among economically desirable options.

In the traditional formulation of the cost–benefit approach, first outlined by Otto Eckstein,[12] the resource allocation problem is clarified through identification of (1) an objective function, (2) constraints, (3) externalities, (4) time dimensions, and (5) risk and uncertainty.

Selecting an *objective function* involves the identification and quantification (in dollar terms, to the extent possible) of the costs and benefits associated with each alternative. *Benefits* are the net outcomes, both tangible and intangible, of a program or project. The specification of benefits is sometimes relatively straightforward, as in many technical and industrial projects. For social programs, however, benefits are often diffuse, intangible, and difficult to define and measure.

Costs are somewhat easier to identify. They are the direct and indirect inputs— the resources required to carry out the program or project. The concept of opportunity costs—the value of foregone opportunities—is an important consideration in determining project costs. The actual evaluation of opportunity costs may be complex, however, even for programs for which extensive impact data are available.

Constraints are the "rules of the game"—that is, the limits within which a solution must be sought. Frequently, solutions that are otherwise optimal must be discarded because they do not conform to these imposed rules. Constraints are incorporated into mathematical models as parameters or boundary conditions.

Projects may have external or spillover effects—that is, side effects or unintended consequences that may be beneficial or detrimental. These *externalities* may be difficult to identify and measure, and initially they may be excluded from the analysis in order to make the problem statement more manageable. The long-range effects of these phenomena must ultimately be considered, however, usually after the objective function and model have been tested and the range of feasible alternatives has been narrowed.

Costs and benefits occurring at different points in *time* must be made commensurable—that is, translated into a common unit of measurement. It is not sufficient merely to add the estimated benefits and subtract the estimated costs. The impact of deferred benefits and future costs must be taken into account. In so doing, the analyst encounters the problems of risk and uncertainty.

Discounting Future Costs and Benefits

In developing a cost analysis, it is important to recognize that dollar values are not equal over time. Benefits that accrue in the present are usually worth more to their recipients than benefits anticipated some time in the future. Similarly, resources invested today cost more than those invested in the future, since one option would be to invest the same funds at some rate of return that would increase their value.

Therefore, the equivalent *present value* of future streams of both costs and benefits must be determined by multiplying each stream by an appropriate *discount factor*. If the alternative is to invest available funds at some interest rate (i), then an appropriate discount factor can be expressed as:

$$\frac{1}{(1 + i)^n}$$

where i is the relevant interest rate per year and n is the number of periods into the future that the benefits and costs will accrue. If, as is the usual case, i is positive, the farther an event is in the future, the smaller is its present value. High discount rates mean that the present is valued considerably over the future; that is, there is a significantly higher regard for present benefits than for equal future benefits and/or a willingness to trade some larger amount of future benefits for smaller current benefits.

The choice of the discount rate may make the difference between acceptance and rejection of a project. Unfortunately, no simple guidelines are available for determining an appropriate discount rate for public investments.

Two common bases for discounting, reflecting both local conditions and the marketplace for investments, are: (1) the cost of borrowing the capital necessary to finance a project or program and (2) the rate of return that could be realized if an equivalent amount were invested for the same period of time. Thus, if a project could be financed by borrowing the necessary capital at 11 percent, or if an investment of equivalent funds could be expected to yield 10 percent, either of these percentages might appropriately be used to discount future costs and benefits.

Although the choice of a particular discount rate may be difficult to justify, the procedures for discounting are quite simple. Once an appropriate rate has been chosen, a table of discount factors can be consulted to determine the appropriate figure to apply to each year in the stream of costs and benefits. As the data in

Exhibit 6-3 illustrate, however, the selection of the discount rate can significantly affect the final decision.

Exhibit 6-3   *Discounting $10,000 Annually Over Ten Years*

Year	Discount Factor @ 8 Percent	Value	Discount Factor @ 10 Percent	Value
1	0.925926	$ 9259.26	0.909090	$ 9090.90
2	0.857339	8573.39	0.826446	8264.46
3	0.793832	7938.32	0.751315	7513.15
4	0.735030	7350.30	0.683013	6830.13
5	0.680583	6805.83	0.620920	6209.20
6	0.630170	6301.70	0.564472	5644.72
7	0.583490	5834.90	0.513156	5131.56
8	0.540269	5402.69	0.466505	4665.05
9	0.500249	5002.49	0.424095	4240.95
10	0.463193	4631.93	0.385541	3855.41
Total		$67100.81		$61445.53

Criteria for Analysis

Once an objective function has been identified, the next step in cost–benefit analysis is to select an indicator of "success"—that is, an index that will yield a higher value for more desirable alternatives.[13] Conceptually, such an indicator involves the *maximization* of something. Businesses, for example, seek to maximize profits. Public officials are presumed to seek maximum benefits for their constituencies. An inability to quantify overall benefits, however, has led to the identification of *cost minimization* as the most important goal in many analyses.

It is frequently suggested that the goal of cost–benefit analysis should be to maximize benefits *and* minimize costs. In reality, however, both cannot be accomplished simultaneously. Costs can be minimized by spending nothing and doing nothing, but in that case, no benefits result. Benefits can be maximized within a particular project or program by committing organizational resources until marginal benefits are zero. But such action may require far more resources than are available. Therefore, some composite criterion is needed. Three obvious choices are:

1. Maximize benefits for given costs.
2. Minimize costs while achieving a fixed level of benefits.
3. Maximize net benefits (benefits minus costs).

A *benefit/cost ratio* is defined as the present value of benefits divided by the present value of costs (or average annual benefits over average annual costs). Thus, for example, if the discounted stream of benefits over the expected duration of a program or project equals $800,000 and the discounted stream of costs equals $600,000, the benefit/cost ratio is 1.33.

A variation on the basic benefit/cost ratio emphasizes the return on invested capital by segregating operational costs and subtracting them from both sides of the ratio. In the previous example, assume that the present value of operational costs represents $200,000 of the total stream of costs. Subtracting operational costs from both benefits and total costs results in the following *net benefit/cost ratio*:

$$\frac{\$800,000 - \$200,000}{\$600,000 - \$200,000} = \frac{\$600,000}{\$400,000} = 1.50$$

As operational costs account for an increasingly larger proportion of total costs, the net benefit/cost ratio becomes larger.

Net benefit/cost ratios may be preferable for private enterprises in which capital is a greater constraint than operational expenses, especially when taxes are considered. However, a number of economists argue for the use of gross ratios in public sector applications. Their contention is that legislative bodies should consider operational costs as well as capital costs and should give agencies credit for savings on operational costs by permitting them to spend more on capital costs.

The criterion recommended, if not used, most frequently in contemporary cost–benefit analysis is *net benefits*. Net benefits measure *difference,* whereas benefit/cost calculations produce a *ratio.* The results of these two techniques are not always interchangeable. The fact that the net benefits of alternative A are greater than those of alternative B does not imply that the benefit/cost ratio of A is greater than that of B. For example, suppose the benefits in alternative A have a present value of $300,000, and the costs have a present value of $100,000. The net benefits of this alternative would be $300,000 minus $100,000, or $200,000; the benefit/cost ratio would be $300,000 divided by $100,000, or 3.0. If the present value of benefits in alternative B were $200,000 and that of costs $40,000, alternative B would have lower net benefits ($200,000 − $40,000 = $160,000), but a higher benefit/cost ratio ($200,000 ÷ $40,000 = 5.0). In addition to knowing the benefit/cost ratio for a given project or program, it is also necessary to know the size of the project or program.

Project size is important in another respect. Suppose that two projects each offer net benefits of $10,000. One project involves a present value of benefits of $2 million and a present value of costs of $1.99 million; the other has a present value of benefits of $100,000 and a present value of costs of $90,000. Now suppose that something goes wrong, so that the calculations of costs and benefits are off by 10 percent. The first project might have a negative benefit of as much as $200,000, whereas the second would do no worse than break even.

Limitations of Cost–Benefit Analysis

Cost–benefit techniques do not purport to solve all problems relating to the allocation of scarce organizational resources. They are of limited usefulness, for example, in the evaluation of programs of relatively broad scope or in the comparison of programs with widely differing objectives. Cost–benefit analysis provides only limited assistance in establishing priorities among various goals.

The basic objective of cost–benefit analysis is not simply to maximize the ratio of benefits to costs. At times, the "equalization" of benefit/cost ratios may serve as a necessary condition for achieving a desired goal. More often, however, other factors must be considered in selecting an appropriate or "best" decision. These factors include: (1) the time stream of costs and benefits, and the time preference for present as opposed to future consumption of goods or services; (2) limitations imposed by revenue (budgetary) constraints; and (3) the question of whether goals and objectives can be specified in sufficient detail to permit a fuller identification of direct and indirect costs and benefits.

It is virtually impossible to eliminate the need for subjective judgment in the process of making decisions for any organization. Nonetheless, a more systematic approach to the comparison of costs and benefits, including consideration of time preference and of the marginal productivity of capital investments, can contribute significantly to providing a more rational basis for such decisions. This is particularly true when compared with the uncoordinated, haphazard, and intuitive nature of many more traditional methods. Important contributions of cost–benefit analysis include the examination of expenditures in terms of programs and objectives, instead of merely by spending entities, and the consideration of total benefits of expenditures alongside total costs of inputs for alternative programs.

Cost–Effectiveness Analysis

Cost–benefit analysis is designed to pursue *efficiency,* often at the expense of *effectiveness.* The effectiveness of a program is measured by the extent to which, if implemented, some desired goal or objective will be achieved. Since a goal can usually be achieved in more than one way, the analytical task is to determine the most effective approach from among several alternatives. The preferred alternative either (1) produces a given level of performance at the minimum cost or (2) achieves the maximum level of performance possible for a given level of cost. Although costs can ordinarily be expressed in monetary terms, levels of achievement are usually represented by nonmonetary indexes, or *measures of effectiveness.* Such indexes measure the direct and indirect effects of resource allocations.

Output Orientation

Techniques of cost–effectiveness analysis originated in the early 1970s and have yet to reach full maturity. Cost–effectiveness studies initially were used in situations where benefits could not be measured in units commensurable with costs. In these early applications, the level of performance or output was usually taken as a given. Several alternative methods of achieving this level were then examined in order to identify the alternative with the lowest costs. These initial studies revealed many important aspects of decision making with respect to the allocation of scarce resources.

In contemporary applications of cost–effectiveness analysis, the emphasis is on program objectives and on the use of effectiveness measures to monitor progress toward these objectives. The extended time horizon adopted in cost–effectiveness analysis leads to a fuller recognition of the need for life-cycle costing—that is, analysis of costs over the estimated duration of the program or project.

Cost–effectiveness analysis can be viewed as an application of the economic concept of *marginal analysis*. The analysis must always move from some base that represents existing capabilities and existing resource commitments. The objective is to determine what additional resources are required to achieve some specified additional performance capability. Thus, the focus is on *incremental costs*.

Effectiveness measures involve a basic scoring technique for determining increments in output achieved relative to the investment of additional increments of cost. Effectiveness measures are often expressed in relative terms—for example, percentage increase in some measure of educational attainment, percentage reduction in the incidence of a disease, or percentage reduction in unemployment. These measures facilitate comparisons and rank-ordering of alternatives in terms of the costs involved in achieving identified goals and objectives. However, since benefits are not converted to the same common denominator, the merit of any single project cannot be ascertained. Nor is it possible to compare which of two or more projects with different objectives will produce the better return on investment. It is only possible to compare the relative efficacy of program alternatives with the same or similar goals.

Types of Analyses

Three supporting analyses are required under the cost–effectiveness approach:

1. *Cost–goal studies* are concerned with the identification of feasible levels of achievement.
2. *Cost–effectiveness comparisons* assist in the identification of the most effective program alternative.
3. *Cost–constraint assessments* determine the cost of employing less than the most optimal program.

The objective of a cost–goal study is to develop a cost curve for each program alternative. This curve approximates the sensitivity of costs (inputs) to changes in the level of goal achievement (outputs). Costs may change in direct proportion to the level of achievement; that is, each additional increment of cost may produce the same increase in output. However, if output increases more rapidly than costs, then the program alternative is operating at a level of *increasing returns*. This is represented by a positively sloped curve that rises at an accelerating rate, as illustrated by the initial segment of cost curve B in Exhibit 6-4. If costs increase more rapidly than output, the program alternative is operating in an area of *diminishing returns* (as in the upper segment of cost curve B).

Cost–effectiveness analysis requires a model that can relate incremental costs to increments in achievement. For some types of problems, practical models can be developed with relative ease. For other problems, cost curves can be approximated from historical data. As the input–output relationships associated with various alternatives are better understood, the construction of cost curves and effectiveness scales should become increasingly more sophisticated.

Assuming that the costs associated with different achievement levels can be determined for each alternative, the problem remains of how to choose among these alternatives. In principle, the rule of choice should be to select the alternative that

Exhibit 6-4   *Cost–Effectiveness Analysis in Graphic Form*

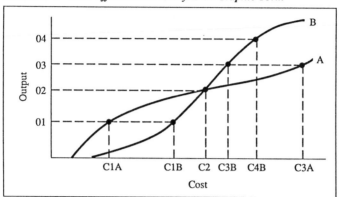

yields the greatest excess of positive effects (attainment of objectives) over negative impacts (resources used, costs, and negative spillover effects). In practice, however, this ideal criterion is seldom applied, as there is no practical way to subtract dollars spent from the nonmonetary measures of effectiveness.

The best approach, therefore, may be a *cost–effectiveness comparison* of program alternatives, as illustrated in Exhibit 6-4. Alternative A achieves the first level of output (O1) at a relatively modest level of cost (C1A), whereas nearly twice the amount of resources (C1B) would be required to achieve the same level of effectiveness using alternative B. Both alternatives achieve the second level of output (O2) at the same level of cost (C2). Alternative B requires a lower level of resources (C3B) to achieve the third level of output (O3). And only alternative B achieves the fourth level of output (O4), since the program cost curve of alternative A is not projected to reach this level of effectiveness.

Which of these two program alternatives is more desirable? To answer that question, it is necessary to define the *optimum envelope* formed by these two cost curves. If resources in excess of C2 are available, then alternative B is clearly the better choice. However, if available resources are less than C2, alternative A provides greater effectiveness for the dollars expended.

In general, it may not be possible to choose between two alternatives simply on the basis of cost–effectiveness unless one alternative dominates at all levels of goal attainment. Usually, either a desired level of performance must be specified and costs minimized for that effectiveness level, or a cost limit must be specified and achievement maximized for that level of resource allocation.

In practice, organizations may adopt programs that are not the most effective technically available. Among the more obvious reasons for this are legal constraints, employee rights, union rules, technical capacity, and community attitudes. The purpose of a *cost–constraint assessment* is to examine the impact of these factors by comparing the cost of the program that might be adopted if no constraints were present with the cost of the constrained program.

Once this cost differential has been identified, decisions can be made as to the feasibility of eliminating the constraints. This assessment gives decision makers an estimate of how much would be saved by the relaxation of a given constraint. By the same token, the cost of the constraint suggests the amount of resources that might be committed to overcoming it. In some cases, however, maintaining a constraint may be more important for social or political reasons than implementing a more effective program.

Summary

In the allocation of limited fiscal resources, it may be assumed that most organizations consider both the payoffs and the pitfalls associated with various program requirements. These assessments, however, are often haphazard and uncoordinated, with little systematic effort to quantify benefits or to include all costs appropriate to the particular alternatives under consideration.

Various techniques of financial ratio analysis—such as liquidity measures, leverage ratios, measures of profitability, and asset utilization ratios—have been widely used for many years to indicate the relative well-being of business organizations. These ratios, however, tend to be retrospective and static in nature and are of only limited application in public resource management.

Strategic funds programming is a more future-oriented approach that can be helpful in determining where discretionary funds to implement new programs and strategies may be available within the financial structure of an organization. The techniques used in programming strategic funds help to identify feasible options under various financial assumptions. The financial manager, however, must still make an assessment of risks and payoffs before the "best" option is selected.

In recent years, interactive computer software has become a significant analytical tool for financial planning, making possible on-line, real-time decision support systems. Traditional methods of financial analysis use hindsight to determine why things went wrong. Computer-assisted methods of financial planning provide a basis on which to anticipate (and accommodate) change before its full impact occurs. Most computer-based systems for financial planning can also be used to analyze risk and uncertainty.

A basic objective of financial management is to reduce uncertainty and bring risk within tolerable limits. This is accomplished through the generation of management information that clarifies critical relationships among elements in the decision process. Various methods for converting uncertainty to risk—including the use of objective and subjective probabilities and the techniques of sensitivity analysis, contingency analysis, and a fortiori analysis—have been outlined in this chapter. The concept of expected utility has also been touched upon, in an effort to provide the reader with a broader understanding of the critical dimensions of strategic decisions.

Factors influencing future costs must be examined as part of the financial planning process. Monetary costs—research and development costs, investment costs, and the costs of operations, maintenance, and replacement—are commonly reflected in financial accounts. In financial planning, however, it often is necessary to look beyond these monetary costs to opportunity costs, associated costs, and social costs.

A thorough cost analysis must also distinguish (1) fixed and variable costs, (2) recurring costs, and (3) marginal or incremental costs. These costs should be examined over the life of the project or program under analysis. The need to adopt an extended time dimension in such cost assessments has led to the development of cost–benefit analysis.

Cost–benefit and cost–effectiveness analysis can be applied at two pivotal points in the evaluation of resource commitments. In the planning stage, cost–benefit analyses are based on *anticipated* costs and benefits. Such analyses are not necessarily empirically based. After a program or project has been implemented and shown to have a significant impact, cost–benefit and cost–effectiveness analyses can be used to assess whether the costs of the program are justified by the magnitude of net outcomes. Such after-the-fact analyses should be based on detailed studies of available empirical data.

Cost–benefit and cost–effectiveness models need not be adopted "whole cloth." A number of subroutines may be introduced into ongoing program analysis procedures. Decision inputs can be developed to include considerations of time preference and marginal productivity of capital investment. The techniques of cost curve analysis can be applied to a variety of decision situations. The examination of expenditures in terms of program objectives and the evaluation of total benefits for alternative program expenditures can be important derivatives of cost–benefit techniques. The extended time horizon adopted in these analytical methods leads to a fuller recognition of the need for life-cycle costing and benefits analysis. The importance of incremental costing, sunk costs, and inheritable assets is also highlighted by this extended perspective. Cost–goal and cost–constraint analyses add other important dimensions to the information available to the decision maker. As the complexity of the resource allocation problem becomes more evident, other subroutines may be adopted, depending on the availability of data and the needs and capabilities of the analyst.

Endnotes

1. Alan J. Rowe, Richard O. Mason, and Karl E. Dickel, *Strategic Management and Business Policy: A Methodological Approach* (Reading, MA: Addison-Wesley, 1982), p. 102.

2. Stephen H. Archer, "The Structure of Management Decision Theory," *Academy of Management Journal* 8 (December 1964): 283.

3. For a basic discussion of Monte Carlo techniques, see E. S. Quade, *Analysis for Public Decisions* (New York: American Elsevier, 1975).

4. L. Sommer (Trans.), "Specimen Theoriae Novae de Mensura Sortis," *Comentari Academiae Scientiarum Imperiales Petropolitanae* 5 (1738); in *Econometrica* 22 (1954): 46.

5. Sheen Kassouf, *Normative Decision-Making* (Englewood Cliffs, NJ: Prentice-Hall, 1970), p. 46.

6. For a broader discussion of this point, see Jack Hirshleifer and David L. Shapiro, "The Treatment of Risk and Uncertainty," in Robert H. Haveman and Julius Margolis (Eds.), *Public Expenditures and Policy Analysis,* 2nd ed. (Chicago: Rand McNally, 1977), pp. 180–203.

7. Edith Stokey and Richard Zeckhauser, *A Primer for Policy Analysis* (New York: Norton, 1978), p. 252.

8. For a more detailed discussion of decisions under uncertainty, see Howard Raiffa, *Decision Analysis* (Reading, MA: Addison-Wesley, 1968). For more about dynamic equilibrium, see Stuart Nagel and Marian Neef, *Operations Research Methods* (Beverly Hills, CA: Sage, 1976). For an introductory discussion of Markov chains, see Stokey and Zeckhauser, *A Primer for Policy Analysis,* chap. 7.

9. U.S. Congress, House Subcommittee on Evaluation Standards, Report to the Interagency Committee on Water Resources, *Proposed Practices for Economic Analysis of River Basin Projects* (Washington, DC: U.S. Government Printing Office, May 1958), p. 9.

10. Ronald H. Coase, "The Problem of Social Cost," *Journal of Law and Economics* 3 (October 1960): 1–44.

11. A. R. Prest and R. Turvey, "Cost Benefit Analysis: A Survey," *The Economic Journal* 75 (1965): 583.

12. Otto Eckstein, *Water Resource Development* (Cambridge, MA: Harvard University Press, 1958).

13. Leonard Merewitz and Stephen H. Sosnick, *The Budget's New Clothes* (Chicago: Markham, 1971), p. 85.

CHAPTER 7

Budgeting

Budgeting is a cyclical decision-making process involving the allocation of limited financial resources to meet organizational goals and objectives. Budgeting also involves the systematic evaluation of prior commitments and their consequences in terms of anticipated achievements. Properly applied, budgeting can contribute significantly to greater efficiency, effectiveness, and accountability in the overall management of an organization's financial resources.

Principles and Practices of Budgeting

A budget is much more than a fixed document, presented annually for review and approval by a governing body. Budgeting represents a complex decision process whereby (1) organizational policy is formulated, (2) action programs are put into effect, and (3) both strategic and management controls are established. The annual cyclical nature of this process should not be misinterpreted as an inflexible routine. Budgets must have the capacity to adapt to changing needs, interests, and available technology in the delivery of organizational services.

Changing Perspectives on Budgeting

Contemporary perspectives on what constitutes prudent fiscal policy differ considerably from those of the past. The appropriate role of government in providing public facilities and services has also come in for considerable reevaluation, as has the question of what government can or should do to foster sound economic development. These shifts in perspective have both emerged from and resulted in changing attitudes toward budgeting in the public sector. As Charles Beard once observed, "Budget reform bears the imprint of the age in which it originated."

Historically, the fiscal aspects of budgeting have received the greatest emphasis. The budget has been viewed primarily as an accounting and management control device, in which expenditure estimates for various programs are reviewed in monetary terms. Under this approach, budget requests are supported by detailed *objects of expenditure*—tabulations of the myriad items required to operate each program, including salaries and wages, rent, office supplies, travel, equipment, and other inputs. The validity of requests is judged primarily through comparisons with previous levels of expenditure.

By the early 1920s, the object-of-expenditure approach to budgeting was widespread. This budget format, with its detailed recording of spending requirements and subsequent commitments, provides a most effective basis for fiscal control. The expenditure of budget allocations can be controlled within relatively narrow, predetermined limits. Financial accounting systems—developed in parallel with the object-of-expenditure budget—support the objectives of fiscal control admirably. This period in public financial administration was marked by a preoccupation with forms and actual and recommended procedures for budgeting and accounting.

As more reliable systems of accounting were installed, the budget was gradually freed from its primary role as fiscal watchdog. If the main function of budgeting is to keep spending in check, then program outputs are seen primarily in terms of limited and fixed values. However, if program accomplishments are examined in terms of benefits, the task of budgeting must be redefined to include the effective marshaling of fiscal and other organizational resources to achieve those benefits.

Recognition of this gradual change in orientation led the Hoover Commission, in 1949, to call for a budget approach that would

> focus attention upon the general character and relative importance of the work to be done, or upon the service to be rendered, rather than upon the things to be acquired, such as personal services, supplies, equipment, and so on. These latter objects are, after all, only the means to an end. The all important thing in budgeting is the work or the service to be accomplished, and what that work or service will cost.[1]

The commission adopted the term *performance budgeting* to identify this approach.

The principal objective of a performance budget is to help administrators assess the *work efficiency* of operating units by (1) casting budget categories in functional terms and (2) providing work-cost measurements to encourage more efficient performance of prescribed activities. Performance budgeting derives much of its conceptual and technical basis from cost accounting and the scientific management movement of the thirties.

Performance budgeting had its heyday in the late forties and early fifties. It is seldom discussed in any detail in contemporary textbooks, which generally relegate the subject to a historical footnote. Many elements of performance budgeting have survived, however, and to understand how the budget can be used as a more effective tool of financial management, it is important to explore these elements in greater detail. This exploration will be the focus of a subsequent section of this chapter.

The innovation in the budget process that has received greatest attention in recent years is the Planning–Programming–Budgeting System (PPBS). PPBS was brought to full public attention in August 1965, when President Lyndon B. Johnson announced that all federal departments would adopt the budgeting system that had been used for some years in the Department of Defense.

PPBS was an outgrowth of program-based budgeting techniques that had been developed earlier in business and industry.[2] The basic objective of PPBS is to present budget requests in terms of program "packages" rather than the usual object-of-expenditure format. Under the PPBS approach, a conscious effort is made (1) to state end objectives, (2) to seek a wide range of program alternatives, and (3) to link program and financial plans. In short, PPBS recognizes that planning and budgeting are complementary processes.

> The need for planning, programming, budgeting, and scheduling arises from the indissoluble connection between the allocation of resources and the formulation and conduct of governmental policy. When undertaken in the proper "mix," these processes constitute the means by which objectives and resources—and the interrelations among them—are taken into account to achieve a more coherent and comprehensive program of action.[3]

PPBS sought to focus attention on aggregates of expenditures—broad program classifications that may cut across agency lines of responsibility. Such a focus was intended to facilitate the evaluation of alternative courses of action in terms of costs and benefits (or effectiveness).

As with many innovations introduced by dictum, however, inadequate groundwork was laid for the development of PPBS at the federal level, and even less at the state and local levels. Although PPBS received enthusiastic support from proponents of a more rational and comprehensive approach to financial management, it was met with corresponding skepticism by many who had experienced previous experiments with performance and program budgeting. A fairly successful technique for evaluating Defense Department weaponry systems, PPBS proved to have only limited immediate application in other public agencies.

The past twenty years have been a period of experimentation in the processes of public budgeting. At the federal level, PPBS—the major budgetary reform of the mid-sixties—gave way to zero-base budgeting (ZBB) under the Carter administration, only to be replaced by mission budgeting and supply-side economics in the 1980s. Each of these approaches represents an attempt to provide a more comprehensive and longer-range perspective to the budget process—to incorporate a *planning perspective.*

Need to Integrate Planning and Control Objectives

An evident shortcoming of these new budgetary approaches has been the failure to integrate these systematic procedures fully with other basic components of financial management. In particular, more recently developed budgeting techniques—such as program budgeting and zero-base budgeting—have not been well aligned with appropriate accounting procedures. These new budgetary formats tend to emphasize the planning function. Far less attention is given to the equally important techniques and procedures for financial control. As a result, these new approaches, in many cases, have failed to produce the desired improvements in terms of more efficient, economical, and effective governmental operations.

Introduction of these budgetary techniques in the private sector has usually been accompanied by parallel improvements in accounting procedures—in particular, the fuller application of managerial and cost accounting techniques. Applications of managerial accounting in government are still in the formative stages.

Purposes and Objectives of Budgeting

Based on this brief historical overview, it is possible to define more clearly what the basic objectives of budgeting can and should be. A budget can be defined as "a comprehensive plan, expressed in financial terms, by which an operating program is effective for a given period of time. It includes estimates of: (a) the services, activities, and projects comprising the program; (b) the resultant expenditure requirements; and (c) the resources usable for their support."[4] A budget provides the legal basis for spending and accountability. Especially in not-for-profit public organizations, budgeting is integrally linked to the accounting process. Through the budgeting/accounting process, revenue and expenditure information is structured to facilitate the continuous monitoring, evaluation, and control of financial resources. Financial authority and responsibility can be delegated throughout the organization, while appropriate central control is maintained.

Budgeting also involves decision making under conditions of uncertainty, where such decisions may have significant long-term consequences. The purposes of budgeting should include both *policy formulation* and *program management.* Before a budget is prepared, goals and objectives should be formulated, policies analyzed, and plans and programs delineated. The financial commitment to organizational programs is (or should be) a clear declaration of policy. The fiscal stewardship that builds on the budget is a principal responsibility of management. Public budgeting also serves as a substitute for mechanisms of the economic market system. It is the process by which decisions are made regarding the allocation of scarce resources— the politics of "who gets what."

Two Types of Budgets

A distinction is made in most public organizations between the annual operating budget and the capital budget. An *operating budget* serves to justify the allocation of financial resources to be expended during the fiscal year. It provides the basis upon which the governing body may authorize organizational units to incur obligations and to pay for them. These obligations and payments are for personal services (salaries, wages, and related employee benefits), contractual services (such as travel, computing services, and consulting services), materials and supplies, certain types of equipment, and other recurring expenses.

A *capital budget* is based on estimates of expenditures to be made over a period of years for capital facilities (major equipment, buildings, and other fixed assets). The means of financing these longer-term commitments during the current fiscal year are identified in the capital budget. The capital budget is often the first year of a program statement that documents improvement needs over a longer time period (usually five to six years). The *capital improvements program* may provide an analysis of anticipated financial resources to support debt commitments that may be incurred through bond issues or other forms of borrowing to finance public improvements.

Different budgeting and accounting principles and procedures are associated with each of these budgets. The balance of this chapter will focus on operating budgets. The next chapter is devoted to the planning and budgeting of capital facilities.

The Annual Operating Budget

The annual operating budget includes an estimate of expenditures which, in turn, must be balanced against the recommended revenue program. It provides information to each successive level of management as a basis for evaluating competing requirements for limited financial resources. Although the budget sets limits on spending, adoption of the budget should be viewed as a positive act. Emphasis on the control aspects of budgeting often results in a negative perception of the process, which can adversely affect the execution of the budget.

The operating budget provides a basis for articulating goals and objectives and, subsequently, for measuring their attainment within a given fiscal period. A budget also facilitates the coordination of personnel and nonpersonnel service requirements and the scheduling of work assignments. Thus, all parties involved in the process can gain a better understanding of the operational plans proposed for the ensuing fiscal year. Once the budget has been approved, organizational units can adjust their activities for the upcoming fiscal year to conform to budget appropriations. Finally, the budget provides a basis for a financial audit and, as appropriate, an evaluation of performance both during the fiscal year and after its close.

The Budget Cycle

Budget making requires careful scheduling to ensure adequate time and information for sound decisions. The budget process commonly involves four major steps:

1. Executive preparation.
2. Review and adoption by the governing body.
3. Budget execution.
4. Post-audit and evaluation.

If the required mass of detail is to be coordinated and important deadlines are to be met, steps in this process should be undertaken in a logical sequence. Responsibility for performing each specific step must be clearly assigned. Well-designed forms should be developed to ensure that budget requests are submitted in as uniform and complete a manner as possible. Guidelines for the preparation of the budget should also be set forth in writing (as a *budget manual* or other form of written instructions).

The Budget Calendar

Key dates and assignments of responsibility for preparing the budget should be established in advance and set forth in chronological order. Controlling dates of the budget calendar for local governments are often set by state law, city charter, or local ordinance. The budget calendar should identify important deadlines, such as those for submitting the budget to the governing body, for legislative adoption of the budget, and for setting the annual property tax levy and rate.

The total time for the annual budget preparation cycle will vary from four to six months in large cities and from two to three months in smaller municipalities and other public organizations. The time required for each step will also vary with the size of the jurisdiction, established legal requirements, and the type of budget format applied.

The Executive Budget

The chief executive has primary responsibility for the preparation of budget estimates and the development of a preliminary budget document. The executive budget is then presented to the governing body for review and adoption. In larger jurisdictions, the chief executive may rely on a budget office, a finance department, and financial planning analysts to develop the background information and financial details necessary to support the budget document.

A *budget guidance memorandum* should be issued to all organizational units, along with a set of instructions for completing the required forms and supporting justifications. The guidance memorandum should outline (1) anticipated fiscal policies, (2) agreed-upon goals and objectives, and (3) performance expectations of the current administration. Statements outlining the overall programs of the organization should establish appropriate levels of program activity or service for the various component units. These service levels should be further specified in the budget submission of each unit. *Budget targets* may be set forth to reflect preliminary estimates of anticipated revenue.

The required budget forms should be completed by each unit, reflecting the most appropriate assignment of resources—personnel, equipment, materials and supplies, and so forth—to carry out its program responsibilities. Broad goals and objectives identified in the guidance memorandum may have to be further refined in order to place specific agency programs within this broader perspective. Various performance measures and measures of effectiveness may be required in the budget justifications. These justifications may also include a priority listing of all programs. Major policy issues or administrative problems, if any, should be identified. Requirements for new organizational policy or legislation should also be outlined, as appropriate.

These submissions must be checked for completeness and accuracy by the central budget agency. Budget requests are then compiled into a preliminary document providing an overall summary of total dollar needs. Preliminary estimates may also be prepared by the budget staff to reflect changes in employee compensation and benefits, estimates of debt service requirements and interfund transfers, and any policy changes inherent in agency budget requests.

The Budget Document

Balancing expenditure requests against total anticipated revenues is a major budgeting task for the chief executive and his or her staff. Since department heads are concerned primarily with the operations of their own units, the budget requests they submit, in the aggregate, usually exceed estimated revenues. State laws generally prohibit local governments from making expenditure commitments that exceed expected revenues. Thus, the process at this stage is often one of budget cutting to bring the total budget into line with overall fiscal constraints. It may be necessary and appropriate, however, to identify new or modified fiscal policies to provide the resources necessary to meet justified program needs.

Department heads should be given an opportunity to meet with the chief executive to explain or defend all, or selected portions, of their budget submissions. Such meetings may be wide-ranging in scope, or they may be restricted to a few points requiring further clarification prior to a final executive decision.

The executive budget document should present a clear picture of the programs to be carried out and the financial basis to support these activities. This document must be designed so that it can be readily understood by members of the governing body and program managers, as well as by financial experts. It should give particular attention to necessary policy decisions. The enthusiasm of technicians for complete detail may need to be curtailed in the interest of clarity and simplicity. Simplicity can be achieved without omitting important facts, however, with the help of (1) a well-constructed budget message; (2) carefully chosen summaries; and (3) charts and tables that explain service programs and the relationships among various proposed expenditures.

Budget Adoption

Every effort must be made to provide a full explanation of the budget, in terms of the range and scope of services it represents. The governing body should receive more than a thick document, with page after page of exhibits, offering little or no explanation of the services to be provided or the intent of the administration. Handed such a document, members of a governing body tend to focus on details of expenditures, such as the amount requested for office supplies, publications, and so forth. Such nitpicking over details arises from the absence of any broad explanation of the programs to be undertaken. As a consequence, important policy decisions—for example, determining appropriate levels of service—may never be directly addressed. The governing body may wish to consult with the chief executive and budget staff for detailed explanations of the proposed programs and the means of financing them.

In local government, public hearings are held so that citizens may express their sentiments on the budget. These hearings should be widely publicized. Although relatively few citizens attend unless they are irate over some aspect of the budget, public officials should be prepared for surprises. The turnout may be much larger than anticipated, and officials must be prepared to answer any and all questions.

The budget may be discussed again in executive sessions following the public hearings. On the basis of these discussions, the expenditure portion of the budget may be amended and the proposed revenue measures modified by the governing body. The budget may be approved by *resolution,* or the governing body may adopt a separate *appropriation measure* that lists specific amounts for specific units by specific categories of expense. An appropriation measure provides a more effective benchmark for administration and auditing. However, care must be taken not to limit the ability of organizational units to adjust to changing conditions in the implementation of programs during the fiscal year.

Budget Execution

The preceding steps in the formulation and review of the budget are of relatively little consequence if the budget is not properly administered. Budget execution is both a financial process and a substantive operational process. This stage of the budget cycle involves the initiation of authorized projects and programs within an established time schedule, within monetary limits, and ideally, within standard cost limits. Budget execution is the longest stage in the budget cycle, covering the full fiscal year and overlapping both the formulation and review stages of the budget for the succeeding and prior years, respectively.

Allocations and Allotments

Budget execution procedures vary considerably from one public organization to the next. In some cases, these procedures consist of little more than a cash flow bookkeeping system that records expenditures in accordance with predetermined item accounts.

In more advanced systems, however, the steps in budget administration are (1) allocation, (2) allotment, (3) expenditure control, and (4) adjustment. Under these procedures, the budget is viewed as both a mandate for and a limit on expenditures. The fiscal period begins with the effective date of the budget. The budget contains estimates of revenues to be collected, and the operating and accounting cycles are based on the budget.

In government, an *appropriation* represents the legal authority to spend. As a rule, such authority is very specific about how much each agency can spend, and for what. The budget is formally recorded by the initial accounting entries for the fiscal period, at the level of detail specified in the appropriations.

The budget is further subdivided through an *allocation* process. Allocations may be identified in the budget document or may be made administratively in executing the budget. Allocations can be made according to objects and/or character of expenditure, activity, organizational units, programs, and/or functions. The budget of the Health Department, for example, might be subdivided through the allocation process to stipulate amounts for outpatient clinics, public health nurses, a community mental health program, and so forth. Allocations are often made for personal services (salaries, wages, and fringe benefits) and for operations, with further subdivisions by major line-items (such as travel, materials and supplies, and fixed assets or equipment).

Provision may also be made for an *allotment* system, whereby budget allocations are further subdivided into time elements—for example, monthly or quarterly allotments for personal services or for some items in the nonpersonal service categories. An allotment system is particularly appropriate when expenditures are contingent upon some future event, such as the availability of a federal or state grant or the projected opening of a new public facility. For example, assume that provision is made in the Fire Department's budget for utility services in a new fire station. These funds should not be made available before the new station is completed and opened. Under this approach, the portion of the budget in question remains unallocated until it is required for actual commitment. Thus, if the facility is not completed on schedule or if the grant is not received, monies initially earmarked for these purposes are restricted until required for the originally approved use. The basic function of the allocation and allotment processes is to assign elements of the overall budget to specific categories of expenditure to ensure that the funds are reserved for those categories.

Encumbrances

Budgetary accounting, as presented in Chapter 2, provides the principal control mechanisms for enforcing allocation, allotment, and appropriation limits. Specific allocations may be encumbered—reserved from the appropriation at the outset of the fiscal year. They are then *liquidated* on an "as billed" basis—for example, payments for employee benefits, legal services, or consulting fees. The purpose of an encumbrance is to ensure that these funds will be available at the time needed—that they will not be spent for other purposes. In addition to all actual expenditures, commitments for goods and services that have been ordered but not yet received must be recorded in an encumbrance system. An encumbrance simply records the placing of a purchase order or the letting of a contract against the appropriation or allocation.

The basic function of an encumbrance is to preclude the incurring of fiscal obligations in excess of appropriated or allocated funds. Suppose, for example, that sizable maintenance agreements are required on computer hardware and software leased from vendors, payable in four quarterly installments. The director of the computing center may schedule these payments so that the final quarter can be deferred until the next fiscal year, thereby freeing up additional operating funds to meet the day-to-day expenses of the center. Such deferred bills become a burden on the next period, however. The appropriation/allocation for that fiscal period may become exhausted prematurely, thus encouraging further deferrals. Although the center may appear to stay within its budget for any given fiscal period, eventually the accumulated debt must be funded. An encumbrance system is designed to prevent this type of problem.

Other Expenditure Controls

Other mechanisms through which the local governing body can control specific expenditure are (1) line-item appropriations, (2) detailed controls on specific funds, (3) periodic budgetary reports, and (4) the independent audit at the close of the fiscal year. Line-item appropriations—funding for specific, detailed spending purposes—became so commonplace in the era of fiscal control that the budget format has come to be known as a *line-item budget* (see Exhibit 7-1). Some control in the budget execution stage may be retained by requiring that proposed transfers between major appropriation items (usually above some arbitrary percentage) receive the approval of the governing body. Mandatory expenditures may be imposed on local governments by the state legislature (for example, for education), and a state supervisory authority may need to be satisfied that the legal aspects of budgeting have been met.

Budget Adjustments

Appraisals of current performance and changing conditions often necessitate significant adjustments in the budget during the fiscal year. Midyear reviews may be scheduled, in addition to a comprehensive review during the time that the budget for the succeeding year is being prepared. The budget should be reappraised and revised at many points during the fiscal year to ensure adequate flexibility in operations.

Sufficient information should be maintained—through the accounting process and other sources—to anticipate requirements for formal budget amendments during the fiscal year. Some amendments require immediate attention; others can be handled more efficiently through a single *omnibus amendment,* ordinarily made during the final three or four months of the fiscal year. Such amendments may require legislative action by the governing body, especially if a supplementary appropriation is involved. Departmental officials should take the initiative when problems come to their attention. Ultimate responsibility rests with the budget staff to recommend any actions necessary to avoid fiscal crises, such as missed paydays or a lack of funds to buy critical materials or equipment.

Revised estimates must be made during the final quarter of the fiscal year to determine the *closing status* of any unallocated fund balances. Specific allocations are often limited as to their fiscal year carry-over; that is, unspent budget allocations may revert to the general treasury at the end of the fiscal year. Year-end reversion of funds is often cited as a major shortcoming of traditional budgeting procedures. This practice offers no incentive for conserving resources and, in fact, promotes year-end spending.

Some allocations may lapse at the end of the fiscal year only if they are not encumbered. Even if the funds have been encumbered, the National Council on Governmental Accounting suggests, the governmental unit may either honor the contracts in progress at the end of the year or cancel them.

Exhibit 7-1   *Current Line-Item Budget Commitments*

FUND	DEPARTMENT	FUNCTION
General	Financial Management	General Government

Budget Comments

The current budget for the Financial Management Department is 7.14% (or $30,339) higher than the level of expenditure for the previous fiscal year. The projected budget request for the next fiscal year represents a 25.2% increase over the current budget. The major increases anticipated are in Personal Services (31.24%), Employee Benefits (30.86%), and Contractual Services (20.49%). Staff increases (nine new positions are requested) are required to accommodate the additional work load brought about by proposed changes in budget format and accounting procedures. These additional positions account for $61,440 (69.4%) of the $88,480 increase in salaries. The remaining increase is the result of scheduled salary adjustments. The major increase under Contractual Services is for data processing (25%). A decrease in data-processing equipment costs is anticipated, however.

Object Classifications	Last Fiscal Year	Current Budget
Personal Services		
1110 Salaries	$278,020	$363,760
1120 Wages	0	0
1130 Special Payments	0	0
1140 Overtime Payments	5,250	7,990
Subtotal: Personal Services	$283,270	$371,750
Contractual Services		
1210 General Repairs	$ 700	$ 755
1220 Utility Services	3,600	3,900
1230 Motor Vehicle Repairs	500	540
1240 Travel	2,100	2,270
1250 Professional Services	5,725	6,185
1260 Communications	6,780	7,320
1270 Printing	1,000	1,080
1280 Computing Services	64,725	80,900
1290 Other Contractual Services	3,000	3,240
Subtotal: Contractual Services	$ 88,130	$106,190
Supplies and Materials		
1310 Office Supplies	$ 29,440	$ 32,200
1320 Fuel Supplies	0	0
1330 Operating Supplies	1,000	1,060
1340 Maintenance Supplies	900	955
1350 Drugs and Chemicals	0	0
1360 Food Supplies	0	0
1370 Clothing and Linens	0	0
1380 Educational and Recreational Supplies	0	0
1390 Other Supplies	1,500	1,590
Subtotal: Supplies and Materials	$ 32,840	$ 34,805

Equipment		
1410 Office Equipment	$ 770	$ 845
1420 Electrical Equipment	250	270
1430 Motor Vehicles	0	0
1440 Highway Equipment	0	0
1450 Medical and Laboratory Equipment	0	0
1480 Data-Processing Equipment	15,000	12,000
1490 Other Equipment	0	0
Subtotal: Equipment	$ 16,020	$ 13,115
Current Obligations		
1510 Payments to Sinking Funds	$ 0	$ 0
1520 Interest on Temporary Loans	0	0
1530 Rental Charges	0	0
1540 Insurance	300	350
1550 Dues and Subscriptions	5,000	5,300
1560 Electrostatic Reproduction	1,640	1,740
1590 Other Obligations	0	0
Subtotal: Current Obligations	$ 6,940	$ 7,390
Employee Benefits		
1610 Retirement and Pension Benefits	$ 8,780	$ 11,495
1620 Social Security Contributions	8,229	10,768
1630 Federal Old-Age Insurance	1,168	1,529
1640 Group Insurance	724	945
1650 Medical/Hospital Insurance	8,899	11,643
Subtotal: Employee Benefits	$ 27,800	$ 36,380
TOTALS	$455,000	$569,630

If the governmental unit intends to honor them (a) encumbrances outstanding at year end should be disclosed in the notes to the financial statements or by reservations of fund balance and (b) the subsequent year's appropriation should provide authority to complete these transactions.[5]

A comparable amount of funds must be reserved in the subsequent appropriation to cover the estimated expenditures for the unperformed portions of existing contracts.

In attempting to "zero out" budget allocations as the end of the fiscal year approaches, agencies must exercise caution to ensure that the items of expenditure or encumbrances will withstand the test of a post-audit—that is, they are eligible items of expenditure for the agency to incur. If allocations do not revert at the end of the fiscal year, or if only the unencumbered portions lapse, "encumbrances outstanding at year end should be reported as reservations of fund balance for subsequent year expenditures based on the encumbered appropriation authority carried over."[6]

Internal and External Audits

There are two basic types of audits: internal and external. *Internal audits,* conducted periodically by in-house staff, result in reports for internal control purposes. The *external audit,* normally required by state law, is conducted by independent accountants after the fiscal year has been completed. The external audit is submitted to the regulating state agency (such as the auditor of public accounts), as well as to the local governing body. The governing body, in turn, should review the audit to ensure that revenue and expenditure activities have been conducted in accordance with the intentions of the budget and the appropriation ordinance.

The traditional emphasis of the post-audit has been on financial compliance—on an assessment of financial transactions for accuracy, legality, and fidelity. Emphasis has been placed more recently on *management audits,* which seek to assess efficiency and economy of resource utilization. Management audits may also examine the adequacy of management information, administrative procedures, and organizational structure. This emphasis has been further expanded to include an assessment of *program results.* Such audits seek to determine whether program objectives have been met and the desired benefits achieved. An effort may also be made to examine alternative approaches that might yield the desired results at lower costs in the future.

These three major components—financial and compliance, economy and efficiency, and program results—when taken together, have been designated by the U.S. General Accounting Office as a *performance audit.*[7] Such an audit is generally undertaken when a program or project has been completed or has reached a major milestone in its funding. In some instances, auditors must review the performance of agencies or programs because standards of performance accountability are spelled out in legislation, regulations, or other governmental guidelines. Thus, the scope of auditing as an accountability device is expanding because accountability has been expanding. The force behind these developments is an increased awareness of the need for greater economy, efficiency, and effectiveness in public organizations and programs.

Management Emphasis on Performance

Efforts in the mid-thirties to use budgeting for management purposes culminated in the concept of *performance budgeting.* Performance budgeting is distinguished by two key components: (1) identification of performance units and (2) measurement of performance costs.[8] A *performance unit* is a team of workers assigned the responsibility of carrying out a specific task or series of tasks. *Performance costs* are those costs directly associated with carrying out these activities.

The Budget as a Work Program

The performance budget is built upon a series of *work programs* related to particular processes or functions carried out by governmental agencies or units within not-for-profit organizations. The principal focus of a performance budget is at or below the departmental level, where the work efficiency of operating units can be assessed. Work-cost data are reduced to discrete, measurable units to determine the performance efficiency of prescribed activities. Cost accounting techniques provide the conceptual and technical basis for the objectives of efficiency and economy.

Major limitations in the implementation of performance budgeting in the forties and fifties were the inability to achieve a uniform and consistent basis for identifying performance units and a reluctance to adopt cost accounting procedures to assist in measuring performance. As a consequence, many applications of performance budgeting focused only on selected components. However, these components—including workload and unit cost measures—remain as major contributions to financial management procedures.

Performance Measures

In developing a *unit cost measure,* all relevant costs associated with the delivery of a particular service are identified, and these costs are divided by the total units of service provided. The unit cost for the administration of a rubella immunization program, for example, would include salary costs of the medical personnel involved as well as the cost of the vaccine, other supplies, and equipment. These costs may vary with the number of children inoculated and with the method of delivery (through public health clinics, in schools, or by private practitioners). Unit costs are likely to decrease as the size of the program increases (economies of scale), but at some point they may increase again as hard-to-reach cases are encountered.

A *workload measure* relates to the volume of work performed during some defined time period. In a public welfare department, for example, it may be possible to determine the number of cases in various categories that can be handled by a caseworker on a daily, weekly, or annual basis. With this information and an estimate of the total number of cases to be processed, the agency head can calculate the personnel required during any fiscal period. Other common workload measures are number of customers served, tons of trash collected, number of children vaccinated, number of hospital patients served, number of inspections made, number of library books circulated, number of emergency calls responded to, and number of full-time equivalent university students. Each of these measures must include a time dimension—per day, week, month, or year. Workload measures provide basic budget-building information and, retrospectively, often indicate the adequacy of previous resource allocation decisions.

Workload measures are *output measures.* In the aggregate, they indicate the volume of goods and/or services delivered by a program or agency. Unit cost measures, on the other hand, are *input measures;* they indicate the resources used to operate a program. When workload (output) measures are related to unit cost (input) measures, the resulting index is often called a *performance measure.*

Such measures are often used as indicators of operating efficiency—for example, the cost per patient-day of hospital service, the number of cases successfully prosecuted per law enforcement officer, or the response time involved in handling emergency calls. As can be seen from these examples, not all performance measures are expressed in terms of costs. Performance measures examine the relationship between initial resource allocations (inputs) and the delivery of services (outputs), thereby providing basic management information on program economies.

Performance measures can be overemphasized, however, resulting in pseudo-efficiency. Organizations may undertake the easy assignments first, deferring or neglecting the more difficult ones in order to meet such measures of efficiency. This practice is known as *creaming*. For example, if a forensic laboratory is evaluated in terms of the number of tests performed, priority may be given to the simple tests, leaving the more involved ones until the "volume" tests have been completed.

Performance measures—along with the concept of performance levels, or levels of service, discussed in a later section of this chapter—have been incorporated into many contemporary financial management approaches that seek greater efficiency and economy. The focus of performance budgeting on cost-efficiency has its parallel emphasis in current budget and accounting formats. Cost accounting systems are beginning to receive wider application in public organizations, particularly in support of the techniques of cost–benefit and cost–effectiveness analysis.

Planning and Budgeting

The budget affords an opportunity to reevaluate the broad goals and objectives of an organization on a regular cycle. It also provides a basis on which to compare programs and their costs in light of these longer-range goals. The planning potential of the budgetary process, however, has largely been overshadowed by the traditional focus on fiscal controls.

Planning–Programming–Budgeting Systems

The object-of-expenditure budget seeks to control expenditures. Performance budgeting provides mechanisms for assessing efficiency. The Planning–Programming–Budgeting System (PPBS), introduced at the federal level in the mid-sixties, sought to provide a broader basis for policy analysis and decision making within the context of a central review by the chief executive and legislative body.

PPBS was never fully integrated, however, with the "bottom-up" informational flow that characterizes more traditional accounting and budget formats. As a consequence, operating agencies were often left on the periphery of the process. Required to provide new responses to policy directives (such as measures of effectiveness), these operating agencies had little understanding or appreciation of how these responses would affect their resource allocations.

Line personnel tended to be suspicious of the consequences of PPBS. These suspicions were reinforced by the threat of reorganization implied in the PPBS emphasis on "across-the-board" program structures. The focus of budgeting had shifted from the traditional emphasis on fiscal control to one of planning for an uncertain future. Many agencies were unprepared for (and unwilling to participate in) the transition.

By the early seventies, even the proponents of PPBS were eulogizing its demise. Both operating agencies and policy makers were disoriented by the emphasis on long-range planning to the near exclusion of management and control functions. Decision makers often did not fully understand or absorb the implications of the more abstract information about broad organizational programs.

Program Budgeting

In recent years, the techniques of *program budgeting* have been adopted (and adapted) by some localities and public organizations. Program budgeting offers the potential of a more appropriate interface between long-range planning and decision making, on the one hand, and the day-to-day operations of complex organizations, on the other. It also provides a foundation for an accounting system that is more fully attuned to the basic goals of accountability, efficiency, and effectiveness.

In the terminology often adopted by program budget guidelines, a *program* is a distinct organization of resources directed toward a specific objective: (1) eliminating, containing, or preventing a problem; (2) creating, improving, or maintaining a condition affecting the organization or its clientele; or (3) supporting or controlling other identifiable programs. A program is concerned with a time span of expenditures that extends beyond the current fiscal period.

In identifying program objectives, an effort should be made to specify the results to be accomplished within a specific time period. Program objectives must be consistent with the resources available (or anticipated). The formulation of precise, qualitative statements of objectives is often difficult. The tendency is to describe what the organization does, instead of addressing the question of why these activities are appropriate to achieve the long-range goals of the organization.

To avoid this pitfall, the analyst must describe specific objectives, indicating how and where specific organizational resources (personnel, equipment, materials, capital expenditures, and so on) will be used. These statements, in turn, should be related to performance measures. Such measures provide the mechanisms for evaluating the success (or lack thereof) of a program and its efficiency in achieving agreed-upon objectives. Appropriate measures of efficiency and effectiveness provide a baseline against which to test the notion of adequacy. In the absence of such measures, the traditional "least cost" compromise is likely to prevail.

A cornerstone of more effective financial management is the systematic *analysis of program alternatives*. The same dollars spent on different program objectives (or on alternative approaches to the same program objective) may yield greatly varied results. In any organization, the best policy is to spend resources where they can produce the greatest net benefits. A systematic analysis of costs and benefits may be undertaken during the preparation of the budget, or on an ongoing basis, in an effort to determine optimal resource allocations and fiscal policy recommendations.

Program analysis can be used (1) to determine whether particular programs or proposals are justified, (2) to rank various alternatives appropriate to a given set of objectives, and (3) to ascertain the optimal course(s) of action to attain those objectives. Program analysis operates within an extended time horizon. Insofar as possible, it includes explicit consideration of both direct and indirect cost factors involved in the allocation of resources.

The feedback from programs that have been formulated to meet agreed-upon objectives should be analyzed, as should any subsequent revisions to these programs. Thus, program analysis must be an iterative process, involving continuous refinement and modification as dictated by changing circumstances in program delivery. The probability that program revisions will be required increases significantly as the time span of decisions increases.

In practice, the time frame of programs formulated under a program budget is between five and ten years. *Multiyear program plans* often are developed to identify the anticipated outputs of services and facilities according to the objectives outlined in long-range, or strategic, plans. Program plans indicate what accomplishments can be expected from a given commitment of resources.

Program costs are obtained from the organization's accounting system. These costs are projected to match revenue projections, enabling planners to determine the adequacy of revenue sources to support proposed programs. Future cost commitments generated by current programs can also be projected. After the budget has been developed in program terms, total costs can be disaggregated by type of inputs (salaries and wages, materials and supplies, equipment, and so forth). In short, multiyear program and financial plans serve as the critical link between program objectives and other outputs, on the one hand, and resource inputs, on the other.

Once programs have been implemented, *evaluation techniques* should be applied to determine needed improvements and modifications. Program analysis is prospective, or future-oriented. Program evaluation, on the other hand, focuses on the actual performance of ongoing or recently completed activities. Program analysis and program evaluation together form an iterative cycle: analysis precedes program commitments, and evaluation assesses the impact and effectiveness of these decisions and commitments which, in turn, may result in new or changed program commitments. The purposes of evaluation are (1) to suggest changes in resource allocations, (2) to identify needed improvements in current operations, and (3) to plan for future activities. Program evaluation seeks to measure the overall success of a program and to identify areas where improvements might be made.

The "output" of many organizational activities may be difficult to define and measure in direct terms. As a consequence, secondary measures of effectiveness—called *surrogates*—often must be used to test alternative approaches and evaluate costs. The direct benefits of a program that seeks to reduce the incidence of dropouts from high school, for example, may be difficult to measure. A surrogate measure might be derived by comparing the anticipated lifetime earnings of individuals who complete high school with those of individuals who drop out. Such figures, available in terms of national averages, can be applied as a rough measure of program benefits.

Service Delivery Accountability

The incremental aspects of the budget process have been criticized as arbitrary and irrational. The lack of coordination and neglect of important values in traditional budget-building procedures have been the targets of critics for more than sixty years. *Incremental budgeting,* they suggest, produces only small changes in the status quo by examining only the differences between requests for the next fiscal year and budget appropriations for the previous year. Since the results of previous allocations are accepted as the primary decision criteria, existing programs are continued into the future without being subjected to intensive reexamination. A comprehensive analysis of previously allocated resources—the budget base—is effectively precluded by the incremental approach. Therefore, incremental budgeting is limited in its ability to allocate scarce resources in the most efficient, economical, and effective manner.

Service Level Analysis

Budget procedures have been formulated that subject all programs—new or old—to the same mechanism of evaluation. This more comprehensive budget format is sometimes referred to as a *zero-base* approach, because the incrementally established budget base is not accepted as being fixed or permanent. In more recent applications, however, detailed analyses of programs "to the zero base" have been replaced by the concept of *service levels*—that is, the analysis of resources required to deliver various levels of service.

Traditional budgeting procedures focus attention on proposed dollar increases in the budget. Under service level analysis, attention is drawn to the elements of the budget base along with proposed changes in the level of services to be delivered. Service level analysis is applicable to all *actionable* programs or activities—those in which there is some discretion as to the course of action pursued. All activities of local government that compete for general fund revenues (or the equivalent in other public organizations) should be included in the service level analysis. Other special funds, such as intergovernmental grants and formula-funded programs, often excluded from traditional budget analyses, should also be identified to determine their importance to organizational activities.

One objective of service level analysis is the identification of *essential service levels,* so that an agency can maintain, deliver, and be held accountable for such programs in a more efficient and effective manner. Defining a public service as essential is not the same as labeling its supporting expenditures as fixed. Essential services can be provided more efficiently (at less cost) or more effectively (with greater benefits).

The three basic components of a service level analysis are:

1. Identification of budget units.
2. Analysis of decision packages.
3. Priority ranking and evaluation of services.

Budget units are the basic building blocks within the organizational structure responsible for the delivery of services. Budget units usually correspond with established divisions within the established departments or agencies of the local or state government or other public organization. Large multifunctional units may be further subdivided to reflect more specific functions. Since it is unlikely that budget units will change significantly from one year to the next, the identification of these units is generally a one-time task. Minor adjustments may be required in subsequent years as new programs are initiated or existing programs are revised.

The goals and objectives of each budget unit should be identified, and the current purposes and methods of operation of each unit should be examined. Methods for measuring performance and effectiveness, as well as relations with other budget units, should also be delineated.

Decision packages are discrete sets of services, activities, and resources required to carry out a given operation or accomplish a program objective. Decision packages may involve alternative methods for delivering a service (for example, using outside contractors versus carrying out the functions in-house) or alternative approaches that use "more" or "less" of the same basic resource inputs (for example, assigning full-time salaried personnel versus hiring part-time wage personnel on an as-needed basis). A decision package should be described in such a way that it can be evaluated and ranked against other packages competing for the same limited resources.

For some essential services, only one decision package may be readily evident. Continuation of the current approach at the current level of commitment may be the only feasible alternative. One of the underlying sources of waste and inefficiency in organizational operations, however, is the maintenance of existing programs simply because "that's the way it has always been done."

Minimum Service Levels

A minimum level of service should be identified for each decision package. By definition, the maintenance of an existing program or the initiation of a new program would not be feasible below this minimum level. Minimum service levels include only the most essential elements or activities within chosen decision packages.

It often is difficult to identify a level of service/funding below the present level of support. In such cases, a percentage of the current level may be arbitrarily set as the minimum level—typically, 65 to 80 percent of the current appropriation. The budget unit manager is asked to identify the level of service that could be provided at this reduced funding level and what current activities might have to be eliminated to accommodate this funding level.

Additional levels of service should then be identified. Each succeeding level should expand the services available until the level of service equals or exceeds current service standards (see Exhibit 7-2).

The resources required to deliver each level of service should be summarized for each budget unit. This summary should include detailed costs to be met from

Exhibit 7-2 *Service Level Impact Summary*

FUND General	DEPT/PROGRAM Fire Safety	DIVISION/ELEMENT Operations

Current Operations and Resources

Free ambulance service is provided to all people in the city. Calls for emergency transportation are dispatched over the fire emergency communications network. Vehicle responds to the scene of need. One vehicle, three drivers, and three paramedics provide around-the-clock service 365 days a year.

Alternative Methods of Operation

Contract with Digger O'Dell's Mortuary: save about $10,000 per year, but risk not having dedicated vehicle.

Contract with City-County Hospital: hospital ambulance is sometimes dispatched to remote parts of the county or to other medical facilities outside the county.

Service Level Summary	Service Level		Cumulative		Cum. Percent	
Service Level Title	Total	Pos.	Total	Pos.	Total	Pos.
1. Volunteer Service	$ 7,660	0	$ 7,660	0	8.6%	0%
2. Assigned Drivers	$41,025	3	$ 48,685	3	54.7%	50%
3. Add Paramedic Team	$40,360	3	$ 89,045	6	100.0%	100%
4. 2nd Paramedic Team	$24,220	2	$113,265	8	127.2%	133%
5. 2nd Ambulance Unit	$57,345	4	$170,610	12	191.6%	200%

	Program Objectives
1	10-minute response time; no medical or first aid assistance
2	7-minute response time; no medical or first aid assistance
3	Add medical assistance and reduce complications from lack of first aid assistance
4	Paramedic services provided around the clock
5	Response time less than 10 minutes to all parts of city

all funding sources and a listing of personnel, equipment, and other major resource requirements. The mechanisms of the object-of-expenditure format can be reintroduced at this point. Once the detailed cost data have been established for the minimum level of service, these data can be built upon in cumulative fashion for each successive level.

Ranking Service Levels

Peter Drucker has defined *efficiency* as "doing things right" and *effectiveness* as "doing the right things."[9] Formulating levels of service involves a determination of how to do things right. Deciding to do the right things is the objective of the ranking process.

Ranking establishes an order or priority among service levels for various activities or programs. Service levels are listed in descending order of importance, until all levels have been included. This process of ranking, or "prioritizing," should be familiar to governments with established procedures for programming capital improvements.

In all likelihood, more service levels will be presented than can be funded from available resources. Three approaches can be used to bring proposed expenditures and projected revenue into balance:

1. Funds can be withheld from the lowest priority service levels.
2. Efforts can be made to reduce the cost of providing one or more levels of service.
3. Resources can be increased (for example, by increasing service fees, raising taxes, or liquidating assets).

Funds are allocated to the service levels in order of priority until anticipated resources are exhausted. A funding "cutoff line" is drawn at this point, and those services below the line are not funded. Unfunded service levels should be re-examined, and if deemed necessary to the well-being of the organization or community, efforts should be made to reduce costs or increase resources.

Without a ranking process, budgeting is little more than a juggling act. Decision makers may try, in a hit-or-miss fashion, to find the proper pieces that will add up to an acceptable whole. Unable to discern which programs or activities are of lower priority, decision makers are often forced to make across-the-board cuts. By creating an explicit priority listing, service level analysis minimizes this need.

Service level analysis can also be helpful in driving accountability for budgeting and budget execution deeper into the organization. Program managers must be involved in the analysis from the outset, thus tapping a larger reservoir of program knowledge and analytical skills. Direct involvement of program managers in budget making, in turn, often increases their concern for the proper implementation of organizational policies and programs.

Summary

The traditional object-of-expenditure budget serves well the purposes of *internal fiscal control*. It offers two distinct advantages over other budget formats: (1) a detailed set of accounts is established through which expenditures can be recorded, controlled, and audited; and (2) the close linkage between personnel and other budgetary requirements permits the use of position controls to control the entire budget.

Performance budgeting sought to strengthen the management aspects of the budget process by focusing on operating economies and performance efficiencies. Two key components distinguish performance budgeting from other approaches: (1) the identification of *performance units* within *work programs,* and (2) the measurement of *performance costs* through the use of cost accounting techniques. Workload and unit cost measures provide detailed information useful to operating managers in assessing the efficiency of their programs and organizational units.

The focus of program budgeting is on *policy analysis* and *planning.* The extended time horizon of the program budget shifts the decision focus from the one-year budget cycle to a multiyear time frame, thus providing a more comprehensive basis for annual budget deliberations.

Service level analysis seeks to overcome the shortcomings of incrementalism that characterize traditional budget formats. The identification of *budget units* is analogous to the specification of cost and responsibility centers under managerial accounting procedures. *Decision packages* provide a rough parallel to programs and subprograms in the program budget format. By arranging levels of service in descending order of importance and determining a funding cutoff point, the analyst can rank alternative approaches according to their capacity to meet program objectives.

The information input and output requirements of program budgeting and service level analysis differ significantly from those of more traditional budget practices. Contemporary budget formats provide important managerial feedback—soundings, scannings, and evaluations of changing conditions resulting from previous program decisions and actions. This feedback, in turn, can be strengthened significantly by the adoption of managerial accounting procedures.

Information feedforward is also generated by these budgeting procedures, providing a basis for more informed decisions and actions over a range of time periods, locations, and perspectives. Feedforward information emerges from projections and forecasts; goals, objectives, and targets to be achieved; program analyses and evaluations; and the projection of outcomes and impacts of alternative programs.

Each of these budget formats has obvious strengths and weaknesses. By combining the positive points of each format in a hybrid approach, governments and other public organizations should be able to develop budget systems that better serve sound financial management objectives.

Endnotes

1. U.S. Commission on Organization of the Executive Branch of the Government, *Budgeting and Accounting* (Washington, DC: U.S. Government Printing Office, 1949), p. 8.

2. David Novick, often credited for the formulation of PPBS, has observed that the concepts of program budgeting "have rather ancient and hoary origins." Large corporations, such as DuPont and General Motors, were applying program

budget techniques in the early twenties. For a further discussion of the roots of PPBS, see David Novick (Ed.), *Program Budgeting: Program Analysis and the Federal Budget* (Cambridge, MA: Harvard University Press, 1967).

3. Alan Walter Steiss, *Public Budgeting and Management* (Lexington, MA: Lexington Books–D. C. Heath, 1972), pp. 154–155.

4. Committee on Budgeting of the Municipal Finance Officers Association.

5. National Council on Governmental Accounting, *Statement 1. Governmental Accounting and Financial Reporting Principles* (Chicago: Municipal Financial Officers Association, 1979), p. 14.

6. *Ibid.*, p. 14.

7. U.S. General Accounting Office, *Standards for the Audit of Government Organizations, Programs, Activities, and Functions* (Washington, DC: U.S. Government Printing Office, 1972), p. 2.

8. Jesse Burkhead, *Government Budgeting* (New York: Wiley, 1956), pp. 153–155.

9. Peter F. Drucker, "The Effective Decision," *Harvard Business Review* 45 (January–February 1967): 95.

CHAPTER 8

Planning and Programming of Capital Facilities

The term *capital facility* refers to a project that (1) has a relatively long life (usually a minimum of fifteen to twenty years), (2) involves a significant investment of resources of a nonrecurring nature, and (3) yields a fixed asset for the community or organization. Because of this extended time frame and substantial commitment of resources, a comprehensive approach should be taken in the planning, programming, and financing of capital facilities. The primary focus of this chapter will be on the first two components; financing considerations will be introduced only as they bear upon the planning and programming processes. The next chapter will be devoted to long-term debt financing and administration.

Capital Facilities Planning

Two key elements in the planning of capital facilities are: (1) the formulation of goals and objectives and (2) the provision of quantitative data on which to base specific program commitments. Goals and objectives must be related to demographic and economic trends and projections of future demand for services and facilities. By comparing anticipated needs with the capacity of existing facilities, it is possible to determine the additional supply necessary to meet the anticipated demand.

Formulating Objectives and Determining Needs

Data on future client/community needs must be sufficiently reliable to justify decisions that involve relatively large, long-term commitments of financial resources. Capital facilities planning should be built upon a continuous assessment of client/ community preferences, demographic estimates, economic forecasts, and projections of development expectations. The following elements should be included in this planning framework:

1. *External factors* that may influence the service programs of the community or organization. Such factors include shifts in demographic characteristics, changes

in economic activities, social trends, scientific and technological change, emerging land use patterns, and so forth.

2. *Total service demands.* Assumptions, standards, and criteria used to quantify and project facility and service needs must be clearly identified and tested against available trend analyses.

3. *Service delivery responsibilities.* Present and future roles of various levels of government, as well as private enterprise, in the provision of facilities and services must be examined. Such an evaluation may include recommendations regarding the elimination of overlapping responsibilities through coordination or realignment.

Modeling and simulation techniques have been used effectively in various aspects of capital facilities planning. Computer-assisted models can provide general direction to financial management decisions in the initial iterations, and more detailed specifications in subsequent cycles. Such models should:

1. Take full advantage of readily available data.
2. Take into account those variables in the broader environment that affect or are affected by the variables of direct concern to resource management.
3. Enable decision makers to influence the "final states" of the model through the use of controllable variables.
4. Use goals and objectives to test various trial inputs in order to identify optimal policies.
5. Recognize constraints, especially those concerning the operation of the system, that must be met in order to achieve given goals and objectives.
6. Synthesize or "invent" situations that may lead to feasible states at some specific future stage of development.
7. Measure performance at the specified future stage. Such measures should be sensitive to changes in goals or constraints and to variations in the setting of controllable (decision) variables.

Demographic Estimates and Projections

The demand for public improvements is a function of growth. This emphasis on meeting growth demands does not imply a "self-fulfilling prophecy," however. In situations of service crisis, local governments and other public organizations may be panicked into uneconomical investments and overdevelopment. Comprehensive capital facilities planning can help avert these crises, thereby contributing to more realistic and rational patterns of growth.

In capital facilities planning, it is necessary to identify the segments of the population, or client groups, in which growth is occurring. To anticipate the types of improvements required, the population to be served should be disaggregated to the fullest extent possible. For example, an aging population will require specialized health facilities and housing. Young adults just starting families, on the other hand, will require schools, day-care centers, and recreational facilities. Income levels, household size, and other demographic and economic characteristics also provide vital information as to facility needs and service expectations.

Demographic projections are often based on an *age-cohort survival* model, which analyzes the population by narrow age categories (cohorts) according to vital statistics on births, deaths, and net migration patterns (inflow or outflow of population). Further breakdowns can also be made by race, sex, income, and so forth. These forecasts are not merely linear projections of past conditions. Many factors may cause a leveling or even decline in population as particular demographic patterns change. It is important to understand the current demographic composition of the community in order to identify any unique characteristics that may influence future population structure. For example, the transient student population of a college town is influenced by factors other than typical demographic elements and cannot be "aged" in the cohort structure with the resident population.

The basic age-cohort survival model must be applied simultaneously to a number of five-year cohorts (one-year cohorts are often used for children under five years of age). These cohorts, in turn, are "stepped up" through each iteration (see Exhibit 8-1). The results of this "aging" of cohorts are then modified by adjustments for births, deaths, and net migration. The basic mathematics of the age-cohort survival model are fairly simple. Making good assumptions about migration is not easy, however, and for this reason, many projections turn out to be inaccurate or unrealistic in terms of actual demographic data.

Mistakes in projecting population can be costly. Many school districts are still paying off the bonds on facilities constructed in the late 1960s and early 1970s, when enrollments were at peak levels as a consequence of the "baby boom." Some of these school districts are now faced with underutilized facilities as a result of significantly declining enrollments.

Economic Forecasts and Projections

Economic forecasts are an important factor in the preparation of demographic projections, since assumptions concerning population growth or decline are based in part on economic activities. A locality experiencing rapid industrial growth, for example, will likely experience a wave of worker in-migration. The age and socioeconomic characteristics of these new groups must be forecast to ensure adequate provision of basic public facilities and related services.

Economic projections and forecasts, in turn, must be translated into public improvement needs. The attraction of young workers and their families to an area experiencing industrial growth will likely result in increased demands on the educational system. If the municipality is not responsive to these demands, the momentum of economic activities will be adversely affected.

Future economic conditions also determine the financial capacity of a community to pay for capital improvements. Economic indicators—including data on employment, cost of living, disposable income, building activity, and bank

Exhibit 8-1   *Age-Cohort Survival Model*

Age Cohorts Base Year	Population Base Year	Survival Rates*	Age Cohorts Plus 5 Years	Surviving Population Plus 5 Years
			Under 5	6656**
Under 5	6047	0.99173	5–9	5997
5–9	6782	0.99780	10–14	6767
10–14	6705	0.99777	15–19	6691
15–19	7543	0.99537	20–24	7508
20–24	9689	0.99382	25–29	9629
25–29	6398	0.99299	30–34	6353
30–34	4608	0.99136	35–39	4568
35–39	4124	0.98795	40–44	4074
40–44	4233	0.98127	45–49	4153
45–49	4081	0.97099	50–54	3962
50–54	3564	0.95468	55–59	3402
55–59	3239	0.93271	60–64	3021
60–64	2939	0.89949	65–69	2643
65–69	2400	0.85451	70–74	2051
70–74	1776	0.78990	75–79	1403
75–79	1272	0.69571	80–84	885
80–84	757	0.54790	85–89	415
85–89	371	0.37028	90–94	137
90–94	108	0.17810	95–99	19
95–99	20	0.08608	100+	2
100+	3	—		
Totals	76660			80336

*Application of Reed–Merrell tables on the probability of dying to actual mortality data.
**Children under 5

Age Cohorts	Females of Childbearing Age		Fertility Rate (per 1000 females)	Children Under 5
	Percent Base Year	Number Plus 5 Years		
10–14	48.78	3301		
15–19	48.84	3268	220	719
20–24	43.80	3289	280	921
25–29	43.29	4168	594	2476
30–34	49.44	3141	544	1709
35–39	50.30	2298	195	448
40–44	51.89	2114	181	383
Total				6656

deposits—can be used to analyze trends and to suggest the future revenue capacity of the community.

Economic base studies, widely applied in capital facilities planning, divide the local economy into two broad categories: (1) *basic,* or *export, industries*—those industries producing goods and services (and capital) for distribution to markets outside a defined local economic area; and (2) *nonbasic*, or *service, industries*—those producing goods and services that are consumed within the local economic area (see Exhibit 8-2). Thus, a distinction is made between those economic activities that bring new money into the community (basic industries) and those that simply result in the recirculation of money (service industries). The underlying assumption of this approach is that expansion of basic activities usually results in growth of service activities and, thus, growth in the total economy. Forecasts of economic growth are based on *multipliers* that relate local activities to exports.

Exhibit 8-2 *Economic Base Structure Classification by Market Location and Consumer Commodity*

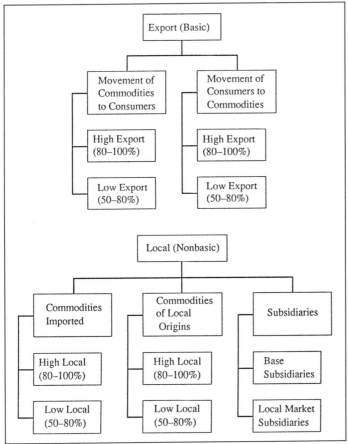

I. Export (Basic)
   A. Movement of commodities (goods, services, and/or capital) to consumers or purchasers.
   B. Movement of consumers or purchasers to commodities.

II. Local (Nonbasic)
   1. Importation of commodities (goods, services, and/or capital) for local distribution or local fabrication and distribution.
   2. Local origination of commodities for fabrication and local distribution.
   3. Subsidiaries may be either class 1 or 2 firms that enter into sales arrangements with firms of either basic or local market; no or few sales to final or household consumers.

As suggested in Exhibit 8-2, employment data of some industries or firms must be apportioned between the basic and nonbasic sectors. Once these data have been sorted, ratios can be calculated to reflect current conditions in the local economy. Various assumptions can be tested, using these ratios to determine the impact of increases or decreases in employment in the basic sector.

Assume, for example, that the current basic-to-nonbasic ratio is 1 to 1.5 (each job in a basic industry generates 1.5 jobs in the service sector). In that case, a new economic activity that adds 100 jobs to the basic sector will increase total employment by 250 jobs. If 35 percent of the total population is in the labor force, the ratio of basic employment to total population will be approximately 1 to 7.

Economic base multipliers and location quotients can be generated for various units of measurement, including (1) employment data, (2) payrolls, (3) value added, (4) value of production, (5) physical production, and (6) dollar income and expenditure accounts.[1] Since each of these measures has shortcomings, Andrews recommends that all feasible measuring techniques be used in any economic base study. The capacity of the analysis to predict future conditions can be further extended and refined by adding other measures and indexes. As additional indexes are considered, however, computational requirements increase, making the computer an essential tool of analysis.

Financial Analysis and Fiscal Policy

The demand for public services and facilities increases as a function of growth and changes with the social and economic characteristics of the community. Local revenues tend to increase at a slower rate than demand, creating an ever-widening fiscal gap in many localities. In economic terms, the revenue sources available to local governments are relatively *inelastic*; that is, they are not very responsive to changes in the overall economy. This inelasticity is attributable, in part, to the heavy reliance of local governments on property taxes. Under fiscal pressures, property taxes have proven relatively unresponsive in meeting increasing demands for public services and facilities.

Other taxes have not been very productive at the local level. Unilateral taxation of income, sales, or business by local governments often results in a shrinkage of the local tax base. That is, if one municipality introduces such taxes, economic activities tend to locate beyond the taxing jurisdiction (for example, major shopping facilities located just outside the taxing jurisdiction of cities).

Property taxes may play an important role in the initial location decisions of commercial and industrial firms. Real property is relatively immobile, however. Differential taxes seldom induce migration out of a locality. Workers must live close to their work; retail outlets tend to locate close to consumers; once committed, manufacturing establishments tend to stay put, since property taxes are a modest part of their total costs. In the administration of the property tax, the tendency is to underassess certain property values and to defer increases in the tax rate between property assessments.

Sources of revenue should be separated into appropriate categories. The analysis of each category must include not only the estimate of dollar receipts, but also the percentage of total revenues that each category represents. Trends in both absolute and relative increases and declines can be calculated based upon these disaggregated figures. Some assumptions must be made about inflation and interest rates. Inflation is important because it affects the magnitude of revenue sources, such as sales and property taxes. Interest rates are important because they affect the cost of borrowing. Although these assumptions involve considerable uncertainty, there is no good alternative to the use of such projections. Using the computer, "best case" and "worst case" scenarios can be run to provide an "envelope" in which to plan.

Expenditure analysis also requires disaggregation of data into major expenditure categories. Data from past fiscal years provide a basis for the calculation of rates of increase or decrease. Subsequently, these data assist in the computation of multipliers appropriate to each expenditure category. Future levels of expenditure can be derived from these multipliers, which can also be adjusted for changes in demographic characteristics, inflation rates, and so forth.

A sound revenue policy must be based on a thorough assessment of public service and capital facilities needs. Estimates should include an analysis of the revenues to be collected if existing fiscal policies are maintained. New revenue sources or shifts in yields from current sources under alternative policies should also be analyzed.

Programming Capital Facilities

Limitations on the resources available to any level of government or other public organization give rise to the need for careful programming of capital facilities. Programming should be based on a system of priorities which, in turn, should be tied to the goals and objectives set forth in the capital facilities plan. Procedures must also be developed for the continuous evaluation of services and facilities.

Analysis of the Infrastructure

The following tasks should be undertaken in the programming of capital facilities:

1. Basic inventory of the community's infrastructure to determine current conditions and range of potential improvement needs.

2. Analyses of the maintenance, repair, and replacement options for different improvement proposals.
3. Identification of risks and uncertainties associated with the various investment choices.
4. Evaluation of financing options.
5. Ranking of the investment proposals based on the preceding analyses.

Solid information and sound analytic procedures are required for effective programming of capital facilities. The need is especially critical in local government, where increasingly constrained resources must be allocated among competing investment alternatives. The application of advanced tools of analysis, however, often must be balanced off against technical limitations and political considerations.

Task 1: Inventory of Current Infrastructure Conditions

Programming must begin with an assessment of major components of the local infrastructure—streets, bridges, public buildings, recreational facilities, transit vehicles, water distribution and sewer collection networks, and so forth. Priorities among investment projects can be more readily established once conditions in the various segments of the infrastructure have been identified. Specific analysis of repair and replacement alternatives combines information on the condition of the existing infrastructure with cost accounting data on maintenance spending.

Three categories of indicators should be considered for each of the basic systems:

1. *Engineering-type assessments*—for example, measures of water pipe capacity loss, bridge condition ratings, or insulation values in public structures.
2. *Performance measures*—for example, number of sewer line stoppages, frequency of bus breakdowns, or service calls for water line repairs.
3. *Service impact indicators*—number of citizen complaints and losses arising from system failures, such as water main breaks or basement flooding from sewer backups.

Appropriate indicators should be drawn from a wide variety of sources, including engineering practices and federal and state rating schemes. A small group of indicators, for which reliable information can be obtained over time, should be selected for each system to provide valid measures of conditions. Efforts should be made to identify other means of assessment that are both reliable (minimizing dependence on subjective judgments) and practical (minimizing extensive data gathering or use of expensive equipment). Indicators must be tested under conditions appropriate to selected capital projects in each component of the infrastructure.

Where possible, *benchmarks* should be established for performance measures, such as system failures and breakdown rates. Standardized definitions should be prepared for each indicator. For example, frequency of emergency road calls in the public transit system may be defined to include only those calls attributable to mechanical failures, and not minor maintenance repairs. On this basis, the mean and range of performance levels can be determined. Performance of the local infrastructure can then be evaluated through the application of appropriate standards and rules of thumb developed by practitioners.

The product of this task should be a description of appropriate *condition indicators* and procedures for obtaining indicator information on an annual or other regular basis. Estimates should be made of the cost of data collection and the reliability and validity of the assessment procedures.

Task 2: Replacement Analysis

The condition indicators identified in Task 1 should (1) point out problems in the existing capital facilities inventory, (2) suggest the current extent of these problems, and (3) indicate likely candidate projects for improvements. This type of analysis, however, will not indicate whether a facility should be repaired or replaced. Nor will it identify the costs and service level impacts of choosing either option.

Local governments have four options: (1) replace the facility or equipment; (2) rehabilitate or undertake a major overhaul; (3) continue to provide current maintenance, with emergency repairs as required; or (4) cut back maintenance spending and defer repairs. The fourth option may be the least costly in the short run, but is usually the most costly in the long term.

The purpose of replacement analysis is to assess the trade-offs among these options. Officials should be provided with information on the likely costs, impact on service levels, and risks of the choices involved. Some typical choices are:

- Should certain street segments be resurfaced or seal-coated now, or should spending be deferred at the risk of more costly reconstruction in the future?
- Should a deteriorated bridge deck continue to be repaired, receive extensive rehabilitation, or be entirely replaced?
- Should a sewer line repair program be continued, or should existing infiltration and inflow into sewers be accepted, with consequent backups and basement flooding incidents?
- Should a break in the city's water supply system be repaired, or should the main be replaced?
- Should buses that break down considerably more often than the industry standard be replaced, be given major overhauls, or continue to receive regular maintenance and repair?

Although each of these questions involves its own technical considerations, the appropriate type of analysis is quite similar.

Depreciation curves should be developed for different components of the infrastructure. Such curves show the rate of deterioration as a function of such factors as age, original construction material, climates, and intensity of use. Although some general guidelines have been developed concerning useful service lives, unfortunately these do not typically relate to individual segments of the local infrastructure.

In the private sector, the output of an investment, as well as the cost, can be expressed adequately in dollar terms. In the public sector, consideration must also be given to nonmonetary impacts, such as water quality, transportation delays, or number of sewer stoppages and backups. Under certain circumstances, issues related to the maintenance of the public infrastructure can be discussed primarily in dollar terms. Even in these cases, however, it is usually necessary to analyze levels of service to ensure that these will not be reduced by an otherwise economically preferable option.

Equipment replacement models should be explored, using methods of operations research. These models generally aim at minimizing future net costs by estimating the time at which operating and maintenance costs (plus loss of resale value) of existing equipment will exceed the cost (annualized) of replacement plus the operating and maintenance costs of the replacement equipment. Thus, the cost of keeping the equipment another year can be compared to the cost of buying and operating new equipment.

Applications of *cost–benefit* and *cost–effectiveness analysis* should be considered. Cost–benefit analysis has been popular in the examination of transportation alternatives. The utility of cost–benefit analysis is likely to be limited by problems of imputing dollar values to service level impacts and, secondarily, of handling distributional effects. In cost–effectiveness analysis, outputs are usually expressed in nonmonetary units, with the results presented in the form of trade-offs rather than cost–benefit ratios.

In addition to these basic techniques of economic analysis, more detailed procedures might include:

1. *Estimation of costs.* Maintenance records, engineering estimates, and bids are major sources of information. Procedures for the explicit consideration of full costs—operating and maintenance costs, as well as investment costs—should be developed when feasible. The use of statistical cost analysis techniques should be explored to make better estimates of future costs. Such techniques may be applicable to major facilities and equipment for which firm bids cannot be obtained, such as for new types of buses or water treatment plants.

2. *Discount rates.* Discounting is an important analytical technique for considering the time stream of expenditures and benefits (and the opportunity costs of benefits forgone). Often these measures will not be monetary, or if stated in monetary terms, will represent dollar imputations rather than actual dollar outlays.

3. *Distributional effects.* Procedures should be developed to examine the distributional effects of investment choices within a jurisdiction. Distributional consequences are of considerable concern to public officials and, of course, to the public. Considerations should include the number of citizens affected, their location, and their demographic and socioeconomic characteristics. In most cases, the condition indicators can be disaggregated by neighborhoods, districts, or other relevant groupings, and estimates can be made at these levels.

Task 3: Consideration of Risk and Uncertainty

The risk and uncertainty involved in selecting specific options are key elements in choosing among investment alternatives. In making such choices, the following procedures (discussed in previous chapters) should be considered:

- Use of *sensitivity analysis* to assess the relative magnitude of changes in costs and output indicators if key elements in the replacement analysis have values different from those considered most likely.
- Use of *contingency analysis* to construct alternative future scenarios (for example, a substantial buildup in traffic on a road segment or bridge) and examine the effects of each scenario for each maintenance or replacement option.
- Application of *probabilities* to uncertain events so that an "expected value" and/or a distribution of likely total costs and outcomes can be generated for each alternative.
- Inclusion of an uncertainty factor in the *discount rate,* primarily where costs and benefits are both expressed in monetary terms, to reduce net benefits computed for future years.
- Inclusion of *qualitative statements* about the relative amount of uncertainty and risk involved in each alternative.

The field of *risk analysis* has recently begun to receive national attention, arising primarily out of concern over major national health and safety hazards and their attendant risks. Analysis and modeling of the situation are used to estimate the probability of major consequences of certain governmental actions. Such sophisticated and resource-demanding techniques are applicable only to major investment decisions. More heuristic procedures must be developed for making explicit the trade-offs involved in local investment decisions.

Task 4: Consideration of Financing Options

Financing constraints ultimately play a major role in most capital investment decisions. Therefore, financing alternatives must be integrated into the initial assessment of capital projects. Capital facilities can be financed in a number of ways—on a pay-as-you-go basis, from reserve funds, through long- or short-term borrowing, and so forth. These financing methods must be evaluated in terms of the fiscal policies of the community/organization and in light of the particular capital facility needs.

"Pay-as-you-go" financing encourages government to "live within its income." It minimizes premature commitment of funds. The government's credit is conserved for times of emergency, when ample credit may be vital. This approach avoids the added cost of interest payments and, therefore, costs less than borrowing.

On the other hand, the pay-as-you-go approach may place an undue burden on present taxpayers to finance future improvements from which they may not fully benefit. Thus, it may be argued that public projects providing services over many years should be paid for by people according to their use or benefit—should be financed on a "pay-as-you-go" basis. Achieving *user-benefit equity* may require financing a facility by borrowing, spreading repayment over the life of the improvement.

Excessive commitment to pay-as-you-go financing may prevent a municipality or other public organization from doing things that really need to be done. Projects may be too costly to be carried out using only annual revenues. Few governments today have the capability to finance vital public facilities strictly on a pay-as-you-go basis. Therefore, the power to borrow is one of the most important assets of government. Through borrowing, taxpayers are relieved of part of the immediate tax burden, which is shifted to future taxpayers. At the same time, tax liabilities are increased because of the interest charges on the monies borrowed. The assumption is that future economic and population growth will offset the increased liability and make the payment of debt service (principal and interest) more feasible.

Like all governmental powers, the capacity to borrow must be used with critical regard for its justifiable purposes and with a clear understanding of its safe and reasonable limits. A sound borrowing policy is one that seeks to conserve rather than exhaust credit. The ability to borrow when necessary on the most favorable market terms is an objective that applies to governments just as it does to business and industry.

Financing capital facilities through a *reserve fund* (sometimes called a capital reserve) can be thought of as the opposite of borrowing, in that the timetable is reversed. A portion of current revenue is invested each year in order to accumulate sufficient funds to initiate some project in the future. The amount (S) of a reserve fund created by a fixed investment (N) placed annually at compound interest (r) for a term of n years can be expressed by the following formula:

$$S = N \frac{(1 + r)^n - 1}{r}$$

Thus, an investment of $10,000 each year for ten years at 6 percent interest will yield a reserve fund of $131,800. Conversely, the amount (N) that must be placed annually at compound interest (r) for a term of n years to create a reserve fund (S) can be calculated by means of the following formula:

$$N = S \frac{r}{(1 + r)^n - 1}$$

Should the objective be to develop a reserve fund of $2 million at the end of ten years, an investment of $151,736 per year at 6 percent would be required. Simple computational routines using these basic formulas can test various assumptions as to appropriate investment periods under different interest rates.

To illustrate this point, assume that a municipality is considering a major addition to its community health center. Construction costs are estimated to be $500,000 (in current dollars), with an additional $50,000 for site preparation and $150,000 for equipment. Construction costs are increasing at a rate of 12 percent a year, and the cost of equipment is estimated to be increasing 15 percent a year. Four different financing approaches that the municipality might consider are outlined in Exhibit 8-3. Given the cost assumptions, the fourth alternative turns out to be the "least cost" approach. Achieving the least cost, however, is not necessarily the only consideration, for there are pros and cons to any financing strategy.

The availability of federal and state aid programs will influence both the feasibility and net cost of local improvement projects. Federal grants provide a

Exhibit 8-3 *Cost Analysis of Funding Alternatives*

Alternatives

1. Fund the project from general tax revenues over a period of four years, with site preparation in year 1, construction in years 2 and 3, and equipment acquisition in year 4.

2. Fund site preparation out of current revenues and issue bonds for the $650,000 in equipment and construction costs.

3. Build a capital reserve fund over four years until the total project costs have been accumulated, at which time the project can be constructed.

4. Establish a capital reserve fund with annual payments made from this fund to cover the project schedule outlined under alternative 1.

	Alternative 1	
	"Pay-As-You-Go" Funding From General Revenues	
Year	*Project Phase*	*Cost Calculations*
1	Site Preparation	= $ 50,000
2	Construction: First Phase	$250,000(1.12) = $250,000
3	Construction: Second Phase	$250,000(1.2544) = $313,600
4	Equipment Acquisition	$150,000(1.52) = $228,130
	Total Cost	$871,730

Alternative 2
Bond Issue—Five-Year Annuity Serial
(6 Percent Annual Interest)

Annual Debt Service $= \dfrac{\$650,000 \ (0.06) \ (1.06)}{(1.06) - 1} =$

	$154,300
	$\times$ 5
	$771,500
Site Preparation	$ 50,000
Total Cost	$821,500

Exhibit 8-3   *(continued)*

Alternative 3
Capital Reserve Fund (8 Percent Annual Interest)

Project Phase	*Cost Calculations*	
Site Preparation	$ 50,000(1.12)	= $ 70,246
Construction Costs	$500,000(1.2544)	= $ 702,464
Equipment		
Acquisition	$150,000(1.52)	= $ 228,130
Total Reserve Required		**$1,000,840**

$$\text{Annual Payments} = \frac{\$1,000,840 \ (0.08)}{(1.08)^4 - 1} = \$222,107$$

Total Cost = $222,107 × 4   = $888,428

Alternative 4				
Capital Reserve Fund				
With Annual Funding of Project				
Year	*Carry Forward*	*Payment to Reserve*	*Cost*	*Reserve Balance*
1		$196,500 × 1.08 ———— $212,220	$ 50,000	$162,220
2	$162,220 × 1.08 ———— $175,198	$196,500 × 1.08 ———— $212,220	$280,000	$107,418
3	$107,418 × 1.08 ———— $116,011	$196,500 × 1.08 ———— $212,220	$313,600	$ 14,631
4	$ 14,631 × 1.08 ———— $ 15,801	$196,500 × 1.08 ———— $212,220	$228,130	0
Total Cost = $196,500 × 4			=	$786,000

tremendous boost to local capital spending, but they can also affect local objectives, particularly for infrastructure repair and rehabilitation. Historically, federal programs for capital projects have been biased toward new construction.

Understandably, local governments wish to leverage their resources. However, providing the local match for such projects can divert funds from vital maintenance-related investments that receive no external assistance. For example, local governments may find their efforts to meet local sewer system needs for pipe rehabilitation and repair frustrated by federal funding realities. Although eligible for intergovernmental grants, in practice these projects are far down the federal and state priority lists. Thus, local governments frequently face the choice of constructing a new interceptor sewer that requires a maximum of 25 percent local funds, or funding sewer line replacement projects that typically require 100 percent local financing.

Bond financing options also affect local investment choices. Many local capital improvements can only be financed through the issuance of tax-supported *general obligation bonds* to provide full project funding or the local match. Faced with increasing rehabilitation needs, spiraling construction costs, and limited bonding authority, many cities may need to consider alternative financing arrangements for projects traditionally funded through general obligation bonds. For example, local governments are exploring increased use of revenue bond financing for projects with identifiable revenues that can be pledged to debt repayment. These options will be discussed in further detail in the next chapter.

Local governments have many possibilities for combining and substituting funding sources. The use of revenue bonds to finance capital construction in one area—such as a water system—may free up general obligation bonds for financing other portions of the capital plant—such as streets—in which service pricing is not feasible. Restricted funds may be used to free up block grants for other capital purposes. These financing alternatives should be made explicit in the initial evaluation and ranking of capital investment projects.

Task 5: Ranking Multiple Projects

The ranking of capital improvement proposals is of major importance to management and the governing body. A set of ranking criteria should be identified against which each proposed capital project is rated. Values derived from the previous tasks (infrastructure condition assessments, repair and replacement cost options, service impacts, risk considerations, and financing alternatives) can be used to provide information for priority ratings. Procedures should also be considered for combining criteria to provide an overall summary score, without losing the backup information on each individual criterion for each proposal.

Ranking procedures are not intended to make decision making on capital improvement proposals "automatic." They are not a substitute for judgment and consideration of the political environment. Rather, they provide more substantive information—in effect, making explicit issues and trade-offs that are always present but often hidden. In view of the importance of this phase of the capital facilities programming process, the balance of this chapter will be devoted to an examination of these evaluation and ranking procedures.

Evaluation Criteria

In all likelihood, for any given budget period, the overall cost of the proposed capital projects will exceed the available financial resources. Therefore, proposed projects must be evaluated and ranked in some manner, preferably through the use of an explicit set of evaluation criteria. Various approaches have been developed in an effort to rank projects in some objective fashion. Economic costs and benefits can often be quantified in such priority systems. With few exceptions, however, social benefits and costs have yet to reach this level of quantification. Various "political factors" are seldom included among such criteria but are brought to bear on the final rankings.

Hatry, Millar, and Evans have suggested eleven criteria for the evaluation of capital projects.[2] These criteria are summarized in Exhibit 8-4. Most cities require a description or justification of each project as part of the departmental submissions. Often these statements are so general, however, that the process of comparing and selecting among competing projects becomes very subjective. For these evaluation criteria to be useful, information should be provided on each of the relevant factors.

Exhibit 8-4 *Suggested Evaluation Criteria*

---

1. Fiscal impact on costs and revenues.

2. Health and safety effects.

3. Community economic effects.

4. Environmental, aesthetic, and social effects—impact on the quality of life.

5. Disruption and inconvenience caused by the project—impact on the quality of service.

6. Distributional effects—who is affected and how.

7. Feasibility, including public support and project readiness.

8. Implications of deferring the project.

9. Amount of uncertainty and risk.

10. Effects on interjurisdictional relationships.

11. Advantages accruing from relationships with other capital proposals.

Adapted from Harry P. Hatry, Annie P. Millar, and James H. Evans, "Guide to Setting Priorities for Capital Investments," *Guides to Managing Urban Capital,* Volume 5 (Washington, DC: The Urban Institute Press, 1984), p. 9.

Fiscal impact. In addition to data on the expected costs of each capital project, information should also be provided on the operating and maintenance (O&M) costs of the proposed project. Often capital projects, particularly those involving the rehabilitation of existing facilities, are intended to reduce future O&M costs. Therefore, estimates of such reductions may be an important factor in justifying these projects. Explicit consideration of both initial costs of development (site acquisition and preparation, construction, and capital equipment acquisition) and subsequent costs of operation, maintenance, and repair of the capital facility is sometimes referred to as *life-cycle costing.*

Other fiscal impact considerations include:

1. *Changes in revenue.* Capital projects may generate new revenues (for example, when charges are levied for public services) or may result in a reduction in revenues (for example, when private land is taken off the tax roll for a capital project site).
2. *Impact on energy requirements.* Estimated changes in energy requirements (increases or decreases) should be included as part of a project's O&M cost impact.
3. *Legal liability.* Estimates should be made of any potential cost liabilities of undertaking (or not undertaking) a capital project, such as for flood damage resulting from the diversion of a natural stream.

Health and safety effects.   Project justifications should include an assessment of health- and safety-related effects, such as anticipated reduction in traffic accidents, elimination of health hazards arising from sewer problems or poor water quality, or long-term health hazard effects of asbestos in public buildings. Data should be provided on the estimated number of persons affected and the severity of the effect. These data should indicate anticipated improvements in such conditions if the proposed project is implemented.

Economic effects.   Information on the economic effects of proposed projects should include the likely impact of the project on (1) property values, (2) the tax base, (3) employment opportunities, (4) personal income, (5) business income, and (6) the stabilization or revitalization of declining neighborhoods. These impacts may be more evident in capital projects proposed in response to community growth and expansion. However, projects aimed at maintaining or upgrading the existing infrastructure may also have significant economic effects.

Quality of life and service.   Both beneficial and adverse effects on the quality of life—environmental, aesthetic, and social—should be considered. Though perhaps not resulting in major health problems, the potential for noise, air, or water pollution should be taken into account. Increased travel times and other inconveniences to the public should also be evaluated. Some projects may involve lengthy disruptions of service and inconvenience to users during construction. Repair or reconstruction of bridges, streets, or water and sewer lines may involve rerouting of traffic, temporary interruptions of service, or even relocation of households. Estimates should be provided as to the duration and severity of such disruptions and the number of persons likely to be affected.

Distributional effects.   Capital projects vary with respect to the number of citizens affected, and inevitably, projects affect various sectors of the community differently. Depending on the particular type of project, estimates should be provided by the proposing agency or central staff as to the number of persons likely to be affected. Where appropriate, these data should be broken down by age groups, economic status, neighborhoods or districts, residential or commercial areas, handicapped persons, and so forth.

Project feasibility. Projects should be evaluated for any special problems that may arise in implementation (for example, the need for permits or other authorization), including legal issues. The compatibility and compliance of the project with the capital facilities plan should be assessed. If the project is a continuation of previous improvements, the impact on prior investments should be identified. And finally, the degree of public support for or opposition to the project should be evaluated, and any special interest groups involved should be identified. Efforts should be made to explore the availability of needed staff, the time required to obtain federal or state approvals, the time required to ensure necessary citizen support, and lead times for architectural and engineering plans, construction bidding, material acquisition, and the like.

Implications of project deferral. The impact of deferring the project should be examined in terms of each of the previous criteria. What will be the added costs? What and who will be disbenefited, and how? Is intergovernmental assistance more or less likely to be available in the future? What are the trends in the bond market? Deferring projects is especially tempting for public officials when the locality is financially hard-pressed in the current fiscal year. Before the decision to defer is made, however, local officials should obtain an estimate of the possible effects of such a decision, such as higher future costs and the extent of inconvenience or harm to the citizens of the community.

Risk and uncertainty. All capital projects involve some risk and uncertainty. Uncertainty can arise, for example, from cost estimates (especially in projects involving new technologies or procedures) and in the quality of service (because of uncertainties about the durability and reliability of new materials). There are always risks in the bond market. When such risks and uncertainties are substantial, the consequences should be included in the overall project evaluation.

Interjurisdictional relations. Special coordinating activities may be required if a proposed project has significant adverse or beneficial effects on other jurisdictions or agencies that serve the same area. Examples include water supply projects where the source (reservoir or aquifer) is outside the municipality, or a landfill project in one jurisdiction that may handle waste disposal for other jurisdictions.

Advantages accruing from other proposals. The relationship between capital projects should be identified, particularly if the initiation of one project will affect the costs or benefits of another project. An obvious example is improvements to water mains that can be undertaken at less cost if coordinated with street improvements in the same area. If two or more projects can be undertaken together at a lower cost than if done separately, the combined effort may rate a higher priority.

Priority Classification Systems

Decisions regarding capital project requests should be based on measurable and defensible criteria that establish priorities among needs. Approaches to the assignment of priorities can be divided into two classes: (1) those that stress intangible values, and (2) those that seek to quantify various criteria into a numerical scoring system. Each of these approaches has its merits and its shortcomings, and to the extent possible, elements from each should be incorporated into a sound priority system.

Priority systems developed under an *intangible approach* begin by giving preference to projects that contribute to "the protection of life, health, and public safety." A second order of priority goes to projects designed to meet current deficiencies in existing facilities based on some standard of service. Deficiency criteria are often expressed in rather general terms. It may be possible, however, to establish some quantitative measures based on these general statements. These criteria can then be applied to determine the essential level of service and the harm arising from a deficiency of service. It is often difficult, however, to develop measures that are comparable across functional lines (for example, parks versus schools).

Priority consideration may also be given to projects designed to conserve or maintain existing properties, investment, or resources, or those that demonstrate some substantial economic or social benefit to the community. Projects on which established facilities depend to realize their full potential may also be given a high priority, along with projects that are self-liquidating or self-supporting. Special consideration may also be given to projects for which substantial state or federal subsidies are available. Finally, special consideration is given under the "intangible" approach to emergency situations.

A priority system reflecting the intangible approach is summarized in Exhibit 8-5. A six-way breakdown of priorities is suggested, along with criteria for assigning capital projects to each of these categories. The last category—deferrable—is largely reserved for the adjustment of priorities following the initial review. Examination of the various suggested criteria will reveal several areas in which quantitative indexes might be developed.

Numerical priority systems involve the development of weighted scores that reflect the relative importance of the various "intangibles" set forth in the previous discussion. The criterion judged to be most important or most significant as a determining factor in establishing the priority of capital projects is given the highest score (frequently based on units of 10 or some multiple of 10). All other factors are then ranked in relation to this score. Thus, "protection of life and maintenance of public health" may be ranked as the most important criterion and given a score of 100. "Conservation of resources" may be judged to be nearly as important and, thus, given a score of 90. On the other hand, "aesthetic and cultural values" may be ranked relatively low, scoring only 20 points. These categories are often further divided into a number of subcategories, and scores are accumulated for any given period. It should be evident that any effort to develop such an "objective" approach must be based, to a large degree, on subjective judgments.

Quite obviously, such a point system cannot be applied rigidly, but rather must be used as a guide for priority decisions. The priority system, whether developed on a more subjective, "intangible" basis or on a numerical system, must be tailored to the particular goals and objectives of the individual jurisdiction. One locality may

Exhibit 8-5 *General Criteria for Capital Facilities Priority System*

Category	General Criteria
1. Urgent	Projects that cannot reasonably be postponed; projects that would remedy conditions dangerous to public health, welfare, or safety; projects required to maintain a critically needed program; projects needed to meet an emergency situation.
2. Essential	Projects required to complete or make fully usable a major public improvement; projects required to maintain minimum standards as part of an ongoing program; desirable self-liquidating projects; projects for which external funds for more than 65 percent of costs are available for a limited period.
3. Necessary	Projects that should be carried out within a few years to meet clearly demonstrated anticipated needs; projects to replace unsatisfactory or obsolete facilities; remodeling projects for continued use of facilities.
4. Desirable	Adequately planned projects needed for the expansion of current programs; projects designed to initiate new programs considered appropriate for a progressive community; projects for the conversion of existing facilities to other uses.
5. Acceptable	Adequately planned projects useful for ideal operations but which can be postponed without detriment to present operations if budget reductions are necessary.
6. Deferrable	Projects recommended for postponement or elimination from immediate consideration in the current capital facilities plan; projects that are questionable in terms of overall needs, adequate planning, or proper timing.

Adapted from Alan Walter Steiss, *Local Government Finance: Capital Facilities Planning and Debt Administration* (Lexington, MA: Lexington Books, 1978), p. 38.

be interested primarily in furthering industrial growth and development. Another may rely on tourism and development of the recreation industry. A third may place primary emphasis on the preservation of a well-maintained residential atmosphere.

Finally, it must be emphasized that no written or mathematical formula can be substituted for human judgment. In the final analysis, the capital facilities planner must exercise his or her best professional judgment in working with the various operating agencies in assigning priorities. At the same time, it must be recognized that in government "the actual choice and establishment of final priorities are still accompanied by the political process of compromise, a give-and-take between all groups concerned."[3]

Capital Improvements Program

When all proposed projects have been examined and analyzed, a composite capital improvements program should be prepared for presentation to the chief executive.

A capital improvements program (CIP) represents the more immediate and more detailed portions of the long-range capital facilities plan, usually spanning a five- to six-year period. Governments have found with experience that six years is a convenient period for the detailed programming of capital expenditures, permitting sufficient lead time for the design and other preliminary work required by such projects. Projects included in the CIP should be arrayed according to their priority rating/ranking.

The capital improvements program is then reviewed and adopted, with appropriate modifications, by the chief executive and the governing body. When adopted, the CIP should be made available in report form to civic groups and interested citizens, in addition to being distributed to the operating departments. The capital program report should cover three main topics:

1. Explanation of the various considerations and policies brought to bear on the development of priorities—legal requirements, magnitude of projected capital needs, fiscal resources of the jurisdiction, and so forth.
2. Listing of the major projects now under construction or for which funds have been appropriated.
3. Detailed description of the capital improvements program and budget for (a) the next fiscal year and (b) the following five years, with a listing of projects by agency and by priority.

The detailed description of each project should include a brief statement as to its general purpose and reason for its inclusion in the CIP. Capital costs, operating costs, source of funds, method of financing, and financing schedule should be set forth in the report for each project.

Even after legislative action has been taken in adopting the CIP, funds must still be made available. Therefore, although a capital budget may be adopted, there still is another opportunity for review at the time appropriations are made, or in the case of an issuance of general obligation bonds, at the time the referendum is placed before the voters. Of course, even after appropriations are made, changes and adjustments are still possible prior to construction or acquisition. If the original project requests are based upon a sound planning foundation, however, the need for such changes should be minimal.

Endnotes

1. Richard D. Andrews, "Mechanics of the Urban Economic Base," *Land Economics* 29 (November 1953): 344–349; "Urban Economics: An Appraisal of Progress," *Land Economics* 37 (August 1961): 223–225; "Economic Planning for Small Areas: An Analytical System," *Land Economics* 39 (May 1963): 143–155.

2. Harry P. Hatry, Annie P. Millar, and James H. Evans, "Guide to Setting Priorities for Capital Investment," *Guides to Managing Urban Capital,* Vol. 5 (Washington, DC: Urban Institute Press, 1984).

3. William B. Rogers, "Fiscal Planning and Capital Budgeting," in *Planning 1954* (Chicago: American Society of Planning Officials, 1954), p. 96.

CHAPTER 9

Debt Financing and Administration

Most state and local governments, at one time or another, find it necessary to issue long-term bonds to finance capital projects. A *bond* is a promissory note ensuring that the lender will receive periodic payments of interest (at some predetermined rate) and, at the bond's maturity, repayment of the original sum (principal) invested. Although referred to as "municipal bonds," this broad investment category includes bonds issued by any political subdivision—cities, counties, school districts, or special purpose districts—public agency, authority, or commission, or by a state, territory, or possession of the United States.

Interest earned on municipal bonds is exempt from federal taxation, and usually from state taxes in the state in which the bond is issued. As a consequence, municipal bonds carry lower interest rates than taxable corporate bonds. This tax exemption is, in effect, a federal subsidy that reduces borrowing (debt service) costs for local governments. In April, 1988, the Supreme Court overruled a major 1895 precedent, by holding that the Constitution does not protect state and local governments against federal taxation of the interest received by holders of their bonds. Thus ruling upheld a relatively minor tax provision passed by Congress in 1982. However, the chairmen of the Senate and House tax-writing committees immediately went on record that the decision was not expected to prompt Congress to impose any new taxes on such bonds.

Choice of Debt Form

Municipal bonds possess three significant features in addition to their tax-exempt status:

1. The *security* of municipal bonds is generally considered second only to that of federal government bonds.
2. Municipal bonds have high *marketability,* assuring that investors can always sell them if they wish to do so.
3. The *diversity* of municipal bonds enables investors to obtain bonds in a geographical area and at maturities of their preference.

Long-term borrowing is appropriate for projects that (1) will not require replacement for many years; (2) are financed by service or user charges to pay off revenue bonds; (3) are urgently needed for public health and safety or other emergency reasons; (4) can be financed only by means of special assessment bonds; or (5) are needed to serve newly annexed or rapidly expanding areas where demands on municipal resources are comparatively large and unforeseen.

Types of Bonds

General obligation bonds are backed by the "full faith, credit, and taxing power" of the issuing government. General obligation bonds are viewed by many investors as the most secure municipal issue, since the issuing authority has the power to levy taxes to meet debt service requirements. There are practical limits in the levying of taxes, however. In effect, the security of general obligation bonds is based upon the economic resources of taxpayers in the issuing jurisdiction.

Revenue bonds are backed by a pledge of revenues to be generated by the facility being financed and do not carry the "full faith and credit" pledge. Revenue bonds are often used to construct toll roads and bridges, parking structures, sewage treatment plants, and other facilities that have fairly predictable revenue-generating capacities.

Special tax or *special assessment bonds* are payable only from the proceeds of a special tax (such as highway bonds payable from a gasoline tax) or special assessments levied against those who benefit from the improvements (such as special assessments for curbs and gutters in residential areas). In recent years, to offset rising costs, the great majority of special assessment bonds have been secured by a pledge of full faith and credit, making them general obligation bonds.

Municipal bonds can also be classified into two general types according to the method of redemption. *Term bonds* become due in a lump sum at the end of the term of the loan. All bonds in the issue reach maturity and must be paid off at the same time. *Serial bonds* are retired by annual installments directly from tax revenues, or, in the case of revenue bonds, from earned income. Serial bonds have simpler retirement requirements and offer greater flexibility in marketing and in arranging the debt structure of the jurisdiction or public organization.

The lump-sum principal payment on term bonds is met by making annual payments to a *sinking fund*. When invested at compound interest, these annual payments should produce the amount of principal required at maturity. Frequent actuarial computations are required to determine the adequacy of sinking funds to meet principal payments at maturity. Some states do not permit the issuance of bonds whose principal is funded solely through a sinking fund. With proper investment safeguards, however, term bonds do offer some advantages. Term bonds may serve to finance public utilities and other enterprises that do not have established earning records.

There are two types of serial bonds: annuity serials and straight serials. With *annuity serials,* the debt service payment is approximately the same each year (as with a home mortgage). The portion of the annual payment devoted to interest is higher in the early years of the issue but declines as payments toward principal are made (as the outstanding principal is retired). *Straight serial bonds* require annual payments of principal of approximately equal amounts. Interest payments are large in the early years and decline gradually as the bonds approach maturity. A payment schedule for straight serial bonds, with interest calculated at 6 percent over ten years on a declining principal, is shown in Exhibit 9-1. Also shown in this exhibit is the payment schedule for an annuity serial bond, with interest calculated at 6 percent on the outstanding principal for the life of the loan. Note that the total debt service cost of the straight serial is less than that of the annuity serial.

Exhibit 9-1   *Debt Service Charges on $1 Million for Ten Years*

Straight Serial Bonds (6 percent on declining principal)			
Year	Outstanding Principal	Principal Payment	Interest Payment	Total Debt Service
1st	$1,000,000	$ 100,000	$ 60,000	$ 160,000
2nd	900,000	100,000	54,000	154,000
3rd	800,000	100,000	48,000	148,000
4th	700,000	100,000	42,000	142,000
5th	600,000	100,000	36,000	136,000
6th	500,000	100,000	30,000	130,000
7th	400,000	100,000	24,000	124,000
8th	300,000	100,000	18,000	118,000
9th	200,000	100,000	12,000	112,000
10th	100,000	100,000	6,000	106,000
Total		$1,000,000	$330,000	$1,330,000

Annuity Serial Bonds (6 percent on outstanding principal)			
Year	Outstanding Principal	Principal Payment	Interest Payment	Total Debt Service
1st	$1,000,000	$ 75,868	$ 60,000	$135,868
2nd	924,132	80,420	55,448	135,868
3rd	843,712	85,420	50,623	135,868
4th	758,467	90,360	45,508	135,868
5th	668,107	95,782	40,086	135,868
6th	572,325	101,528	34,340	135,868
7th	470,797	107,620	28,248	135,868
8th	363,177	114,070	21,791	135,868
9th	249,100	120,922	14,946	135,868
10th	128,178	128,178	7,690	135,868
Total		$1,000,000	$358,680	$1,358,680

Callable bonds are issued with the provision that they can be paid off—"called in" for payment—prior to their maturity date. The call normally is exercised with appropriate notice only on interest payment dates. Callable bonds can afford greater flexibility in the jurisdiction's debt structure. Bonds may be recalled and refunded at more favorable terms if (1) the market or the jurisdiction's credit rating improves, (2) the initial retirement schedule proves too rapid, or (3) a period of declining revenue is encountered. The callable feature can be used to avoid overly rigid fiscal responsibilities, while at the same time permitting more rapid retirement if the project's revenue capacity expands. Since most investors insist on a premium for callable bonds, the resultant savings must be carefully considered. For example, a 1 percent premium on a 7 percent callable bond would eliminate the net savings if the bonds were refunded at 6 percent.

Revenue Bonds

In general, revenue bond financing is best suited to projects that (1) can operate on a service charge or user-fee basis; (2) have the potential to be self-supporting, previously demonstrated under public or private operation; and (3) can produce sufficient revenue without jeopardizing other important economic or social objectives of the community. Problems of social equity may arise when traditionally tax-supported functions are placed on a service charge basis. Facilities supported by service charges also frequently produce benefits to individuals who do not pay for them—for example, an enhancement in land values that may accrue to speculative holders of unimproved real estate.

Revenue bonds are not ordinarily subject to statutory or constitutional debt limitations. Revenue bonds should not be issued to pursue speculative projects or merely to evade sound and reasonable debt limits. When a jurisdiction has an adequate borrowing capacity, the primary consideration should be which type of bonds can be marketed at the lowest cost.

The general provisions usually included in revenue bond laws are outlined in Exhibit 9-2. *Covenants* are often incorporated in the bond ordinance or resolution and made a part of the bond contract to protect the project from political interference, as well as to save money and help assure its success.

User charges are the oldest and most common source of support for revenue bonds. In financing utility systems, many localities issue bonds payable solely from such revenues. When debt service payments are guaranteed by the municipality in the event these resources are insufficient, the bonds are sometimes referred to as "double-barreled" securities.

Turnpikes and other transportation facilities are often financed by bonds payable from the *tolls and fees* collected and from the marginal income of *concessions* (for example, service facilities and restaurants along turnpikes, space lessees and parking lots at airports). *Special taxes* are those derived from an additional levy on such items as tobacco, alcoholic beverages, and other goods and services considered semiluxuries.

Exhibit 9-2 General Provisions of Revenue Bond Laws

1. Identification of the governmental units authorized to borrow and the types of utilities to which the enabling legislation applies.

2. General grant of power to acquire, construct, improve, or extend the specified improvements, to issue revenue bonds, and to pledge revenues to the payment of these bonds.

3. Requirement that the issuing body establish sufficient charges or rates to operate and maintain the project and to meet principal and interest payments.

4. Guarantees that revenue bonds have all the qualities of negotiable instruments under the appropriate laws of the state.

5. Provisions governing the authorization and sale of revenue bonds (including regulations relating to public referenda).

6. Provisions designed to secure the successful operation of the project.

7. Remedies to be initiated in the event of default.

Under a *leaseback arrangement,* bonds are usually issued by an authority to finance construction of a facility that is then leased to the city, school district, or state at a rental level sufficient to pay interest and retire the indebtedness. Funds for the rental payments are obtained by the lessee from various sources, including direct taxes, special taxes, and legislative appropriations.

Since 1936, local governments (mostly in the southern United States) have issued *industrial revenue bonds* to finance the construction or purchase of factories or other business facilities that are then leased to private business. The use of public credit to "buy" the location of new businesses in a community has been strongly opposed by many financial organizations. In their haste to find a lessee for the property, public officials may fail to investigate the financial stability of the enterprise thoroughly or to insist that the lease extend over the life of the bonds. As a consequence, the jurisdiction runs the risk of having a contingent liability become an actual one, or of becoming saddled with debt for special facilities for which another lessee cannot be found. Nonetheless, a growing number of states have authorized this type of debt as a means of attracting new industry.

Revenue bonds can play an important role in the long-range planning of capital facilities. It must be clearly established, however, that revenues generated by the proposed project are sufficient (1) to cover the cost of operations, maintenance, and debt service; (2) to provide a comfortable margin of working capital; and (3) to create a reserve fund to meet emergencies and to cover possible declines in income. In short, revenue bonding must be approached with the principles of sound management and debt administration firmly in mind.

Comparison of Bonding Strategies

Simple computational routines can be used to assess the impact of different bonding strategies—that is, different maturity periods and interest rates. Exhibit 9-3, for

Exhibit 9-3   *Total Debt Service Costs for Annuity Serial Bonds Under Different Maturities and Interest Rates (Face Value = $1 Million)*

Rank	Maturity	Interest Rate (r)	$(1 + r)^n$	Total Debt Service
1	10 years	5.5%	1.70814	$1,326,686
2	10 years	6.0%	1.79085	$1,358,680
3	10 years	6.5%	1.87714	$1,391,043
4	10 years	7.0%	1.96715	$1,423,777
5	10 years	7.5%	2.06103	$1,456,862
6	10 years	8.0%	2.15893	$1,490,289
7	15 years	5.5%	2.23248	$1,494,378
8	10 years	8.5%	2.26098	$1,524,081
9	15 years	6.0%	2.39656	$1,544,440
10	10 years	9.0%	2.36736	$1,558,205
11	10 years	9.5%	2.47823	$1,592,659
12	15 years	6.5%	2.57184	$1,595,293
13	10 years	10.0%	2.59374	$1,627,457
14	15 years	7.0%	2.75903	$1,646,921
15	20 years	5.5%	2.91776	$1,673,584
16	15 years	7.5%	2.95888	$1,699,306
17	20 years	6.0%	3.20714	$1,743,688
18	15 years	8.0%	3.17217	$1,752,443

example, shows the total debt service for $1 million annuity serial bonds with various interest rates and terms of maturity.

Such computations can provide considerable assistance in determining the appropriate method of financing a given project or series of projects. How much could be saved, for example, by investing in a sewer expansion project now, rather than delaying the project for three years? Assume that the current project cost is $3 million. An annuity serial bond issued for twenty years at 8 percent interest (alternative A) would cost $305,556 annually in debt service, or more than $6.1 million over twenty years. If construction costs were to increase by 10 percent per year, three years hence the project would cost $3,993,000. A twenty-year annuity serial bond would have to be available at 4.5 percent to "break even" when compared to the current option at 8 percent.

As an alternative, if the municipality could invest $305,000 annually in a capital reserve at 12 percent interest (compounded semiannually), a reserve fund of $1,160,000 would accumulate in three years. This reserve could be applied to the project cost of $3,993,000, leaving $2,833,000 to be financed through borrowing (alternative B). An annuity serial bond for this amount, at 8 percent for fifteen years, would cost approximately $330,930 in annual debt service, or $4,963,950 over fifteen years. When combined with the annual contributions to the capital reserve fund, the total cost of this alternative would be $5,878,950.

To complete this decision scenario, of course, it would be necessary to consider the benefits that might accrue from expanding the sewer system three years earlier.

Such a comparison is provided in Exhibit 9-4. It is assumed that benefits will begin to accrue one year after the system expansion is initiated, totaling $100,000 in year 2, $200,000 in year 3, $300,000 in year 4, and $400,000 each year thereafter. Benefits for alternative B would begin in year 5—that is, one year after the deferred project is initiated—and would total $100,000 in year 5, $200,000 in year 6, $300,000 in year 7, and $400,000 each year thereafter. For purposes of this illustration, these benefits may be assumed to represent the "net income" from the project—that is, the funds remaining after operating and maintenance costs have been met.

Exhibit 9-4 *Comparison of Costs and Benefits of Two Financing Alternatives*

		Present Value			
		Costs		Benefits	
Year	Discount Factor @ 8%	Alternative A	Alternative B	Alternative A	Alternative B
1	0.92593	$ 292,923	$ 282,409	$ 0	$ 0
2	0.85734	261,965	261,489	85,734	0
3	0.79383	242,560	242,118	158,766	0
4	0.73503	224,593	243,243	220,509	0
5	0.68058	207,955	225,224	272,232	68,058
6	0.63017	192,552	208,542	252,068	126,034
7	0.58349	178,289	193,094	233,396	175,047
8	0.54027	165,083	178,792	216,108	216,108
9	0.50025	152,854	165,548	200,100	200,100
10	0.46319	141,530	153,283	185,276	185,276
11	0.42888	131,047	141,929	171,552	171,552
12	0.39711	121,339	131,416	158,844	158,844
13	0.36770	112,353	121,683	147,080	147,080
14	0.34046	104,030	112,668	136,184	136,184
15	0.31524	96,323	104,322	126,096	126,096
16	0.29189	89,189	96,595	116,756	116,756
17	0.27027	82,189	89,440	108,108	108,108
18	0.25025	76,465	82,815	100,100	100,100
19	0.23171	70,800	0	92,684	92,684
20	0.21455	65,667	0	85,820	85,820
Totals		$2,999,990	$3,034,610	$3,067,413	$2,213,847

Benefit/Cost Ratio:

$$\text{Alternative A} = \frac{\$3,067,413}{\$2,999,990} = 1.0225$$

$$\text{Alternative B} = \frac{\$2,213,847}{\$3,034,610} = 0.7295$$

Net Benefits:

Alternative A:	$3,067,413
−	2,999,990
	$ 67,423
Alternative B:	$2,213,847
−	3,034,610
	($ 820,763)

As the calculations show, alternative A has a benefit/cost ratio of 1.0225 and net benefits of $67,423. In short, this alternative "breaks even" in present value terms. Alternative B has a benefit/cost ratio of 0.7295 and negative net benefits of $820,763. Alternative B is not a good investment; the municipality would be "better off" initiating the project now rather than deferring it for three years. By programming basic computational routines to accept various parameters, public officials can assess a wider range of alternatives that might not otherwise be readily apparent.

New Fiduciary and Fiscal Instruments

The municipal bond market traditionally has been supported by large institutional investors, such as fire and casualty insurance companies. In the late 1970s, however, faced with reduced profit margins, many of these institutions curtailed their municipal bond buying, forcing tax-exempt bond yields to unprecedented highs. Interest costs increased significantly as bond issuers were forced to make yields more attractive to buyers. Investors were unwilling to lock into fixed returns, feeling uncertain about inflation, tax liabilities, and yield curves. Governments still needed to borrow, however, and investors still needed to earn returns. As a consequence, a number of new fiduciary and fiscal instruments were devised to meet these needs.

Tax-Exempt Leveraged Lease Financing

Often more versatile and cost-effective in today's market than conventional borrowing, *tax-exempt leveraged lease* (or *TELL*) *financing* can greatly reduce the cost of borrowing on capital projects of $5 million or more. In TELL financing, municipalities generate capital funds by *selling* public facilities. The sale is financed through tax-exempt revenue bonds. Once the buildings have been sold, the private investment is "leveraged" by the municipality's leasing back the facility at subsidized rates. The results are sharply reduced financing costs, a new pool of unrestricted funds for capital projects, and greater financial flexibility for borrowers.

The four main participants in TELL financing are shown in Exhibit 9-5. Any government unit or public agency authorized to issue special purpose revenue bonds or industrial development bonds may take advantage of leveraged lease financing.

Exhibit 9-5 *Tax-Exempt Leveraged Lease Financing Structure*

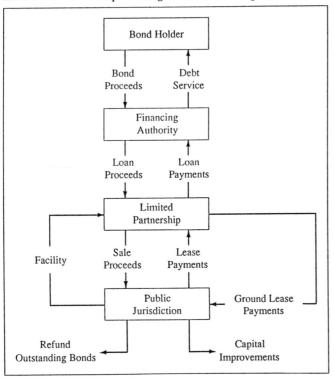

A private investor (special purpose limited partnership) buys a public building by making a down payment and, over a five-year period, contributing equity equal to 25 to 30 percent of the sales price. The municipality then leases back the building on a long-term basis for continued use. The infusion of equity by the investor reduces rents significantly during the first five years.

The balance of the sales price is financed by tax-exempt revenue bonds issued on behalf of the partnership and loaned by a qualified financing authority (such as an industrial development authority). Underwriters arrange the tax-exempt bond financing and structure the sale/leaseback transaction to meet the requirements of the bond market, the private investors, and the government. The lease serves as collateral for the loan which, in turn, secures the bond issue. The proceeds of the sale then finance the intended capital improvement.

In purchasing the facility, the private investors obtain the tax benefits associated with ownership. The subsidized base payments during the initial five years are a reflection of the value of these benefits. Lease payments represent the cost of financing to the governmental unit. In reducing the magnitude of the lease payments, TELL successfully reduces the effective borrowing cost below the issuer's current tax-exempt rate.

Although investors own the building, the facility lease is carefully written to provide the government with maximum flexibility and control over the use and final disposition of the building. Typically, a jurisdiction leases back the building for a period of thirty years on a *net-net basis;* that is, the jurisdiction assumes basic operating and maintenance costs. In so doing, the jurisdiction retains control over day-to-day management and operations. In addition, the lease usually provides the government with several renewal options and with rights to repurchase the facility. As a further protection, the public agency often retains ownership of the land, leasing it to the investors for a period of sixty-five years. At the end of the land lease, the land and improvements automatically revert to the government.

Under TELL financing, the repurchase price cannot be negotiated in advance of the sale. However, lease provisions can shield the jurisdiction from inflated real estate values at the time of repurchase. These safeguards include the land lease, the renewal options, and the method of appraisal that defines the repurchase price at the end of thirty years. The land lease, for example, serves to encumber the facility and to limit its future value in the open market.

Almost any capital project, from new construction to the refunding of outstanding debt, can be financed through leveraged leases. In considering TELL financing, the managing underwriter should assist the government in developing a feasibility study, which should include an analysis of the impact of the project's proposed financing terms on the local budget, an estimated rental schedule, and an outline of legal and financial actions required of the government. Upon completion of this analysis, the managing underwriter, the bond counsel, and representatives of the equity partnership should draft the necessary lease, purchase, and financing documents, followed by the submission of a firm purchase contract within sixty to ninety days.

Stepped Coupon Bonds

In traditional serial bonds, each maturity has a single coupon rate payable over the life of the bond. *Stepped coupon bonds,* on the other hand, use a serial maturity schedule, with coupon rates that start at lower levels and progressively increase to higher levels, even though all the bonds in the issue are sold at par. Stepped coupon bonds are particularly applicable to the financing of projects requiring that interest payments be made from project revenue.

The substantial increase in coupon payments each year is intended to provide a hedge against inflation and thus make the bonds more marketable. The assumption is that, as the purchasing power of paper money goes down each year, stepped coupons give bondholders more paper money to keep pace with inflation. From the perspective of the issuing government, because of the lower coupon rates, more bonds may be scheduled to mature in early years, thereby lowering the average life of the issue.

Zero Coupon Bonds

Zero coupon bonds were introduced into the tax-exempt bond market in the late seventies and quickly became a "hot item" in public finance. As a form of original investment discount bonds, they are especially favored by individual bond buyers.

Federal tax laws entitle bondholders who forego tax-free income over the life of their investment to receive tax-exempt capital gains upon maturity. The result is a sort of tax-free income, accrued annually from the time the bonds are first issued. Zero coupon bonds sell at substantial discounts from the customary face, or par, value of $1,000 because they pay no interest. By paying par upon maturity, however, they offer capital gains that may be as much as 25 times the original investment, depending on the length of the issue. Held to maturity, for example, a seventeen-year zero coupon bond purchased for $150 will provide a tax-free capital gain of $850; or, according to the IRS, $50 in tax-exempt income each year ($850 divided by 17).

Leading brokerage firms have bought traditional coupon-bearing, long-term issues and have stripped the coupons from the bonds. Each component is then sold separately. The bond becomes a zero coupon bond, with the guarantees of the issuing public agency. Without coupons, the value of what is called the *corpus* is much reduced. For example, a 14 percent corpus maturing in the year 2011 could have been bought in the early 1980s for about $40 per $1,000 bond face amount, providing an annual yield to maturity of 11.5 percent compounded. In other words, over thirty years, each $40 invested would increase about 25 times to maturity in the year 2011.

Compound Interest Bonds

Compound interest bonds (sometimes called *municipal multipliers*) are beginning to rival zero coupon bonds in popularity. These bonds do not pay annual or semiannual interest. Instead, the return to the investor at maturity is the principal plus interest compounded at a specified rate. Unlike zero coupon bonds, which sell at a discount, these bonds sell at face value. However, an investor in compound interest bonds still pays much less for the bond than it would be worth at maturity. For example, a 1982 issue of single-family mortgage revenue bonds from the Virginia Housing Development Authority was priced at $250 per $1,000 maturity amount, for an annualized yield of 11.83 percent at maturity in 1994. As with zero coupon bonds, the longer the maturity of a compound interest bond, the higher the yield. The Virginia issue also included bonds priced at $100 yielding 12.45 percent in 2001, as well as some priced at $20 yielding 12.58 percent in 2014.

The main advantages of these bonds over regular coupon bonds is that an investor knows exactly what the total return will be. With a traditional coupon bond, the holder must reinvest the semiannual interest at the then-prevailing rate, thus making the total return uncertain. Compound interest bonds guarantee the current rate of return for fifteen to twenty years. This new type of bond combines the investment-multiplying power of compound interest with the income-sheltering feature of traditional tax-exempt bonds.

Tender Option Bonds

A *tender option bond,* also known as a *put bond,* offers the investor the option of submitting the bond for redemption before maturity. Usually the investor may redeem or "put in" a bond five years after the date of issue or on any anniversary date thereafter. In return for this option, the investor accepts a lower yield. The issuer pays a lower rate of interest (usually about 1 percent less than for conventional bonds of the same maturity), and consequently, the jurisdiction's cost is lower. However, the bond returns more to the investor (about 0.75 percent) than conventional bonds that mature on the first prescribed put date.

Tender option bonds may also be issued with a simultaneous "call" date, on which the issuer can call in and pay off the bonds. Thus, the issuer and the bondholder have equal rights to cash in the bonds when market conditions and interest rates are favorable. If interest rates go down, a put bond will probably be called in by the issuing government. Conversely, if interest rates go up, the bondholder can "tender his option" to be paid at face value by the issuer.

A variation on the tender option bond approach has been used primarily in conjunction with mortgage revenue bonds used to finance low-income housing. Instead of offering a "put" option, the issuer is required to call in the bonds for early payment at face value as sufficient funds become available. The bonds are redeemed by lottery: the individual bondholder does not know when or if his/her bond will be called in for redemption. When all the bonds to be called from this fund are lumped together, the maturity is referred to as a *super-sinker.*

Flexible Interest Bonds

The idea of issuing tax-exempt bonds with a floating interest rate has been adapted from the Eurocurrency market. This approach provides stability for both the issuer and the bondholder throughout the life of the bonds, particularly during times of interest rate volatility. As the name implies, the yield (interest paid by the issuer) on a *flexible interest bond* changes over the life of the bond, based on some interest index printed on the bond itself. This feature stands in contrast to the traditional fixed-rate bond, whose interest rate remains constant but whose market value changes when interest rates rise or fall.

The interest index most often used is the average weekly rate of Treasury bills or bonds issued during the preceding interest period. For example, the floating rate for a short-term bond might be pegged at 67 percent of the average weekly T-bill quote, while the rate for a longer-term issue might be set at 75 percent of the average weekly quote on thirty-year Treasury bonds.

An additional feature of flexible interest bonds is a *swing limit*—a preestablished range within which the interest (cost to the public agency) may vary. Bonds issued in the late 1980s, for example, had floating interest rate limits of 7 percent minimum to a maximum of 12.5 percent over the life of the bonds.

As with other municipal bonds, the maturities of flexible interest bonds vary. Such bonds usually have call and/or put features. These specify the earliest dates at which the bondholder can get his/her money back at par. Some recent flexible interest bonds have been structured so that they can be redeemed at the end of a given calendar quarter. Flexible rate certificates issued in 1981 by the state of Washington, for example, pay interest each month, and bondholders may elect, on the 15th day of each month in which the interest payments are due, either (1) to accept a new interest payment date at the same rate as the previous month, or (2) to tender the bonds for purchase by the state at par. Although they are basically bonds, floating rate bonds with short demand features are often called *notes* or *certificates of indebtedness.*

Since flexible interest bonds have less risk of principal erosion, interest costs are lower than on long-term, conventional bonds. The savings in interest costs to the issuer can be very substantial; the difference between a traditional bond and a flexible interest bond is often as much as 3 to 3.5 percent.

Detachable Warrant Bonds

A *warrant* gives the holder the right, at some future date, to purchase more of the same securities to which the warrant is attached, at the same price and rate of return as the original bond. In exchange for that right, the issuer pays a lower rate of interest (about one-half percent less) than offered on otherwise comparable securities. The marketability of such bonds depends on the opinion of prospective buyers as to anticipated fluctuations in interest rates. If interest rates rise, the savings to the issuer become real because of the initial lower interest cost. If the rates fall, the opposite is true.

The Municipal Assistance Corporation of the City of New York issued the first public tax-exempt detachable warrant bonds in 1982. These bonds gave the holders warrants that could be exercised for two years. The expectation was that, even if interest rates declined during the two-year period, the savings from the lower interest payments over the life of the bond issue would amount to about $11 million. Since interest rates held relatively constant during this period, the long-term savings will likely be even greater.

A Note of Caution

In the dynamic and uncertain period of the 1980s, state and local governments have had to develop capital financing programs that are more responsive to their overall financial conditions and fiscal policies than traditional general obligation and revenue bonds.

The federal tax reform bill passed in August 1986 will have a number of effects on the future supply of tax-exempt financing. Restrictions on the types of projects that can be financed by tax-exempt bonds, along with statewide caps on the volume of new issues, can be expected to reduce municipal bond issuance by about 40 percent. The reduction in the supply of new issues, in turn, can be expected to increase the relative value of municipal bonds, particularly in states that have historically low municipal debt.

The second important effect of the tax bill is the lowering of the maximum federal tax bracket from 50 percent to 28 percent in 1988. Although the new, lower federal tax brackets have already been discounted, municipal bonds continue to be attractive relative to taxable alternatives for the vast majority of investors whose marginal tax rates are at the higher end of the new federal tax schedule. At the same time, since federal tax brackets have been lowered, the state portion of an individual's total effective tax bracket becomes larger. As a consequence, the exemption from state taxes offered by municipal bonds to residents of the state of issue becomes more important.

New financing techniques are not a panacea for meeting local governments' needs for expanded capital facilities. More conventional approaches should not be abandoned unless officials are satisfied that sufficient benefits will accrue compared to the risks. The development of more innovative approaches stems from the willingness and ability of state and local governments to accept and deal with the uncertainty of future markets for financing capital facilities. Practical concerns are also part of the equation, including the political acceptability of such approaches, the ability of government to structure and manage these creative financing mechanisms, and of course, the laws that govern capital financing. Interest payments are still the cost that governments must pay for the use of other people's money. Careful application of new financing techniques, however, may uncover some real opportunities or provide capital resources that otherwise would be unavailable.

Marketing Municipal Bonds

Constitutional provisions, general statutes, special acts, and local charters that regulate the authorization and issuance of municipal bonds vary from state to state. Controlling laws are not always conveniently codified, and as a consequence, the procedural steps necessary to secure bond authorization are often confusing to local officials and administrators. Expert advice is important to ensure compliance with all applicable legal requirements. Even minor errors may result in annoying delays, expensive litigation, and possible invalidation of the bond issue or sale.

Preliminaries to Marketing

Some form of *popular referendum* is required in most states for the authorization of general obligation bonds. In a few states, governing bodies are permitted, within certain limits, to authorize bonds without popular vote. Experience has shown, however, that this option should be exercised sparingly and held in reserve for emergencies.

Municipal bonds must be negotiable instruments; that is, they must contain an unconditional promise to pay. *Bond ordinances* or *resolutions* should be drawn with precision, setting forth the nature and limits of the security offered. Each issue must be approved by an attorney whose legal opinion will satisfy the market where the bonds are to be sold. Since the city attorney or corporation counsel is usually not a bond specialist, the issuing jurisdiction must obtain the services of a bond attorney whose opinion is "marketable." The official notice of sale should specify that the legal opinion will be furnished to the buyer. The bond attorney may make a preliminary assessment of the legal status of the bond, but will not issue a formal opinion until after the bonds are sold to the underwriters. The sale is subject to the satisfactory provision of such legal opinion, however.

Notice of Sale

At least two weeks in advance of the date set for opening bids, an official notice of sale should be published in *The Daily Bond Buyer* and perhaps in regional bond publications. In some states, notices must also be placed in the official state newspaper. Information to be included in the notice of sale is listed in Exhibit 9-6. Adequate publicity gives prospective bidders (underwriters) the opportunity to form their bidding accounts (syndicates) and to secure information regarding the offering. It also eliminates any suspicion of collusion and demonstrates that the jurisdiction is willing to submit its financial condition to careful inspection.

Exhibit 9-6   *Information for Notice of Sale*

1. The correct legal name of the issuing body, the special law (if any) under which it was organized, and the authority for the sale.

2. Types of bonds to be issued.

3. Amount and purpose of the issue, the maturity schedule, call features (if any), denomination, and registration privileges.

4. Date, time, and place of sale; manner of bidding (sealed or oral); and basis for bidding (at par, discounts allowed, and so forth).

5. Interest rate limitations, interest payment dates, and when and where principal will be paid.

6. Amount of the good faith check; that is, the amount each bidding syndicate will have to deposit with the jurisdiction in order to have its bid considered. These checks are refunded to all but the winning syndicate.

7. Name of approving attorney.

8. Provision made for the payment of principal and interest—from *ad valorem taxes*, special assessments, or revenues of a particular enterprise.

9. Total tax rate in the governmental unit, rate for each levying body, and constitutional or statutory limits restricting debts or the taxes levied for their payment.

If the enabling legislation permits, the best practice is to allow the rates of interest to be fixed by the bidding underwriters.[1] When they can determine the coupon rate, underwriters can make a bid that best fits the market. If permissible under controlling state regulations, bidders should be able to bid different rates on various maturities or groups of bonds—known as *split-rate bids*—in order to obtain the most favorable overall net interest cost.

Supplemental coupons have been used to attract dealers where state requirements mandate that municipal bonds be sold at par. Supplemental coupons are additional coupons attached to a municipal bond and covering the same interest period as one or more regular coupons. When a supplemental coupon is in force, the issuing jurisdiction is required to make two interest payments for the period. Supplemental coupons are usually detached by the underwriter at the time of original delivery from the issuer and may be held until the payment date or sold by the dealer at a discount. These coupons, in effect, represent the underwriter's profit on the sale of the bond.

Timing of an Issue

The bond market experiences minor short-term fluctuations brought on by an excess of supply over demand as well as shifting economic and political trends. By consulting investment bankers and following municipal bond publications, the finance officer can often apply these fluctuations to the advantage of the jurisdiction.

The issuer should avoid setting the date of the sale in the midst of a general rush of new offerings (many large school bond issues, for example, reach the market in late spring or early summer) or immediately following large sales by other jurisdictions. It is unwise to enter the market too frequently (hence the advantage of a consolidated issue). And if the distribution of a previous issue has not been completed, a less satisfactory price may be anticipated on a new issue.

Due dates for semiannual interest payments are determined by the date on which the bond is sold. Since there are certain times of the year when a jurisdiction's funds are low, the timing of an issue should be such that interest and principal payments do not come due at a time when funds are not in hand to pay them.

Bond Prospectus

The publication of all essential facts concerning the financial condition of the jurisdiction is fully as important as any other factor in the successful marketing of municipal bonds. With the exception of revenue bond issues, however, no elaborate prospectus is necessary. The four-page statistical form approved by the Investment Bankers Association and the Municipal Finance Officers Association is usually adequate. This form provides the information that most investors seek regarding debt and the provision for payment, the adequacy of the jurisdiction's revenue system and the effectiveness of its administration, recent financial operations, total tax rate and statutory limits restricting debts or the taxes levied for their payment, population according to latest census data, and so forth.

The bond prospectus should be printed and ready for distribution at the time of the notice of sale. It should be sent, without request, to investment bankers and other institutions that are interested in the municipality's securities. Financial papers that publish the paid notice about the sale will usually carry a news story about the community and, therefore, should also receive copies of the prospectus.

Planning the Sale of Revenue Bonds

On the whole, revenue bonds have had good credit ratings. Defaults that have occurred can be traced to mistakes in planning and management, such as:

- Failure to adhere to appropriate state enabling legislation.
- Underestimation of operating costs or overestimation of anticipated revenues.
- Excessive expenditures for property acquisition.
- Failure to segregate and safeguard project revenues in accordance with the covenants of the bond resolution.
- Insufficient care in engineering studies.
- Failure to allow sufficient time for project completion before bond payments begin to come due.

The terms, conditions, and safeguards on revenue bonds should be planned with two objectives in mind: (1) to suit the nature of the project and (2) to attract the investor. The principles to be observed in planning a revenue bond issue can be outlined as follows:

1. Bonds should be scheduled for retirement well within the useful life of the project; that is, the rate of amortization should at least equal an adequate rate of depreciation on the facility.
2. The retirement of bonds, however, should be distributed so as to allow a comfortable revenue margin for debt service without the need to charge abnormal rates or fees.
3. The amount of combined annual interest and amortization should follow an even, or possibly slightly rising, trend in order to coincide with the prospective pattern of revenues. With serial bonds, for example, the maturity pattern should be established to reflect the anticipated income pattern.
4. The first payment on principal should be deferred until the facility's operations have become well established.
5. Assurances must be evident to the investor from the outset, through covenants, as follows:
   a. The project will receive businesslike management.
   b. Bond funds will be properly expended.
   c. Construction will be carefully inspected.
   d. The plant and equipment will be properly maintained after the project is operational.
   e. The rate structure or fee schedule is designed to keep the project self-supporting.
   f. Financial safeguards will assure the maintenance of adequate working capital and reserves.

In a number of states, revenue bond issues can be established through negotiated sales. If possible, financial advisors should be drawn from experienced bond house personnel or from associated financial consulting organizations.

Avoiding the use of qualified fiscal and legal advisors is a false economy usually resulting in higher interest costs many times over the fees involved.

Revenue bonds may be issued as serial maturities or term bonds. In almost all cases, revenue bonds are callable prior to maturity by means of surplus funds or a mandatory sinking fund. This callable provision may apply to all or a portion of the outstanding bonds.

Certain covenants are spelled out in all bond resolutions or trust indentures for the protection of the investors. Exhibit 9-7 summarizes the covenants commonly made in connection with the sale of revenue bonds. Among other things, these covenants establish appropriate and clearly defined fiscal policies. It has been said that "covenants that protect the bondholder give equal protection to the bond issuer." Failure to incorporate these provisions into the basic bond instrument generally results in higher interest rates.

Costs Involved in Marketing Municipal Bonds

The cost of borrowing involves not only the interest payable over the term of the bonds, but also the costs incurred in readying the bonds for market and delivering

Exhibit 9-7 *Covenants on Revenue Bonds*

1. *Rate covenant.* The issuing body pledges to fix rates, with revisions when necessary, sufficient to meet operation and maintenance charges, as well as annual debt service requirements, and to provide for certain reserves. Rates must be sufficient to provide some minimum margin of safety over the charges incurred in the previous period. For example, for toll facilities, the covenant is generally 120 percent of the foregoing charges.

2. *Maintenance and insurance.* The issuing body must maintain the properties in good repair and working condition at all times. Insurance must be carried on the facility corresponding in amount and in kind to that which is normally carried under private enterprise.

3. *Records and financial reports.* The issuing body must keep appropriate records and provide them for audit annually by independent certified public accountants. Revenues must be deposited in a special fund and kept separate from all other funds of the jurisdiction.

4. *Consulting engineer.* When certain types of projects are undertaken, a qualified engineer must be placed on retainer to perform "watchdog" duties over the operations of the facility. This practice is common with sewer and water systems and toll roads (at the state level).

5. *Nondiscrimination covenant.* Neither preferential treatment nor discrimination shall be applied to any groups in the matter of payment of rates for services; that is, charges will be equitable to all users.

6. *Application of revenues.* A series of covenants usually specifies an order of priority in the disposition of funds. A typical order of priority would be: (1) operations and maintenance; (2) interest and principal on bonds; (3) renewal and replacement fund; (4) working capital fund; (5) interest on future bonds, tax equivalent, or other return to the municipality.

them to the initial investors. Such costs include the expense of conducting a referendum; fees for various legal and financial advisors; the cost of publishing bond notices and the bond prospectus, printing the bonds, obtaining a bond rating, and renting signature machines; court fees; registration or recording fees; and certification costs; (see Exhibit 9-8). Some marketing expenditures may result in a broader sale, culminating in lower interest costs; other expenses add little to the marketability of a bond issue.

Exhibit 9-8 *Costs Involved in Marketing Municipal Bonds*

Average Cost per $1,000		
Size of Issue	General Obligation Bonds	Revenue Bonds	Special Assessment Bonds
Under $499,999	$10.66	$13.90	$15.12
$500,000–$999,999	8.69	12.87	9.90
$1,000,000–$1,999,999	6.98	9.98	5.38
$2,000,000–$2,999,999	5.48	7.50	3.50
$3,000,000–$4,999,999	4.00	5.98	3.83
$5,000,000–$9,999,999	3.32	5.44	3.14
$10,000,000–$24,999,999	1.99	2.94	—
$25,000,000 and over	0.80	2.34	—
All issues	$ 1.98	$ 3.84	$ 5.13

Cost per $1,000: Specific Cost Categories		
Cost Category	General Obligation Bonds	Revenue Bonds	Special Assessment Bonds
Election costs	$1.25	$0.36	$0.15
Legal and financial fees	2.02	2.21	3.88
Bond notice	0.06	0.09	0.25
Prospectus	0.10	0.25	0.34
Printing of bonds	0.20	0.19	0.49
Bond ratings	0.09	0.24	0.48
Other costs	0.08	0.11	0.26

Percentage Distribution of Total Costs		
Cost Category	General Obligation Bonds	Revenue Bonds	Special Assessment Bonds
Election costs	12.7%	1.1%	0.1%
Legal and financial fees	62.7%	81.0%	78.5%
Bond notice	2.5%	1.8%	3.7%
Prospectus	3.3%	4.6%	2.7%
Printing of bonds	8.5%	3.6%	6.8%
Bond ratings	2.7%	1.7%	2.0%
Other costs	2.7%	1.4%	2.7%

Based on the annual survey by the Municipal Finance Officers Association.

Although no single cost incurred is large, in the aggregate these costs can amount to a considerable sum. A survey by the Municipal Finance Officers Association of 481 governmental units revealed that in some instances, total marketing costs amounted to 5.5 percent of the value of the bonds. These costs are usually paid from the bond proceeds, reducing the amount available for the project or necessitating increased borrowing to meet capital costs.

Municipal Bond Ratings

Ratings have assumed considerable significance in determining interest rates and the eligibility of bonds for purchase by certain types of investors. Municipal bonds are rated only in terms of credit risk and not in terms of their investment merits. Bond ratings appraise two basic risk factors:

1. Dilution of bond quality by an inordinate increase in debt.
2. Inability to meet principal and interest payments under depressed economic conditions.

The first risk is within the control of the issuing government, whereas the second is related to the impact of general economic conditions on a given locality.

Two major rating services—Moody's Investors Service, Inc., and Standard and Poor's Corporation—classify into broad quality gradations approximately three-fourths of the total dollar amount issued in municipal bonds. These rating services use symbols, arranged in order from bonds with the least credit risk to those with the greatest risk (see Exhibit 9-9). Some issues rated by one service are not rated by the other, and the opinions of the two rating services may differ on specific issues. A third service—Fitch's Investors Service—rates some municipal bonds, using symbols similar to those of Moody's.

Bond ratings are considered valid for one year or until the same issuer comes into the market again, whichever time is shorter. Generally speaking, there is only one rating for all general obligation bonds of a particular governmental unit or for all bonds of a specific revenue project. Some governmental units or revenue projects may have more than one rating because special security has been pledged for some of the bonds. New issues of a previously rated governmental unit or revenue project are usually assigned the same rating as the outstanding bonds unless there have been material changes in the credit situation.

Ratings are very general and are not absolute standards of quality. Though undergoing continual improvements, particularly since the advent of high-speed computers, existing rating systems are not without deficiencies. Since large institutional buyers are often limited by state law in the selection of their investments, it is very important for a jurisdiction that nothing be done to jeopardize its favorable rating if it is now on the legal investment lists of leading investor states.

The Bond Sale and Delivery

All bids on a particular issue should be made in terms that permit comparison of total costs to the issuer. Public officials should insist that all bids comply strictly

Exhibit 9-9 *Municipal Bond Rating Systems*

Moody's	Symbol	Symbol	Standard and Poor's
Best quality; carrying smallest degree of investment risk; referred to as "gilt edge"	Aaa	AAA	Prime: obligation of highest quality and lowest probability of default; quality management and low debt structure
High quality; rated lower than Aaa because margins of protection not as large	Aa	AA	High grade: only slightly less secure than prime; second lowest probability of default
Higher medium grade; many favorable investment attributes; some element of future risk evident	A	A	Upper medium grade: safe investment; weakness in local economic base, debt burden, or fiscal balance
Lower medium grade; neither highly protected nor poorly secured; may be unreliable over the long run	Baa	BBB	Medium grade: lowest investment security rating; may show more than one fundamental weakness; higher probability of default
Judged to have speculative elements; not well safeguarded as to interest and principal	Ba	BB	Lower medium grade: speculative noninvestment-grade obligation; high risk and uncertainty
Lacks characteristics of desirable investment	B	B	Low grade: investment characteristics virtually nonexistent
Poor standing; issue may be in default	Caa	CCC	Default
Speculative in high degree; marked shortcomings	Ca	CC	Default
Lowest rated class; extremely poor prospects of ever attaining any real investment standing	C	C	Default

with the terms of the sale. All bids should be received and opened in public by the governing body at the designated hour, with the bonds awarded on the basis of the lowest net interest cost.[2] All papers required to complete the bond transcript should be forwarded to the bond attorneys as soon as possible.

Before the bonds are delivered, information required to establish the *bond register* (sometimes called the *bond and interest record*) should be recorded. At the time a bond issue is sold, the interest due on each date of maturity should be computed and recorded, as should the required payments of principal or payments into a sinking fund. With such records, a complete schedule of debt service requirements can be readily prepared for the current budget and for all outstanding debt obligations.

Bonds should be delivered at the earliest practical date after the sale (no later than thirty days). The winning bidder usually has the option to cancel the obligations if delivery is not made on or before the date specified in the contract. The purchaser should stipulate where the bonds are to be delivered. Many municipalities prefer to have at least one official sign the bonds at the point of delivery and to have the municipal seal imprinted at that time. Large bond issues are usually signed at the place of delivery because the travel expenses of officials are often less than the insurance required on the delivery of signed bonds.

Summary

The marketing of municipal bonds is a complicated process, the mysteries of which, to the uninitiated, are comparable to those of the stock market. Local officials must know the procedures for marketing bonds, from the planning of the issue through delivery of the bonds to the winning bidder. Failure to adhere to these procedures can result in unnecessary delays, higher interest costs, and possible legal ramifications. As a practical matter, almost any bond issue that is in proper technical form can be sold at any time. However, whether a particular offering is "successful" at the date of sale depends on the congruence of many factors.

The finance officer is caught in the middle—faced, on the one hand, by uncertainties as to the political and economic future of the community and, on the other, by uncertainties of a marketplace that he or she may not fully comprehend. Adherence to accepted marketing procedures can go a long way toward reducing these uncertainties. The success of a given issue may be determined by forces in the marketplace beyond the control of local officials. Awareness of these factors, however, can provide important insights into the overall planning of long-term bonds for capital facilities.

Debt Administration

Debt administration was a relatively routine task when long-term debt was a small part of the overall fiscal commitments of local government. The basic requirement was to ensure that sufficient funds were set aside each year from general revenue sources to cover annual debt service charges or, in the case of term bonds, to cover annual interest charges and build an adequate sinking fund. New and diverse bond offerings, however, have resulted in increased responsibilities for the administration of public debt.

Capital Project Funds

Capital project funds account for the resources required to build or buy specific capital facilities. Thes resources come from the issuance of bonds or other long-term obligations, from intergovernmental grants, or as transfers from other funds. Upon completion of the project, the capital project fund is terminated, and the accounting results are transferred to the *debt service fund*. Good financial management standards dictate that a debt service fund be used to account for the payment of interest and principal on the long-term debt for each capital project.

Bonds often are not sold on the date of issue. Assume, for example, that bonds with an issue date of July 1, 1986, were not sold until September 1, 1986. The purchaser of these bonds receives semiannual interest payments from the date of issue (that is, on January 1, 1987, on July 1, 1987, and every six months thereafter) and not from the date of purchase. Therefore, when the bonds are sold, the *buyer* pays the equivalent of interest for the period from the issue date to the date of purchase.

Accrued interest received on the sale of the bonds cannot be used in the capital project fund to pay for construction. It must be transferred to the debt service fund to be used as part of the resources for the first interest payment—that is, as a partial offset to the amount needed from the general fund for the first interest payment. Therefore, only money sufficient to pay the interest from the purchase date to the interest payment date will have to be transferred from the general fund to the debt service fund.

It is often difficult to determine at the time a bond issue is authorized exactly what the interest rate will be on the date the bonds are sold. The actual date of sale can seldom be predicted accurately. The possibility exists, therefore, that bonds will be sold at either a *premium* or a *discount*—that is, above or below the face value.

Some states do not permit municipal bonds to be issued at a discount (below face value, or par). This prohibition may force the issuing authority to pay a higher interest rate on the bonds to ensure their sale. When a discount is allowed, the full face value of the bonds is still required to complete the authorized project, and the difference may have to be made up from the general fund or the debt service fund. When bonds are sold at a premium, the difference between par and the premium is usually transferred to the debt service fund and used with other resources to pay off the bonds.

The capital project fund often receives proceeds from the sale of bonds or transfers of monies from other sources (such as state or federal grants) before these resources are needed to acquire the capital asset. These resources should be invested to produce additional revenue. This revenue, in turn, is transferred to the debt service fund for payment of the principal or interest of the debt.

The administration of a capital project fund can perhaps be understood best by tracing a typical set of transactions. Assume that a city proposes to buy land and construct a new administration building at an estimated cost of $1,600,000. Matching grants of $300,000 from the state and $500,000 from the federal government are available for this project. Through a referendum, the city's taxpayers have approved a bond issue of $800,000 to meet the local share of the project's financing.

Regardless of the method by which monies are transferred from one governmental unit to another, the results are the same: the capital project fund receives cash from the granting agencies. Assume that the grants are received at the outset of the project and are invested in short-term, sixty-day certificates of deposit at

8 percent interest. The resulting earnings of $10,520 ($800,000 × 0.08 × 60/365) are deposited in the debt service fund.

Land is purchased for the building site. Two landowners agree to purchase prices totaling $90,000. A third landowner cannot obtain his desired price; his land is condemned, with a court-ordered settlement of $35,000. These transactions are not encumbered because of the relatively short time between purchase and payment.

In governmental fund accounting, capital assets are recorded as expenditures in the capital project fund and as fixed assets in the general fixed assets account group. The journal entry to record this transaction in the capital project fund is:

```
August 15, 19X6
Expenditure                           $125,000
    Accounts payable                              $ 90,000
    Judgments payable                                35,000
```

Payment for the land is recorded as:

```
September 1, 19X6
Accounts payable                      $ 90,000
Judgments payable                       35,000
    Cash                                          $125,000
```

The land sales and the judgment are paid on a proportional basis from three sources: the state grant (3/16), the federal grant (5/16), and the proceeds of the bond sale (8/16). The entry to record this transaction in the fixed assets account group is:

```
Land                                  $125,000
    State grant                                   $ 23,438
    Federal grant                                   39,062
    General obligation bonds                        62,500
```

Grant funds are thus reduced to $737,500. This amount, plus previously earned interest, is invested in a thirty-day CD at 7 percent. The resulting earnings of $4,305 [($737,500 + $10,520) × 0.07 × 30/365] are deposited in the debt service fund.

The bonds, dated July 1, 19X6, are issued as twenty-year general obligation bonds with an interest rate of 5 percent, payable semiannually on December 31 and June 30. For illustrative purposes, it will be assumed that the issue is for term bonds. Interest on term bonds is paid on the full amount of principal over the twenty-year period to maturity.

On September 30, the bonds are sold at a premium of 2 percent, or $16,000, plus accrued interest of $10,000 ($800,000 × 0.05 × 3/12). Total receipts of $826,000 are recorded in the capital project fund as follows:

```
September 30, 19X6
Cash                                  $826,000
Operating transfer to debt service fund 16,000
    Due to debt service fund                      $ 26,000
    Proceeds from bonds                             816,000
```

The accrued interest and premium on the sale of the bonds are transferred to the debt service fund. From the sale of the bonds, $62,500 is paid toward land acquisition, and the balance of $737,500 is combined with the balance of the grant funds ($737,500 + $10,520 + $4,305), for a total of $1,489,825. This amount is invested in a ninety-day CD at 9 percent, yielding $33,060 ($1,489,825 × 0.09 × 90/365) on December 29, 19X6.

On October 1, 19X6, a contract is let for construction of the building, which is designed to be built for $1,300,000, including a contingency allowance of $100,000 to accommodate any necessary plan changes. The contract calls for completion of the building by November 1, 19X7. The Public Works Department will make the necessary land improvements and landscape the grounds at the completion of the construction phase. The estimated cost of $75,000 is encumbered at the outset of the project.

The Sunshine Construction Company is to receive quarterly payments on the basis of percentage of completion of the building and approval by the construction supervisor. During the first year of the project, the following payments are approved, based on invoices submitted by the company:

December 31, 19X6	$350,000
March 31, 19X7	225,000
June 30, 19X7	225,000

Individual entries are made to record each of these amounts when the invoices are received and approved. The balance of the grant funds and bond proceeds continues to be available for short-term investment in certificates of deposit or other securities.

Only $575,000 of the accounts payable is actually paid during the fiscal year (the June 30, 19X7 payment is made early in the next fiscal year), in addition to the $125,000 paid for the land. Closing entries as of June 30, 19X7, to close out the revenue, proceeds, and expenditure accounts, are as follows:

Proceeds from bonds	$816,000	
Revenue	800,000	
Expenditures		$700,000
Accounts payable		225,000
Operating transfer to debt service fund		16,000
Reserve for encumbrances		575,000
Fund balance		100,000

The capital project fund still has $900,000 in cash at the start of the second fiscal year (July 1, 19X7), offset by accounts payable of $225,000, a fund balance of $100,000, and reserve for encumbrances of $575,000 ($500,000 on the construction contract and $75,000 for site improvements). Thus, $675,000 is available for short-term investment.

On July 10, 19X7, a contract change is approved that increases the construction contract to $1,350,000. The third quarterly payment of $225,000 is also made on that date. On September 30, 19X7, another payment is approved for $400,000.

The project is not completed until December 1, 19X7, because of the addition to the contract. At that time, an invoice is received for the balance of the contract. The retained percentage on this project (pending final approval) is 5 percent of the contract price, or $67,500. Therefore, the December payment to Sunshine Construction is $82,500 ($150,000 − $67,500).

The Public Works Department completes its work at a cost of only $60,000, releasing $15,000 of the $75,000 encumbrance back to the fund balance. By February 28, 19X8, the corrections to the project needed for final approval have been made by the contractors, and the retained percentage ($67,500) is paid. The fund balance account is then closed, and the balance of cash on hand—the $15,000 unused encumbrance plus $50,000 unused contingency allowance—is transferred to the debt service fund as a *residual equity transfer.*

Debt Service Funds

Debt service funds are used to account for: (1) the accumulation of resources from which the principal and interest on long-term debt are paid and (2) the investment and expenditure of those resources. Whenever possible, several debt issues should be accounted for in a single fund. The fewer the number of debt service funds, the less complicated is the accounting for long-term debt. One fund needs only one set of financial statements; many funds need many sets of financial statements.

The money required for the repayment of debt, as well as the interest on the bonds, may come from several sources. If the locality or authority earmarks a special source for the repayment of bonds, then a special revenue fund may be set up to collect the money and transfer it to the debt service fund. Often revenue is collected from various sources in the general fund and then transferred to the debt service fund. Many bond indentures require that the money needed for servicing the bonds has first claim on the general revenue of the governmental unit.

Since the resources needed to service the principal and interest on serial bonds are received and expended each year, there is no accumulation of resources on which interest can be earned. The resources needed to service the principal on term bonds, however, are not needed until the debt matures and, therefore, can be invested. Thus, the assets and the fund balance increase annually, providing a *sinking fund* that eventually will be used for payment of the debt.

A sinking fund spreads the cost of repayment over the life of the bond issue. In this way, large, irregular demands will not be made on the annual budget. The amount that needs to be earmarked each year for the sinking fund is determined by: (1) the dollar value of the bonds to be retired, (2) the number of payments to be made into the account, and (3) the anticipated rate of earnings on the invested funds. Sinking fund requirements should be recomputed each year. Should a surplus in excess of actuarial requirements develop, it may be possible to lower future requirements. It is sound debt management practice, however, to absorb any significant surplus gradually over several fiscal periods rather than making a large reduction in payments in a single year. Should a deficit arise in the sinking fund, adjustments should be made as soon as possible by increasing the level of payments into the fund. New investment opportunities should also be sought to produce a greater return.

The same example used to explain the administration of a capital project fund can also be used to illustrate the operations of a debt service fund. Term bonds with a face value of $800,000 were issued at 5 percent for twenty years. Semiannual interest payments are $20,000 ($800,000 × 0.05 × 1/2). Since the bonds were sold three months after the issue date, however, only $10,000 is needed for the first payment. The other $10,000 will come from the accrued interest received upon sale of the bonds. Often interest payments are made to bondholders by a fiscal agent on behalf of the locality. In that case, the handling charges made by such agents (usually 1 percent or less) must be included in the annual transfers to the debt service fund for interest payments.

The estimated amount needed to build up the sinking fund can be developed from an annuity table or from the annuity formula, as shown in Chapter 8. For example, if the fund can earn 6 percent each year on its investments, then an annuity table shows that one dollar invested annually for twenty years at 6 percent will return $36.786. Thus it would take $21,747.40 added to the sinking fund each year, invested at 6 percent, to equal $800,000 at the end of twenty years ($800,000 ÷ $36.786 = $21,747.40). No long-term investments are purchased in the first year because the payment, as an annuity, is generally not received until the end of the year. During the second and all succeeding years, however, the transfers as well as any earnings made in prior years will be invested.

The interest earned from short-term investments during the construction period is summarized in Exhibit 9-10. The $65,000 fund balance, transferred to the debt service fund when the capital project fund is closed, is added to the $114,620 in earned interest, for a total of $179,620. These funds, invested on March 1 at 6 percent, earn $3,592.40 through June 30. The year-end balance of $16,960 from the first year of the sinking fund (see Exhibit 9-11) earns $1,017.60 during the second year. Thus, at the end of the second year, the sinking fund has a substantial balance of $201,190. This fund balance invested at 6 percent would total $574,265 at the end of twenty years when the bonds reach maturity. Therefore, the balance that must be accrued in the sinking fund is reduced to $225,735. Annual payments of $7,304, invested at 6 percent over the eighteen-year period, will yield the sum required in the sinking fund to cover the balance of the principal payment, as detailed in Exhibit 9-11.

Exhibit 9-10 *Interest Earnings on Short-Term Investments*

Investment Period	Funds Available	Rate	Interest Earned	Drawdown
7/03 – 8/31	$ 800,000	8%	$ 10,520	$ 62,500
9/01 – 9/30	748,020	7%	4,305	62,500
10/01 –12/29	1,489,825	9%	33,060	350,000
12/30 – 3/31	1,172,885	9%	26,030	225,000
4/01 – 6/30	973,915	8%	19,210	225,000
7/01 – 9/30	768,125	7%	13,260	400,000
10/01 –11/30	381,385	6%	3,760	82,500
12/01 – 2/28	302,645	6%	4,475	127,500
Fund balance	179,620			
Totals			$114,620	$1,535,000

Exhibit 9-II   *Sinking Fund Requirements to Retire $800,000 in Term Bonds: Twenty-Year Maturity*

Year	Estimated Transfers for Bond Payments	Estimated Fund Earnings @ 6%	Estimated Yearly Fund Balance Increase	Estimated Year-End Fund Balance
1	$ 16,000.00	$ 960.00	$ 16,960.00	$ 16,960.00
2	179,620.00	4,610.00	184,230.00	201,190.00
3	7,304.00	12,071.40	19,375.40	220,565.40
4	7,304.00	13,233.92	20,537.92	241,103.32
5	7,304.00	14,466.20	21,770.20	262,873.52
6	7,304.00	15,772.41	23,076.41	285,949.93
7	7,304.00	17,157.00	24,461.00	310,410.93
8	7,304.00	18,624.66	25,928.66	336,339.59
9	7,304.00	20,180.38	27,484.38	363,823.96
10	7,304.00	21,829.44	29,133.44	392,957.40
11	7,304.00	23,577.44	30,881.44	423,838.84
12	7,304.00	25,430.33	32,734.33	456,673.17
13	7,304.00	27,394.39	34,698.39	491,271.56
14	7,304.00	29,476.29	36,780.29	528,051.86
15	7,304.00	31,683.11	38,987.11	567,038.97
16	7,304.00	34,022.34	41,326.34	608,365.31
17	7,304.00	36,501.92	43,805.92	652,171.23
18	7,304.00	39,130.27	46,434.27	698,605.50
19	7,304.00	41,916.33	49,220.33	747,825.83
20	7,304.62	44,869.55	52,174.17	800,000.00
Totals	$327,092.62	$472,907.38	$800,000.00	

Long-Term Debt Control

Accurate debt records—including auditable ledgers as to the identity, purpose, and amount of debt commitments associated with capital projects and the debt service payments made—are vital to short-term and long-term fiscal operations. From these records, it should be possible to determine quickly and accurately the principal and interest requirements on the total debt over the full maturity of all issues. Such computations are needed to determine the financial capacity to meet future capital construction requirements and to plan the retirement schedule for any new borrowing.

Long-term debt can best be controlled through the use of a subsidiary ledger, such as a *bond and interest register.* By collecting in one place all pertinent information regarding individual bond issues, this ledger allows management to trace the complete history of each issue. It also assists in establishing a schedule of debt service requirements and in posting transactions to the general ledger, bonded debt ledger, and interest payable ledger.

A subsidiary *bonded debt ledger* contains a sheet for each bond issue, showing the project title and purpose, amount of bonds originally outstanding, date of bonds, interest rates, amount retired to date, and balance outstanding. A separate sheet is maintained on each bond issue in an *interest payable ledger.* As interest payments come due, they are entered in the "credit" and "balance" columns. As payments are made, the amount is entered in the "debit" column, and the balance payable is reduced by a corresponding sum. An overall schedule of debt service requirements can be readily computed from these records, and a *maturity and interest calendar* for all debt can be compiled to monitor revenue needs for debt service on a month-to-month basis. The calendar must be adjusted and updated as new issues are marketed.

All fixed assets purchased, constructed, or obtained by contract are recorded at cost in the *general fixed assets account group.* Fixed assets obtained by gift should be recorded at the fair market value when donated. Assets obtained through foreclosure should be recorded at the appraised value of the property or the total taxes or assessments plus costs, whichever is lower. Cash or liability transactions involved in the buying or selling of the asset are not recorded in the general fixed asset account group, however. Though not maintained for external reporting purposes, depreciation should be recorded in supplemental records for internal costing purposes.

An asset that is sold, destroyed, or otherwise rendered valueless is removed from the account group by debiting the general fixed assets account for the original amount recorded and crediting the particular fixed asset. Improvements to an asset, adding to its value, require an entry comparable to the original entry, but only for the amount of the improvement. General repairs, needed to keep the asset in the same operating condition, are not considered improvements and should not be added to the value of the fixed assets in the account group.

The *long-term debt account group* is used to maintain records of long-term liabilities, such as serial bonds, long-term notes, and long-term commitments arising from lease or purchase agreements. Separate records of long-term debt are maintained for special assessment funds, proprietary funds, and profit-type fiduciary funds.

Over the years, a sinking fund is built up by transfers from the general fund and interest on investments to an amount equal to that needed to pay off the bonds. The data in Exhibit 9-11 illustrate the final year transactions. At the beginning of the year 20, the fund balance should equal $747,825.83. This fund balance will earn $44,869.55 (at 6 percent), and a transfer from the general fund of $7,304.62 at year-end will bring the total in the sinking fund to $800,000. Upon recording the matured bonds payable in the debt service fund, the amount in the general long-term debt account group would be closed out.

Financial analysts often point out that the development of annual financial reports concerning public debt is a major point of weakness in the management of government resources. Such reports are important to the basic credit rating of the governmental unit and are of major interest to bondholders, public officials, and ordinary citizens. If adequate debt records are maintained, the preparation of such reports can be a relatively simple procedure. Annual financial reports concerning debt should cover three categories of information:

1. A listing of all outstanding debt by type of issue (general obligation, special assessment, or revenue bonds). For each bond issue, the following information should be provided: date of issue, original amount, date of maturity, coupon

(interest) rate, total interest, amount of principal and interest presently outstanding, and the amount carried in sinking funds, if any.

2. The overlapping debt of the jurisdiction—that portion of the debt of the school district, county, township, or special districts payable from taxes levied by the reporting jurisdiction.

3. A computation of the legal borrowing status of the jurisdiction.

Debt arising from the issuance of revenue bonds in proprietary funds must also be shown, including complete information on the facilities that support such debt. Revenue bond indentures may require an annual report by an independent certified public accountant. Special assessment bonds guaranteed by the jurisdiction should also be shown in the schedule of debt.

Accurate and complete reporting on public debt develops confidence on the part of investors and the general public as to the financial management of a jurisdiction or public organization. The relatively small investment of time and expense in preparing such reports is often repaid many times over through lower interest rates.

Distribution of Revenues and Issuance of Additional Bonds

In most cases, a *reserve fund* is established, into which all receipts and income derived from the operation of a self-supporting project are deposited. Monies in the reserve fund are then distributed monthly by the trustee or other handler of funds in the order established by the bond resolution or trust indenture (see Exhibit 9-12). Monies remaining in the reserve fund after the required distributions have been

Exhibit 9-12 *Distribution of Revenues From Self-Supporting Projects*

1. *Operation and maintenance* have first claim on the reserve fund. Without proper O&M funds, a facility may experience severe loss of income. Revenue bonds are commonly payable from net revenues—that is, gross receipts less operating and maintenance costs.

2. The *bond service account* receives monthly payments sufficient to cover the next semiannual interest payment, as well as the next principal payment on serial bonds.

3. A *mandatory sinking fund* is sometimes required in the case of term bonds, in lieu of principal payments on serial bonds.

4. The *debt service reserve fund* is gradually built up to equal a full year's maximum principal and interest in the case of serial bonds, or two years' interest, in the case of term bonds.

5. A *renewal and replacement fund* (sometimes called a *replacement reserve*) is established to replace equipment or provide necessary repairs beyond normal maintenance. Funds are paid into this account in an amount recommended by the consulting engineer and may be cumulative.

6. A *reserve maintenance fund* may be established to meet unusual or extraordinary maintenance charges that have not been budgeted. Some jurisdictions combine the reserve maintenance fund with the renewal and replacement fund.

7. The *working capital fund,* to cover unforeseen contingencies, should be equivalent to about one-tenth of a year's gross revenues.

made may be placed in a *surplus fund,* to be divided among various categories such as:

- *Redemption account,* to retire bonds in advance of maturity.
- *Payment in lieu of taxes.* When an authority purchases a going operation that has been a corporate unit, payments may be made in lieu of taxes either by legislative requirement or to create good will.
- *Other lawful payments,* including improvements and extensions to the facility or support of other bond interest.

When a facility is being constructed, it is not always possible to foresee just what the future will hold. It may be necessary to increase the size of the facility or to make other improvements that will require additional financing. Therefore, sufficient leeway should be provided in the indenture or resolution to permit the issuance of additional bonds.

If bonds of equal rank are permitted, safeguards must be established to prevent the undue dilution of the security of the original bonds. There are two basic types of trust indentures: (1) the *closed-end indenture,* which does not permit the issuance of parity bonds except as necessary to complete the project if initial financing proves insufficient; and (2) the *open-end indenture,* which permits the issuance of additional bonds but provides a formula prescribing the conditions to be met. In the first case, additional bonds must be junior in lien to the then outstanding bonds.

Recording and Canceling Coupons and Bonds

The final step in debt servicing involves the recording and canceling of coupons and bonds that have been paid. Following each scheduled payment, coupons and bonds must be checked to determine if any have not been redeemed. Some will always be slow in coming in, and occasionally, some may be missing permanently. In most cases, records must be maintained for several years after the final maturity date. Canceled coupons and bonds are usually kept for several years, after which they are destroyed by shredding or burning.

Many commercial banks and trust companies that serve as paying agents for municipal bonds include all phases of recording and cancellation as part of their services. These banks and trust companies provide the municipality with a certified list of canceled and destroyed bonds and coupons. Many municipalities mandate that the disposition of these documents take place in the presence of the director of finance or comptroller and at least one other municipal official. The "mortgage burning" ceremony still has considerable significance for many small communities.

Refunding Mature Bonds

The practice of refunding mature bonds should be avoided if at all possible and, if necessary, should be undertaken with great discretion. Refunding may be necessary to eliminate irregularities in the existing debt schedule resulting from overly optimistic retirement schedules or from sudden shifts in economic conditions beyond local control. Refunding may also be preferable to the high cost of emergency borrowing, particularly when a good credit relationship has been established in connection with outstanding debt.

Faced with the prospect of default on bonds or serious disruption of fiscal operations, a municipality may find it absolutely necessary to refund outstanding debts to avoid financial disaster. Unfortunately, such forced refunding often encounters unfavorable market conditions, since the economic factors that give rise to the need for refunding may be widespread. This situation confronted many cities during the Depression years of the 1930s. Under such circumstances, a municipality may be unable to sell refunded bonds to new investors and may be forced to negotiate with existing bondholders to exchange their holdings for new maturities.

Defaults

No matter how satisfactorily resolved, defaults are likely to result in a sharp decline in the credit standing of a municipality. Even temporary defaults, if allowed to extend beyond the normal ninety-day grace period, may result in the removal of a city's bonds from the list of securities approved for fiduciary investments.

Minor or temporary defaults involve temporary postponement of interest payments or failure to meet the maturity payment of a single security. Such minor defaults may be the result of unanticipated declines in revenue collection, the shutting off of normal lines of bank credit, and/or a temporary inability to market refunded bonds. Minor defaults can usually be corrected by various means without disturbing the general debt structure or further interrupting debt service. Adjustment strategies include: (1) payment during the grace period from belated tax receipts, (2) short-term bank loans, (3) small issues of refunded bonds, or (4) exchanges of securities. This last strategy is particularly effective for relatively recent bond issues. Bondholders are contacted, and negotiations are conducted to effect an exchange of outstanding bonds for new securities that more closely fit the community's long-term ability to pay.

Municipalities faced with such fiscal problems as peak debt service in a period of low paying capacity, serious breakdowns in the local economic base, and/or abnormally high tax delinquency may become involved in a second, more serious class of defaults. Under such circumstances, the municipality may experience difficulties in meeting current accounts as well as long-term obligations. Adjustments are usually effected by refunding or partially refunding a few years' obligations in order to free up some fiscal resources to meet current operating costs. It may be possible to accomplish the adjustment without a major disturbance of the general debt structure and without any scaling of debt. Once current obligations have been returned to a more balanced basis, attention can be redirected toward long-term obligations that may require further readjustments to reflect sound principles of debt administration.

Jurisdictions confronted by abnormally high debt, severely curtailed revenues, and a significant accumulation of operating deficits may have little prospect for correction except through a complete restructuring of the entire debt retirement schedule. When the total obligation is clearly beyond the jurisdiction's ability to pay, it may be necessary to scale down interest and even principal payments. Investors are naturally reluctant to forego any portion of their contractual rights, particularly with regard to principal. Unless the situation is hopeless, they tend to prefer extensive postponements, with the expectation that subsequent community growth and development will eventually restore the value of their investment. Thus, when necessary, scaling can be accomplished more readily through a reduction of interest payments than of principal.

Insofar as possible, a municipality should take the initiative in any necessary readjustments and in planning and implementing the refunding plan. By exercising such initiative, the municipality demonstrates good faith and competence and may gain the necessary cooperation from investors to resolve the pending financial crisis successfully. Attempts to cover up a fiscal crisis merely exacerbate the uncertainty, increase expenses, and ultimately may result in the jurisdiction being placed in receivership. At this point, local officials can no longer control the readjustment process.

A complete investigation of all relevant factors—financial, administrative, and economic—is a prerequisite to the planning of corrective action. Reliable experts should be consulted and a competent adviser retained. The relationship between outstanding obligations and normal capacity to pay must be ascertained, and operating costs should be examined to determine if they afford a basis for appropriate adjustments. The municipality must evaluate its financial status in relation to resources and liabilities, both immediate and future. In short, the municipality should approach its creditors with full knowledge of where it stands and with reasonable expectations regarding its capacity to recover from the financial difficulties.

Although a brief hiatus from full debt service obligations may be necessary, such postponement is valid only if it is used as a means of systematically adjusting current accounts. Such refunding should postpone the retirement of as little debt service as possible. The replanning of the debt structure should not trade a difficult immediate situation for an impossible future one. Callable bonds should be used to the extent possible, to permit re-refunding at lower interest rates if justified by market conditions, as well as the possibility of accelerating the retirement process when conditions improve.

Adjustment of serious defaults involves, at best, a process of compromise in which there is little opportunity for impartial settlement. Furthermore, refunding arrangements may contain the potential for recurring financial difficulties for several decades in the future. The experiences of many communities in the 1930s offer ample support for the necessity of sound debt policies. Traces of the consequences of default are still evident in some of these communities even today.

The procedures involved in refunding and the safeguards against default should be clearly understood by local officials. Most states have adopted legislative measures to circumvent the financial catastrophe faced by many governments in the thirties. The ultimate responsibility, however, still rests with local officials to adopt debt administrative procedures that will protect their community from "mortgaging its future."

Endnotes

1. Municipalities seldom deal with the final investor in a bond issue. Rather, municipal bonds are *underwritten* by large investment syndicates that provide the funds to the issuing jurisdiction and, in turn, reoffer the bonds to individual investors. For a further discussion of the underwriting of municipal bonds, see Alan Walter Steiss, *Local Government Finance* (Lexington, MA: D.C. Heath, 1975), Chapter 7.

2. Underwriters of municipal bonds must perform several calculations on the stated interest rates to determine *net interest cost* (the bid that they will make on the bonds). The net interest cost is equal to the total cost of interest over the life of the bond issue (less any premiums that must be paid) divided by the total number of bond years—that is, the sum of the number of years to maturity for each separate bond.

CHAPTER 10

Financial Management Within the Strategic Management Process

Strategic management is a process by which policies are formulated and strategies are selected to achieve the goals and objectives of an organization. In this process, attention must be given to the performance capacity of the organization and the opportunities and challenges of the broader environment. Strategic management offers a framework for adapting to the vagaries of an unpredictable environment and an uncertain future.

The concepts of strategic management have so far been applied mainly in the corporate setting; they have not been extended to more general applications in an organizational context, whether in the private or public sector. Although individual case studies may be drawn from education, health care, and other government fields, the nonprofit sector in general represents a new and virtually untapped area for research in strategic management. The purpose of this final chapter is to suggest an overall strategic management framework within which the concepts and techniques of financial management might be applied.

Organizational Strategy

The term *strategy* is derived from the Greek *strategos,* meaning "general." In a military sense, strategy involves the planning and directing of battles or campaigns on a broad scale—that is, the responsibility of generals. In this context, strategy is distinguished from tactics—the initiation of actions to achieve more immediate objectives. In the business world, however, the term *strategy* is often used to refer to specific actions taken to offset actual or potential actions of competitors. In a more fundamental sense, organizational strategy is any course of action pursued to achieve major goals and objectives.

Strategic Versus Tactical Decisions

Decision making is one of the most pervasive functions of management, whether in business or in government. If an organization is to achieve its objectives, decisions must be made, and action programs arising from those decisions must be implemented. Organizational decisions can be arrayed on a continuum, with *strategic decisions* at one end and *tactical decisions* at the other. Strategic decisions involve the determination of broad goals and objectives and the development of comprehensive plans to attain those goals and objectives. Decisions are made at the strategic level as to what kinds of products or services the organization will provide, who the beneficiaries will be, and what major capital and operating expenditures will be required to produce these products or services. Because managers of complex organizations often deal with an uncertain future, strategic decisions may involve considerable risk.

Tactical decisions deal with matters of more immediate concern and can usually be made with a higher degree of certainty as to their practical results. Such short-term decisions, however, often have important long-term implications. Serious repercussions may arise for the organization and its client groups if those long-term consequences are overlooked or ignored.

A primary objective of strategic management is to broaden the bases for decisions along this continuum. Strategic managers must attempt (1) to identify the long-range needs of the community or organization, (2) to explore the ramifications of policies and programs designed to meet these needs, and (3) to formulate strategies that maximize the positive aspects and minimize the negative aspects of the foreseeable future.

Basic Components of Strategic Management

Strategic management is both a conceptual framework for orchestrating the basic decision-making process of an organization and a collection of analytical tools designed to facilitate the making of decisions. Linking appropriate methodologies to the various stages in the decision process is a key responsibility of the strategic manager.

An objective of strategic management is to strike a balance between the polar pressures for methodological sophistication and ease of utilization. In applying a mixed bag of analytical techniques and methods to a variety of decision situations, the strategic manager must focus on the integration of planning, analysis, and management in productive harmony. In short, the functions of strategic management should be carried out as a balanced blend of objective methods and subjective ability.

Strategic management is concerned with deciding in advance what an organization should do in the future (planning); determining who will do it and how it will be done (resource management); and monitoring and enhancing ongoing activities and operations (control and evaluation). It involves the combined effect of these three basic components in meeting the goals and objectives of an organization (see Exhibit 10-1).

Planning involves an identification of the specific actions required to carry out a given strategy. *Resource management* is concerned with determining the particular resource configuration to be employed and allocating resources to those units that will carry out the plan. Organizational structure and resource allocation provide the means through which proposed strategies are implemented.[1] Control and evaluation

Exhibit 10-1 *The Strategic Management Process*

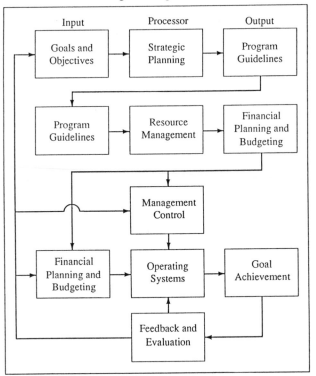

focus on the internal requirements for successful implementation of the strategies selected. Various *control mechanisms* are used to monitor performance; the resulting feedback is used to determine necessary modifications in resource allocations and organizational structure. *Performance evaluation* ties the output of the organization to the requirements of its internal environment. An assessment of the overall capability of the organization, along with certain political considerations, helps to relate the organization (or community) to the demands of its external and internal environment.

This book has focused on the resource management component of the strategic management process and, in particular, on the application of financial management in public organizations. The balance of this final chapter will be devoted to the other two basic components: strategic planning and management control and evaluation.

Strategic Planning

The concepts of strategic planning and strategic management are often used interchangeably. As used here, strategic planning is that component of the strategic management system concerned with (1) clarifying goals and objectives, (2) determining policies for the acquisition and distribution of resources, and (3) establishing a basis for translating policies and decisions into specific action commitments. Strategic planners identify the long-range needs of a community or organization, explore the ramifications and implications of policies and programs designed to meet those needs, and formulate strategies to maximize the positive aspects and minimize the negative aspects of the foreseeable future.

A Model for Strategic Planning

Strategic planning examines broad alternative courses of action and the consequences likely to result from their implementation. Explicit provision must be made for dealing with the uncertainty. The strategic planning model shown in Exhibit 10-2 consists of five basic components. This model assumes that a concentration of systemic data can provide the basis for preliminary goals and objectives. The emphasis is on an orderly evolution—from a broad statement of mission, to goals and objectives consistent with the mission statement, to specific policies and implementation decisions. A major shortcoming of more traditional planning efforts has been a lack of consistency from the general to the specific.

The goal formulation process seeks to avoid the tendency to posit future plans merely on the basis of existing conditions. *Policies* are factual premises representing what can be done. They must be tested against *goals*—value premises representing

Exhibit 10-2 *A Model for Strategic Planning*

1. *Basic research and analysis*
   a. Data collection, inventories, and needs assessments
   b. External and internal environmental analyses to determine system readiness
   c. Identification of planning horizon and levels of client groups to be served

2. *Diagnosis of trends and needs*
   a. Macro-level trends and related considerations
   b. Micro-level technical and applied studies, including facilities analyses and specific needs assessments

3. *Statements of goals and objectives*
   a. Formulation of hypotheses concerning the mission of the organization
   b. Delineation of significant structural changes required to realize the mission statement
   c. Definition of the desired state of the system
   d. Identification of objectives to achieve desired state

4. *Formulation and analysis of alternatives*
   a. Development of an objectives matrix
   b. Redefinition of the desired state of the system in light of more detailed objectives

5. *Policy alternatives and resource recommendations*
   a. Translation of goals and objectives into policies
   b. Formulation of explicit policy sets
   c. Delineation of effectiveness and efficiency measures
   d. Establishment of decision guidelines for the allocation of financial resources

Adapted from Alan Walter Steiss, *Strategic Management and Organizational Decision Making* (Lexington, MA: D.C. Heath and Company, 1985), pp. 76–79.

what should be done. When compromises must be made—as they always must—decisions can be based more clearly on the optimal or normative conditions outlined in statements of goals and objectives.

The Planning Horizon

Basic to the strategic planning model is the use of a planning horizon—the farthest point that can be anticipated based on an interpretation of what is known about existing conditions and emerging trends. The planning horizon can (and should) be changed, revised, or even dismissed as the body of information on which it is based is enlarged and clarified. A strategic plan formulated on the horizon concept yields a series of policy alternatives to guide future activities toward some desired state. The horizon concept offers the basis for a *thesis* rather than merely a *synthesis*. This thesis emerges from a series of hypotheses, or "what if" studies, whereby various mixes of programs and clientele groups (beneficiaries of these programs) are explored within the overall parameters of the planning horizon.

Within the extended time horizon of strategic planning, explicit provision is made for the fact that resource allocation decisions often have significant long-range implications. Multiyear program plans are developed as inputs to each year's budget deliberations. Each plan alternative has different implications for the distribution and management of resources. A number of combinations and permutations are possible, based on a relatively well-defined set of pure alternatives. From these hypotheses, the mix that best fits the mission statement of the community/organization can be identified and set forth as the desired future state. Policies and programs can then be developed to implement this chosen alternative.

Policy Matrix

Policy issues can be arrayed on a continuum, with long-range, general policy concerns anchoring one end and issues of control the other. Between these end points are issues relating to strategic, program, and implementation policies. The other dimension of this policy matrix is defined by (1) what is to be accomplished (objectives), (2) when it is to be accomplished (priorities), (3) where it is to be accomplished (locus), (4) how it is to be accomplished (means), and (5) standards for the evaluation of accomplishments. These five factors relate to and help define the *content* of policy statements (see Exhibit 10-3).

The four quadrants of the policy matrix require the attention of various participants in the policy-making process:

1. *Basic policy* is primarily of a long-range, strategic nature and focuses on objectives and priorities.
2. *Executive policy* establishes operational means and standards within the framework of strategic planning.
3. *Administrative policy* is concerned with the objectives and priorities of implementation and control.

Exhibit 10-3 *A Policy Matrix*

Policy Content	Policy Issues				
	Long–Range General	Strategic	Program	Implementation	Control
Objectives					
Priorities		Basic Policy		Administrative Policy	
Locus					
Means		Executive Policy		Technical Policy	
Standards					

Adapted from Alan Walter Steiss, *Management Control in Government* (Lexington, MA: Lexington Books, 1982), p. 273.

4. *Technical policy and procedures* focus on the means of implementation and standards of control.

Each quadrant suggests a particular realm of policy formulation responsibility, and delimits the focus and emphasis appropriate to each of these realms.

Trade-offs must be made among these four policy quadrants—specifically, between executive and administrative policy, on the one hand, and strategical, managerial, and operational considerations on the other. It is in these areas that conflicts between policies are inevitable.

Strategic planning will not immediately resolve all problems confronting an organization. Nor is its implementation easy to administer; a firm commitment by those involved is essential to its success. The cyclical nature of this process, however, does offer an opportunity to introduce various components in a series of refinements rather than on a whole-cloth basis. Formalization of the process is at the very root of successful strategic planning, as distinguished from forecasting and other piecemeal planning and analytical approaches of the past.

Control and Evaluation

Traditional definitions of management control emphasize the need for corrective action when deviations occur from some predetermined course of events. One of the better-known definitions is that offered by Henri Fayol: "Control consists of verifying whether everything occurs in conformity with the plan adopted, the instructions issued, and principles established. It has for an object to point out weaknesses and errors in order to rectify and prevent recurrence."[2] The administration of such control mechanisms has traditionally fallen within the purview of accountants and auditors.

Internal Control

The concept of *internal control* is sometimes treated as synonymous with management control. Internal control systems, however, are concerned primarily with accounting policies and procedures. Such controls include approval procedures for the commitment of organizational resources; checks and balances among key fiscal duties (for example, the billing function versus receipt of revenue); limited access to assets; and assurance that financial transactions are properly authorized, classified, and recorded on a timely basis, in the correct amounts, and for the proper purposes. Adequate internal controls are the cornerstone of any good accounting system. They can also help management achieve greater operational efficiencies.

The development and continuous maintenance of an adequate internal control system are primary responsibilities of financial management. To meet these responsibilities, management must remain cognizant of changing times and their impact on the organization's control environment. Internal controls must be adapted as circumstances dictate. Flexibility is critical to the continued operations of any entity that seeks to achieve overall success at acceptable levels of risk.

An internal control system comprises those measures taken to provide management with reasonable assurance that everything is functioning as it should. An organizational plan should provide for the segregation of incompatible functional responsibilities for operations (the expenditure of funds), custody of revenue, and accounting. This plan should specify the responsibilities and tasks of the various departments and individuals within the organization. Authorization procedures should ensure reasonable accounting control over assets, liabilities, revenues, and expenses. Adequate controls should encompass proper accountability for assets from the origination of financial transactions to reporting. In addition, appropriate documentation of all tasks and procedures must be maintained.

An objective of internal control is the prompt discovery of unintentional errors or irregularities, so that appropriate corrective action can be initiated on a timely basis. A good system of internal controls provides reasonable (but not absolute) assurance that errors and irregularities will be prevented or detected. This oversight discourages fraud and provides more reliable accounting records.

It is important to recognize, however, the inherent limitations of any internal control system:

1. The extent of the internal controls adopted by any organization is limited by cost considerations.
2. Any established system of internal controls can be circumvented by employee collusion and management fraud.

An internal control system so perfect as to preclude any possible fraud would cost more than it would save and would be impractical to operate. Thus, the concept of *reasonable assurance* must be used in weighing the costs and benefits associated with such controls.

Management Control

Placing greater emphasis on positive action, Robert Mockler defines *management control* as

> a systematic effort to set performance standards consistent with planning objectives, to design information feedback systems, to compare actual performance with these predetermined standards, to determine whether there are any deviations and to measure their significance, and to take any action required to assure that all corporate resources are being used in the most effective and efficient way possible in achieving corporate objectives.[3]

Management control involves four interrelated activities, shown schematically in Exhibit 10-4. Concurrent with the initiation of a program or project, a set of standards must be established against which planned activities can be evaluated as they are carried out. Monitoring devices measure the performance of individuals, activities, and/or programs within the organization. These measurements are then compared with the standards to determine whether the current state of affairs approximates the planned state. Finally, steps are initiated to correct significant deviations or to amplify positive trends to achieve further gains. Corrective action may involve bringing performance more fully into line with plans; in some cases, plans may have to be modified to more closely reflect performance. Positive action may involve the allocation of additional resources for program expansion, new capital investment, diversification, and so forth.

Strategic, predictive, concurrent, and after-the-fact controls can provide a clearer picture of where the organization or program is and where it should be. A proper balance among these various types of controls can vastly improve the overall effectiveness of any organization. Historically, most organizations have relied

Exhibit 10-4 *A Corrective Model for Management Control*

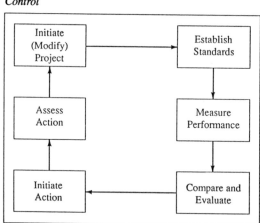

largely on *after-the-fact* control measures—measures that detect problems only after they have occurred.

Using the analytical capabilities of computers, however, it is possible to develop management controls that anticipate problems and make adjustments, often before their impact is fully upon the organization. *Concurrent,* or *real-time,* controls, for example, measure deviations from standards more or less as they occur. Such controls permit a program to be carried out over time within an established range of tolerance. The quality control chart used in production operations is an example of concurrent control techniques in the private sector. Statistical samples of the product are taken periodically and measured against predetermined quality standards. If the samples begin to fall outside the established quality limits, corrective action can be taken before additional items are produced.

Adaptive controls have been used to modify the internal structure and processes of an organization in response to changing requirements in the external environment. These efforts have given rise to *predictive* controls designed to anticipate and identify problems before they occur. For example, if a major expenditure is proposed, the potential impact on budget allocations should be ascertained ahead of time rather than after the fact. Such controls are related to the planning process and generally involve various forecasting and projection techniques.

A *strategic control system* permits changes to be made both in the desired objectives and in the control approach. Donald Harvey defines *strategic control* as

> the managerial function that ensures that actual organizational actions correspond to planned actions. Two aspects are important: First, control and review should take place at many stages of the implementation process; and second, control is closely related to other managerial functions—goal-setting, planning, and decision making.[4]

Complex organizations often require large amounts of data to achieve effective management control. Continuous monitoring of activities is needed if appropriate corrective action is to be taken promptly.

In designing a new control system, it is necessary to determine what features of the existing system, if any, should be retained. It is also important to determine how the transition from the old system to the new is to be accomplished. Often a new control system is implemented on a trial basis in one segment of an organization. In other cases, the system may be designed to serve the specific needs of a particular functional area within the organization (for example, to provide greater accountability for contracts, grants, or other forms of external funding). In such instances, explicit provision must be made to "crosswalk" the data from the new control system to other established formats within the organization. Crosswalks may also have to be developed for other organizations that have grown accustomed to receiving information in certain formats.

Operating managers will have much to learn about any new control system. The new system will seem less strange to them to the extent that it incorporates familiar practices—particularly, familiar terminology—from the existing system. If the new and old systems are permitted to run in parallel, the old system should be discarded slightly before managers become completely comfortable with the new system. Any remaining "holdouts" will then have no choice but to use the new system, as the old data formats will no longer be available.

Performance Evaluation

For the purposes of this discussion, an *evaluation* is (1) an assessment of the effectiveness of ongoing and proposed programs in achieving agreed-upon goals and objectives and (2) an identification of areas needing improvement through program modification (including the possible termination of ineffective programs) that (3) takes into account the possible influence of external as well as internal organizational factors. An evaluation may focus on the extent to which programs are implemented according to predetermined guidelines (*process evaluation*) or the extent to which a program produces change in the intended direction (*impact evaluation*). *Formative evaluations* provide the information necessary to design and/or modify systems for the delivery of services. *Summative evaluations* measure performance and program impact (see Exhibit 10-5).

Standard approaches for conducting an evaluation are: (1) before-and-after comparisons; (2) time-trend data projections; (3) with-and-without comparisons; (4) comparisons of planned versus actual performance; and (5) controlled experimentation. Basic characteristics of each of these approaches are outlined in Exhibit 10-6.

Exhibit 10-5 *A Comprehensive Evaluation System*

Formative Evaluation

1. Needs assessment
2. Goals formulation
3. Consideration of proven alternatives
4. Evaluation of input and intervening variables
5. Consideration of local factors
6. Modification of goals
7. Objectives formulation
8. Design of service-delivery system
9. Design of evaluation method

Decision Making Process

Feedback of Information

Resource Allocation

1. Selection of service mix
2. Adoption of budget
3. Allocation of resources
4. Delivery of services

Summative Evaluation

1. Collection of data
2. Measurement of performance
3. Measurement of impact

Exhibit 10-6 *Approaches to Evaluation*

1. *Before-and-after comparisons.* Identify relevant objectives and corresponding evaluation criteria. Obtain values for the criteria for periods before and after program implementation. Any changes in the "after" data, as compared to the "before" data, are assumed to have occurred as a consequence of the new program or policy.

2. *Time-trend data projections.* Obtain data on each evaluative criterion at several intervals before and after program initiation. Project preprogram data to the end of the evaluation period by means of standard statistical methods. Compare actual and projected estimates to determine the amount of change resulting from introduction of the new program or policy.

3. *With-and-without comparisons.* Identify relevant objectives and evaluation criteria. Identify similar jurisdictions or populations where program is not operating. Obtain data on each of the criteria in each jurisdiction before program implementation and up to the time of evaluation. Compare changes in values of the criteria (rates as well as amounts) for the "with" and "without" groups.

4. *Comparisons of planned versus actual performance.* Establish specific, measurable objectives or targets prior to the initiation of a program or policy. Targets identify specific achievements within specific time periods. At the end of a given time period, compare actual performance against established targets.

5. *Controlled experimentation.* Identify relevant objectives and evaluation criteria. Assign members of the target population (or a probability sample of that population) in a scientifically random manner to experimental and control groups. Measure preprogram performance of each group. Apply the program to the experimental group but not to the control group. Measure postprogram performance of each group, using the selected evaluation criteria. Compare pre- versus postprogram changes in both groups.

Adapted from Alan Walter Steiss, *Management Control in Government* (Lexington, MA: D.C. Heath and Company, 1982), pp. 182–188.

The selection of an appropriate approach will depend on the timing of the evaluation, the costs involved, the resources available, and the desired level of accuracy. These approaches are not either–or choices. Some or all of the methods can be used in combination.

Evaluations can reduce uncertainty but cannot eliminate it totally. As Rossi has observed, "Evaluations cannot influence decision-making processes unless those undertaking them recognize the need to orient their efforts toward maximizing the policy utility of their evaluation activities."[5] The full potential of such evaluation techniques as management and performance audits and sunset legislation has not yet been realized. These techniques, however, provide additional incentives for administrators to undertake evaluations and apply the results to the improvement of program performance.

Management Information

Although vast amounts of facts, numbers, and other data may be processed in any organization, what constitutes *management information* depends on the problem at hand and the manager's particular frame of reference. Traditional accounting data, for example, can provide information when arrayed appropriately in balance sheets and financial statements. Accounting data, regardless of how elaborately processed, may be relatively meaningless, however, if the problem is to evaluate the effectiveness of a new program. To contribute to improved decisions, the information available to management must be both timely and pertinent. In this sense, *information* is incremental knowledge that reduces uncertainty in particular situations.

Basic Components of MIS

The basic components of a management information system (MIS) are presented schematically in Exhibit 10-7. Three specific data areas provide inputs to the formation of strategic decisions: (1) *environmental intelligence*—data about the broader environment of which the organization is a part, including assessments of client needs; (2) *autointelligence*—data about the component elements of the organization, including an evaluation of the organization's resources and its capacity to respond to client needs; and (3) *historical data*—the lessons of past experience. Environmental and internal data are stored in the "memory banks" of the organization, to be retrieved when particular decision situations arise or when a broad assessment of the overall goals and objectives of the organization is appropriate.

In a well-constructed MIS, basic analysis can be carried out using various modeling and forecasting techniques. The results are stored in the database for reference and updating. The diagnosis of trends can be aided, in part, by modeling and simulation programs, by statistical analysis packages, and by programs that perform functions related to operations research, such as network analysis. Probable happenings can be outlined by assuming the continuation of existing trends into hypothetical futures. These probabilistic forecasts, in turn, become important inputs in determining organizational objectives.

Once objectives have been determined (at least in preliminary fashion), and with further inputs from autointelligence, strategic planning can produce two important initiatives: (1) the search for new courses of action to improve the overall performance of the organization; and (2) a framework for resource management and control. The effective storage and query capabilities of the MIS can be used in the formulation and analysis of program and policy alternatives. The results of previous decisions and program actions are combined in policy and resource recommendations. Tactical and technical innovations must also be sought to improve the overall responsiveness of the organization.

The overall intent of strategic plans can be translated through resource management into more specific programs and activities. The budget process provides important managerial *feedback* in the form of evaluations of prior program decisions and actions. *Feedforward* information emerges from the various projections and forecasts required by the financial analysis and budgeting processes.

Management control activities draw on the memory banks of the organization in search of *programmed decisions*—decisions that have worked successfully in the

Exhibit 10-7 *Basic Components of an MIS*

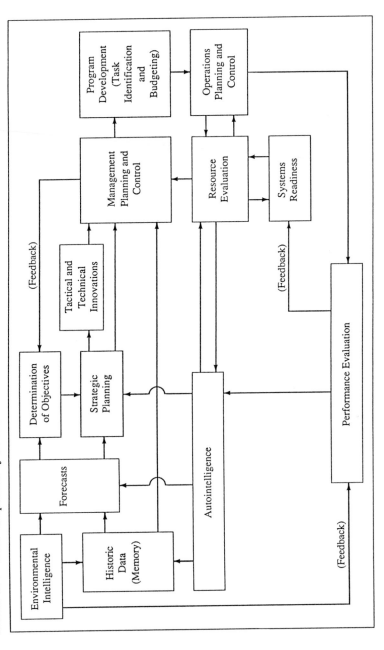

past. *Resource evaluations* include information on the current fiscal status of the organization (accounting data), as well as the overall response capacity of other organizational resources (*systems readiness*).

Program development involves task identification and budgeting. Responsibilities for carrying out operations and the resources required by these operations can be further detailed through operations planning and control, using programming techniques such as Program Evaluation Review Technique (PERT) and Critical Path Method (CPM).

Performance evaluations draw data from the broader environment regarding the efficiency and effectiveness with which client needs are met, problems are solved, opportunities are realized, and so forth. Such evaluations provide feedback from, as well as new inputs into, autointelligence. They also provide feedback on systems readiness, which defines the response capacity of the organization in the short-, mid-, and long-range futures. Sufficient flexibility is required to meet a wide range of possible competitive events.

Feedback

Feedback must be obtained regarding the output of the organization in terms of quality (effectiveness), quantity (efficiency of service levels), cost, and so on. Programs must be monitored to maintain process control. Feedback is provided in the early stages of program implementation through resource (inputs) evaluations. Many decisions based on feedback are made within the management control system. Routine adjustments may be programmed into a set of ongoing procedures, and instructions can be provided to those individuals who must carry out specific tasks. Procedures are modified and files updated simultaneously with routine decision making and program adjustments.

Summary and exception reports generated by the MIS may become part of higher-level reviews and evaluations. These evaluations, in turn, may lead to adaptations or innovations in the organization's goals and objectives. Lags in feedback systems are anticipated by feedforward mechanisms that monitor inputs and predict their effects on output variables. Actions can be taken to change inputs, and thereby bring outputs into equilibrium with desired results, before measurement discloses a deviation from accepted standards.

First and foremost, an MIS involves the organization and timely communication of information needed to resolve management problems. A large, centralized data-processing center is not a prerequisite to, nor a necessary concomitant of, an MIS. The desirability of such large "figure factories" or "number crunchers" depends more on the size and nature of the organization than on the purposes of the MIS. In the late 1960s and early 1970s, many organizations were sold on the notion that "bigger is better," only to find that, with the rapid changes in computer technology, they were saddled with a "dinosaur" that consumed vast quantities of resources but could not serve the expanding information needs of management.

Summary

Effective management must be a dynamic process, involving the blending and directing of available human, physical, and financial resources in order to achieve the agreed-upon goals and objectives of the organization. A basic purpose of management should be to provide focus and consistency to the action programs of the organization. The effectiveness of such an approach must be measured by the results achieved and by the people served—that is, in terms of performance.

The concept of performance suggests a melding of the basic management objectives of *efficiency*—doing things right—and *effectiveness*—doing the right things. Effectiveness must be measured in terms of the response time required to make strategic adjustments when things go wrong. To this end, more systematic and responsive approaches to management are required. The objective is to achieve a coordinative process capable of yielding more rational decisions for the organization.

The following procedural elements define the scope of strategic management:

1. *Strategic planning.* Establish overall strategic goals and objectives; select appropriate policies for the acquisition and distribution of resources; provide a basis for translating policies and decisions into specific action commitments.
2. *Resource management.* Determine requirements to meet identified goals and objectives; determine the available resources (fiscal, personnel, materials, equipment, and time) required for organizational programs; establish the organizational units, procedures, operations, and activities necessary to carry out the strategic plan; judiciously allocate the resources of the organization in accordance with some system of priorities.
3. *Control and evaluation.* Schedule programs from the point of commitment to completion; exercise control by reacting to (and anticipating) deviations between predicted and actual performance; monitor activities to determine whether or not reasonable, feasible, and efficient plans and programs are being executed and if not, why not.

At least three categories of organizational decisions are reflected in this procedural definition: (1) decisions relating to problem recognition, classification, and appraisal; (2) decisions required to convert the intentions of a strategic plan into more specific programs and projects; and (3) decisions that assess the performance of ongoing programs and provide additional inputs in subsequent cycles of the process.

Many of the tasks identified in this procedural definition are presently assigned to various sectors in a complex organization. Planners plan; financial analysts prepare budgets; program personnel schedule and control resources for specific activities; and administrators monitor and evaluate. Some of these tasks are undertaken on a grand scale, whereas others are fairly routine. With increasing complexity of organizational operations, however, the division of labor established to deal with this complexity may well become the major impediment to effective formulation and implementation of policy. Unless a more comprehensive framework is created to provide guidance and coordination, the sum of the management parts may be far less than an integrated whole.

Endnotes

1. Alan J. Rowe, Richard O. Mason, and Karl E. Dickel, *Strategic Management and Business Policy: A Methodological Approach* (Reading, MA: Addison-Wesley, 1982), p. 2.

2. Henri Fayol, *General and Industrial Management* (New York: Pitman Corporation, 1949), p. 107.

3. Robert J. Mockler, *The Management Control Process* (New York: Appleton-Century-Crofts, 1972), p. 2.

4. Donald F. Harvey, *Business Policy and Strategic Management* (Columbus, OH: Charles E. Merrill, 1982), p. 329.

5. Peter H. Rossi, Howard E. Freeman, and Sonia Wright, *Evaluation: A Systematic Approach* (Beverly Hills, CA: Sage, 1979), p. 283.

Index